A Taste of QUEBEC

Julian Armstrong

Macmillan of Canada
A Division of Canada Publishing Corporation
Toronto, Ontario, Canada

Canadian Cataloguing in Publication Data
Julian Armstrong, date.
  A taste of Quebec

ISBN 0-7715-9434-8

1. Cookery, French-Canadian – Quebec style.
I. Title.

TX715.6.A75 1990   641.59714   C90-093380-1

1 2 3 4 5 JD 94 93 92 91 90

Cover and text design by Don Fernley

Front cover photo and food photographs by Fred Bird
Back cover photograph courtesy of Tourism Quebec
Lamb stew photograph
  from New Zealand Meat Co.

Macmillan of Canada
A Division of Canada Publishing Corporation
Toronto, Ontario, Canada

CONTENTS

Introduction   1

Quebec Region   4

Saguenay-Lac St. Jean   24

Beauce   43

Charlevoix   65

Laurentians-Outaouais   84

Côte du Sud   109

Gaspé   128

Montérégie   149

Mauricie-Lanaudière   167

Estrie   191

Index   213

ACKNOWLEDGEMENTS

Many people played a part in this book and deserve my deepest thanks. I'll begin with my editors at The Montreal *Gazette*, who encouraged my culinary exploration of Quebec and in whose pages much of the material originally appeared.

Among those who gave special help were Jehane Benoit, Quebec's late and fondly remembered food communicator, who urged me to search out and record the cooking habits of the generations who passed on their recipes only by example; Suzanne Paré Leclerc, the Quebec agriculture department's dynamo of a public relations officer, who tracked down informed sources for me in every corner of the province; Johanna Burkhard, home economist and *Gazette* columnist, who tested the recipes and developed the microwave versions; Soeur Monique Chevrier , a Montreal cooking teacher from the Congregation of Notre Dame; Soeur Marcelle Boucher, archivist of the Ursuline convent in Quebec City; Nora Dawson, a Toronto teacher who holds a Université Laval doctorate for her research into the folkways of the Île d'Orleans; and many staff members of Montreal's Institut de tourisme et d'hôtellerie du Québec.

Region by region, I received generous help from many home cooks, chefs, innkeepers, cookbook authors, tourist office staff, government officials and others. My special thanks to go to the following:

Quebec: Suzanne Howard Demers, Janet Duplain; Saguenay-Lac St. Jean: Cécile Roland Bouchard, Constance Garneau, Jeannine Renouf; Beauce: Cécile Grondin Gamache; Charlevoix: Rita Dufour Laurin, Jori Smith; Laurentians-Outaouais: Richard Bergeron, Anne Desjardins, Nicole Kretz, Marcel Kretz; Côte du Sud: Edith Martin; Gaspé: Mabel Reynolds Hyman; Montérégie: Thérèse Daigle, Carol Petch; Maurice-Lanaudière: Peggy Lafrenière, Micheline Mongrain-Dontigny; Estrie: Pauline Jacques, Rena Tibbits Marsh.

At Macmillan of Canada, I am indebted to Linda McKnight, who first envisioned a book from my series of newspaper articles; Laurie Coulter, who edited the manuscript; Susan Girvan, production editor; Don Fernley, designer; and Fred Bird, photographer. Tourisme Québec supplied the beautiful photograph of my adopted province.

Finally, I thank my family for having endured many meals of test recipes. My husband, Robert O'Brien, was generous with calming advice and French translation assistance. Our son Charles kept my spirits up through the months at the computer and aimiably funneled trial dishes, in particular dozens of test "Gâteau Jos. Louis" cakes, to fellow law students. Our daughter Claire helped test recipes. Our daughter Jane handled word processing chores. My mother, Polly Armstrong of Toronto, was always game for yet another culinary research trip.

My friend and advisor Suzanne Paré Leclerc delighted me when, upon reading the manuscript, she said, "You really love my province". I do and I hope readers everywhere will be inspired to sample Canada's first and most distinctive cuisine, both in their homes and at the hospitable tables of Quebec.

Julian Armstrong

The following recipes were adapted from these cookbooks and are reprinted with the permission of the publishers:

Québec: "Crêpes à Nicole" from *Recettes de pommes de terre à la mode de chez nous.* Laprairie, Québéc: Club optimiste de Saint-Ubalde, Éditions des Deux Mondes, 1984. "Pâté aux poireaux", "Salade de chou" from *Les Délices de l'Île.* Île d'Orleans, Québéc: privately published, undated.

Saguenay-Lac St. Jean: "Soupe a l'ivrogne", "Tourtière à la ouananiche" from *150 Recettes pour le Saguenay-Lac St. Jean à Cuisiner* by Micheline Mongrain-Dontigny. La Tuque, Québec, privately published, 1988. "Pâté Accaé", "Tarte aux bleuets", "Croustade aux bleuets", "Mains à la mélasse" from *Le pinereau: L'art culinaire au saguenay-lac saint jean* by Cécile Roland Bouchard. Montreal: Les Éditions Leméac, 1971.

Beauce: "Ragoût de pattes de lard aux grands-pères", "Fèves au lard", "Rouleau de boeuf", "Pain de blé entier", "Pouding aux pommes au sirop d'érable" from *Les Plats d'autrefois* by Cécile Grondin Gamache. Scott Jonction, Québec: Imprimerie Bô-Modèle Inc., 1986. "Salade d'hiver" from *Cuisine d'hier et d'aujourd'hui* by Le Cercle de fermières de Ste. Marie. Ste. Marie, Québec: privately published, 1987. "Poitrines de poulet au sirop d'érable" from *Vingt ans de réussite culinaire* by Jeanne d'Arc Nadeau. Ste. Marie, Québec: privately published, 1983. "Oeufs dans le sirop d'érable", "Gâteau Jos. Louis" from *Les meilleures recettes de Maman Mariette* by Mariette Scully Bourque. Notre Dame des Pins, Québec: privately published, 1987.

Charlevoix: "Pâté a l'eperlan" from *La bonne fourchette Charlevoisienne* by Les Filles d'Isabelle du Cercle Madeleine Racine 1159. Baie St. Paul, Québec: privately published, 1985.

Laurentians-Outaouais: "Tarte à la ferlouche" from *Les Recettes de Fermières du Québec.* Chomeday, Laval, Québec: Les Éditions Penelope, Inc., 1978. "Gâteau à la citrouille de Lochaber", "Tire à la mélasse" from *Cent ans de tradition culinaire québecoise* by Le Cercle des Fermières de Thurso. Saint André Avellin, Québec: Les Éditions de la Petite-Nation Inc., 1984.

Côte du Sud: "Langue de boeuf braisée âux légumes", "Esturgeon en ragoût blanc" from *Recettes typiques de la côte du sud* by Mme Charles Gagné. Montreal, Québec: Les Éditions Leméac, 1970. "Crème aux pommes" from *Les meilleures recettes québecoises d'autrefois*, by Suzette Couillard and Roseline Normand. L'Islet Sur Mer, Québec: Diffusion Suzette Couillard Inc., 1986. "Confiture aux mûres" from *Cuisine traditionnelle d'un Québec oublié* by Roseline Normand and Suzette Couillard. L'Islet Sur Mer, Québec: Diffusion Suzette Couillard: 1982. "Pouding aux pommes et à l'érable" from *L'ordinaire 2* by Thérèse Beaulie-Roy. Mont-Joli, Québec: Les Ateliers Plein Soleil Inc., 1979.

Gaspé: "Pouding du chômeur" from *Les recettes de mes amies* by Club Lionnes de Matane. Matane, Québec: privately published, 1982. "Maquereau farci" from *Cuisinons avec les fermières des Îles de la Madeleine.* Îles de la Madeleine, Québec: L'imprimerie Locale, 1986.

Montérégie: "Applesauce bread" from *Recipes* by Hemmingford Branch, Quebec Women's Institutes. Hemmingford, Quebec: privately published, 1972. "Butternutspice cake" from *Old Hemmingford Recipes* by Carol Petch. Hemmingford, Quebec: Imprimie Cyan Printing, 1977.

Mauricie-Lanaudière: "Pâté au saumon", "Soufflé aux navets", "Asperges marinées", "Beignes aux dattes de ma mère", "Tarte aux pommes et au miel" from *Au payes de Laviolette 350 fourchettes* edited by Peggy Lafrenière. Trois Rivières, Québec: Imprimerie St-Patrice enr., 1983. "Potage Livonien", "Oatmeal lace cookies", "Crêpes normandes" from a recipe book published privately by Le Cercle AFEAS de St. Zéphirin de la Tuque. La Tuque, Québec: 1979.

Estrie: "Ragoût d'agneau" from *100 Recettes d'Antan* by Cercle de fermières de Cowansville. Cowansville, Québec: Imprimerie Cowansville, Inc., 1976. "Chaudrée d'hiver", "Salade aux pissenlits", "Crème brulée" from *Nos Recettes Préférées* by Cercle de fermières de Sainte-Edwidge. Compton, Québec: Les Éditions Compton, 1986. "Cream salad dressing" from *Missisquoi Kitchens "Old and New"* by Missisquoi Historical Society. Stanbridge East, Québec: 1985.

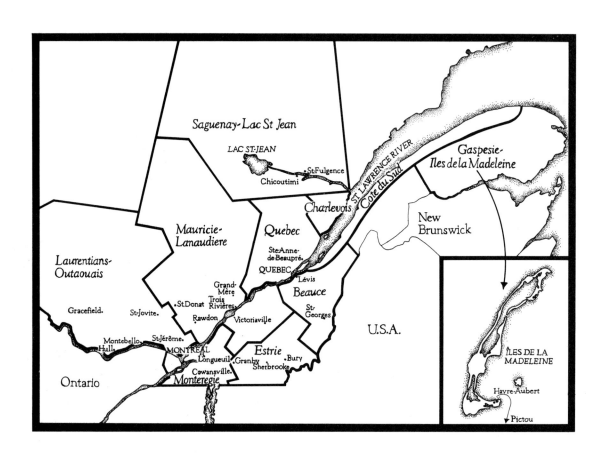

Saguenay-Lac St Jean

LAC ST-JEAN

St-Fulgence

Chicoutimi

ST LAWRENCE RIVER

Côte du Sud

Charlevois

Gaspesie-
Iles de la Madeleine

Mauricie-
Lanaudiere

Quebec

New
Brunswick

Laurentians-
Outaouais

Ste-Anne-
de-Beaupré

QUEBEC

Lévis

Grand-
Mère

Beauce

Gracefield

St-Jovite

St-Donat

Trois
Rivières

St-
Georges

Rawdon

Victoriaville

U.S.A.

ÎLES DE LA
MADELEINE

Montebello

St-Jérôme

Hull

MONTRÉAL

Estrie

Havre-Aubert

Longueuil

Granby

Bury

Cowansville

Sherbrooke

Pictou

Ontario

Montéregie

INTRODUCTION

When the first French settlers arrived in the Quebec region, they brought, along with their baggage load of cast-iron pots and pans, a cooking tradition that makes as much good sense today as it did three centuries ago.

Honest food honestly prepared was their style. Adapting to a wilderness where the luxury of plentiful fish and game was balanced by the penury of long and frigid winters, the colonists developed what culinary historians hail as a regional cuisine that was perfectly in tune with their new land.

Their slow-simmered *ragoûts*, herb-seasoned vegetable soups, hearth-smoked fish, buckwheat crêpes and fruit or maple sugar tarts were prepared using local ingredients, in season when possible or carefully stored when winter closed in.

Foods were used sparingly, for scarcities were constant. Early Quebec cuisine, it's often been stated, was defined by shortages. Fresh foods—meat, fish, fruit and vegetables—regularly ran low and so did products as basic as the grain to make flour, precious spices and oil, sugar and molasses, tea and coffee. Even salt, that most humble of seasonings and preserving agents, was expensive and could become short. Fortunately, the province's pioneer stock had been born frugal, for the homeland of northwestern France was far from rich in many foods we would consider essential.

A century passed before Scots and Irish settlers arrived to add their stamp to food tastes with such favourites as potatoes and oats, dried fruit and nuts. As cooking habits blended, simple recipes continued to be the norm, preparation times short, and cooking times long and easy on the cook. The soup pot could hang for hours, gently bubbling over the embers. If a layered meat and vegetable pie was ready on a trivet, no matter if it had to wait. And a loaf of bread or a pie would not be harmed if the fire happened to die down.

Cooks in the new colony were in as much of a rush to prepare meals as their modern counterparts. Instead of hastening to a job outside the home, mothers had to grow food, harvest and preserve it, make cloth and sew it into the family's clothes, boil up soap and candles, and raise both children and farm livestock. So the time-honoured recipes in this book come largely from French country cooking. Most dishes have a common characteristic—few ingredients, simple assembly, long, slow cooking that requires little or no supervision, and a result that offers substantial nourishment to hard-working settlers.

When I set out to investigate Quebec's culinary past and present, region by region, I had just returned from a food writers' tour of northwestern France. Over and over, through the regions of Normandy, Brittany, Poitou, Bordeaux and Champagne, I had spotted familiar fare on menus or in bakery windows. Normandy's spiced pâté called *rillettes* and cider-flavoured chicken, Brittany's fish stews and plate-sized pancakes and *galettes*, or cookies, *Flamiche aux poireaux* (leek tart) and *Tarte au sucre* (sugar pie) in Champagne country—it was easy to identify the recipes and cooking techniques that have always been part of Quebec cuisine.

Travelling about the province over a period of three years, I found the same core group of dishes wherever I went—pea soup and *tourtière, ragoût de pattes et de boulettes* and *cretons*, pork and beans, sugar pie and *pouding du chômeur*. But, in each region, there were variations in combinations of ingredients, flavour and method. The *pouding du chômeur* is an example: in the Gaspé, the pudding batter is dropped into the hot brown sugar sauce to bake, in comparison with the Saguenay-Lac St. Jean method of pouring the syrup over the batter before baking.

Along the St. Lawrence River, I learned that the similarities are greater than the differences. This is the original New France, where a band of settlements, founded in the 17th century, fanned out along the riverbank. Here were the first seigneuries and—later—Quebec's earliest cities and towns.

The farther I ventured from this long-settled area, north to the Kingdom of the Saguenay, east down the St. Lawrence and around the Gaspé peninsula, the more variations on original themes I found. For example, the *tourtière* of the Saguenay and Lac St. Jean is like no other, the *chiard* or hash of the lower St. Lawrence is made without its usual cooked meat leftovers in the fishing ports of the Côte du sud, and a *cambuse* of the Bay of Chaleurs is a unique braised cod dish made in a way not unlike that of a beef *bouilli* elsewhere.

Suzanne Paré Leclerc, whose job as public relations officer for the provincial department of agriculture, fisheries and food has taken her to every corner of Quebec, points to the isolation in which settlers of these more distant regions lived as explanation for the distinctive character of their recipes.

Marcel Kretz, the classically-trained chef from Alsace who married into a traditional French-Canadian family, discussed Quebec cooking with me one day at his home in Val David. "At the beginning of the colony, most people ate the same basic foods," he said as we studied his mother-in-law's recipes. "Only when they dispersed about the country would different ways of eating appear in the different regions. And what the people of each region would eat would be very much determined by what the particular region had as its native foods, or could produce." The better the cook, Marcel went on, the better and more distinctive a local stamp she would put to the recipes she or her forebears had brought from the old world or the established settlement.

To give each region of the province a distinctive culinary stamp has become a goal of chefs throughout Quebec. With the help of Quebec government funds, the Société des chefs de cuisine et pâtissiers du Québec has embarked on a wide-ranging project to search out each district's best foods, encourage more production of these local specialties, and persuade chefs to serve these foods in light and healthful recipes—dishes that have the stamp of the region without the calories, fat and salt of earlier times. Some of these chefs have contributed their contemporary recipes to this book.

This effort to emphasize regional cuisine started in 1978 at the Montreal chefs' training school Institut de tourisme et d'hôtellerie du Québec.

Up to that time, Quebec was influenced, as was the rest of North America, by commercial food processing and advertising. It was fast becoming a province where pasta was the number one food choice. That opinion belongs to Marcel Bouchard, who hails from Alma on Lac St. Jean and is an innkeeper at Mont Orford southeast of Montreal. But his concern, that the original character of the province's cooking was disappearing and needed to be both identified and preserved, has lately become widespread among chefs, restaurateurs, cooking teachers and gastronomes.

One characteristic that is being accentuated by chefs around the province is the long-established custom of making galantines, aspics, cold stuffed poultry, fish mousses and other elaborate French dishes. As Luc Grand'Maison, born in St. Faustin in the Laurentians and now a chef in St. Sauveur, put it, "The mother cuisine is French—the favourite ingredients, the sauces, the techniques."

This book tells of my explorations as a food journalist in the province I have called home for 34 years. It's a beautiful land with a history both distinctive and fascinating, its people are generous in sharing tales of their family cooking. I hope readers who know Quebec will find old friends among the recipes, and those who visit the province will enjoy seeking out these dishes from its past and present as much as I have. Bon appétit.

QUEBEC REGION

 When Jacques Cartier sailed up the St. Lawrence River in 1535, he described the shoreline east of Quebec City as a "beau pré"—beautiful meadow. When he saw the grapevines on the Île d'Orléans, the French explorer initially named the island Île de Bacchus after the god of wine. Cartier was not the first man to appreciate the fertility of this region, which was the earliest part of the province to be colonized and still one of its lushest market gardening areas.

As I searched for early food customs on the Beaupré shore, I travelled along the old avenue Royale, or Chemin du Roy as Route 360 used to be called. Every few houses, I saw roadside gardens and vegetable stands overflowing with the same trio of vegetables the Indians grew, the corn still labelled Indian corn more frequently than *mais sucré*, or sweet corn—its other name in this province.

Beans continue to be enjoyed too, dried and baked with pork in the traditional *fèves au lard*—or *les binnes*, as I often heard the dish referred to in conversation. And squash still thrives in fields that are as long and narrow as they were in seigneurial times.

Although the old stone and whitewashed farmhouses give an illusion that time halted about 1700, modern agricultural science is improving some of the foods that date back three centuries or more. Game birds bred at the island's Ferme Orléans give a taste of the wild, but with an extra proportion of delicately flavoured meat. I dined on a tender little bird called a *pintadine*, a plump one-serving size guinea hen, before I went to call on Renée Lauzière, the Île d'Orléans bird-breeding specialist.

Her family farm, on a rolling, hilly stretch on the south side of the island, presents quite a sight. This dynamic woman showed me tiny quail in rows of coops, and then walked me around fields of guinea hens, pheasants, partridge, pigeons, duckling and *sauvagines*—her special crossbreed of wild and domestic duck. She stopped on top of a hill to explain that we were looking at the latest members of her feathered family—ducks of the type the chefs of Normandy use to make *Canard à la rouennaise*, Rouen duck.

Strawberries, the island's favourite fruit, are another food that has been improved. Growers André Gosselin and Louis Gauthier have successfully launched a late season strawberry at their farm near the village of St. Laurent.

Such specialties are welcomed by Quebec City chefs, who compete with chefs in the larger gastronomic centre of Montreal in the quality and variety of their restaurants. A few restaurateurs in this region have played a leading role in making sure the dishes of the early settlers are not forgotten. And their chefs have lightened the caloric load of the original cuisine, now that most of us are not chopping down trees or guiding a plough for a living.

Restaurant Aux Anciens Canadiens, located in adjoining Quebec City houses dating back to 1675, serves virtually every well-known early dish, plus new combinations of local foods such as lamb with blueberry wine, breast of turkey with hazelnut sauce and scallops poached in cider. I had a sense of the close community the early settlers must have enjoyed when I went to this restaurant, walking down a narrow sidestreet from one of the comfortable old stone guesthouses behind the Château Frontenac and circling the courtyard of the original Ursuline convent before I ducked in the doorway of the friendly, old restaurant.

At L'Atre, a restored 1680 farmhouse near the Île d'Orléans village of St. Famille, specialties include *cretons*, the pork pâté that is compared to the French *rillettes*; a rabbit terrine; a lean and spicy *tourtière*; and a garlic-flavoured *ragoût de petites boulettes* (meatball stew).

Just how delectable the simplest recipe can be was impressed upon me by L'Atre's most popular dessert, *Tartine d'Antan*. It's nothing more than a thick slab of homemade bread topped with shavings of maple sugar and the island's thick cream. It's also how food ought to taste. When I asked Suzanne Howard Demers, L'Atre's creator, about the cream, she grinned. "Island cows graze well here," she said, and that was as close to the formula as I could come.

Onions are the number one flavouring throughout Quebec but leeks are a characteristic of island cooking, according to older cooks. They add leeks to the staple *soupe aux pois*, the favourite pea soup, to a *bouilli* (boiled dinner) or *pot-au-feu*, to a *sauce blanche* for chicken or vegetables, and to a tart with links to the Flamiche or leek pie found in northern France and Flanders.

Herbs, in particular chives and savoury, are another habit and one that dates back to the Ursulines' first gardens in Quebec City and later on the island too. Those herb plots also included today's big four—parsley, sage, rosemary and thyme, and herbs continue to be used with a generous hand.

Quebec Menu

Crab custard with lemon
butter sauce
(page 6)

Old-fashioned beef in
red wine
(page 18)

Sliced tomatoes with capers

Poached pears with
wine custard
(page 20)

FLAN DE CRABE AU BEURRE CITRONNÉ

Crab custard with lemon butter sauce

In this recipe Quebec snow crab is combined with broccoli, oven-poached and served on a sauce, nouvelle cuisine fashion. The appetizer is the creation of Chef Denis Pelletier of Moulin de St. Laurent, a contemporary French restaurant located in an old stone mill in the village of St. Laurent on Île d'Orléans. Ramekins can be filled ahead and oven-poached at the last minute, or you can reheat the cooked *flan* in a microwave oven for about 2 minutes at Medium (50 percent).

---

1 medium bunch broccoli, cut into small florets
½ pound (250 g) fresh or frozen crab meat, trimmed
   of cartilage
3 eggs
¾ cup (175 mL) whipping cream
¾ cup (175 mL) milk
Salt and ground white pepper
Pinch ground nutmeg
Lemon Butter Sauce (recipe follows)

Cook broccoli florets in boiling salted water just until tender-crisp; drain. Generously brush 6 to 8 ramekins or custard cups with melted butter.

Divide crab meat and broccoli among the ramekins. In a bowl, whisk together the eggs, cream and milk; season with salt, pepper and nutmeg. Fill ramekins three-quarters full with the custard and set in a shallow pan of hot water. Oven-poach at 325°F (160°C) for 1 hour or until set. (A knife, inserted in centre, should come out clean.)

Make Lemon Butter Sauce and pour onto 6 to 8 serving plates. Run a knife around the edge of each ramekin and unmould onto sauce. Six to eight servings.

Lemon butter sauce

½ cup (125 mL) white wine
1 dry shallot, finely chopped
1 cup (250 mL) unsalted butter, cut into pieces
¼ cup (50 mL) whipping cream
Juice of 1 lemon

In a small saucepan, heat wine and chopped shallot. Bring to a boil and reduce over medium-high heat until only 2 tablespoons (25 mL) of liquid remain. Reduce heat to low and whisk in butter, a few pieces at a time, until sauce is smooth and all the butter is incorporated. Whisk in cream and lemon juice. Keep warm in the top of a double boiler set over hot water until serving time. Makes about 1½ cups (375 mL) sauce.

MICROWAVE METHOD

Crab Custard: Rinse broccoli florets in cold water and place in a 4-cup (1 L) casserole. Cover and microwave at High (100 percent) for 2 to 3 minutes or until just tender.

Divide crab and broccoli among 6 to 8 lightly buttered ramekins or custard cups.

Prepare custard as directed in recipe and divide among the ramekins, filling each three-quarters full. Cover each ramekin with plastic wrap and place in microwave, arranging in a ring formation. Microwave at Medium (50 percent) for 12 to 14 minutes or until custard has set, rearranging once during cooking. Let stand for 5 to 10 minutes before unmoulding.*

* Test for doneness: Edges of custard are set and centres are barely moist.

Auberge La Goéliche

Staying in this turreted and gingerbread-trimmed inn is like staying in a family-owned château, or maybe an early riverboat. A Victorian landmark on the western tip of Île d'Orléans, it's being renovated by new owners. Already, its dining room at water level serves some of the finest contemporary cuisine in the region. Ocean-bound craft pass so close that guests can wave to passengers from the verandahs or many of the comfortable white-painted bedrooms. Explore the pretty old village of St. Pétronille, swim in the outdoor pool, or golf nearby. Cross-country ski on the island, or try downhill skiing a short drive across the Felix Leclerc bridge and east to Mont St. Anne. Moderate rates. (Rooms: 27, most with private bath; address: 22 du Quai Ave., St. Pétronille, Île d'Orléans, Québec, G0A 4C0; telephone: (418) 828-2248.)

China pie explained

A meat pie named *pâté chinois* is found on menus throughout Quebec. It has no connection with Chinese cuisine. Instead, it's a French-Canadian term for shepherd's pie, the combination of ground-up roasted meat, gravy and mashed potatoes. The name has been traced by Quebec food historian Claude Poirier to a town in the state of Maine called China. In the late 19th century, thousands of Quebecers migrated to the northeastern United States to work in the mills. Those who settled in the town of China eventually returned to Quebec with a recipe for shepherd's pie which they called *pâté chinois*.

Lemon Butter Sauce: In a 4-cup (1 L) glass measure, combine wine and shallot. Microwave, uncovered, at High (100 percent) for 7 to 8 minutes until all but 2 tablespoons (25 mL) of liquid has evaporated. Whisk in a quarter of the butter at a time and microwave at Medium (50 percent) for 20 to 30 seconds, whisking well after each addition, until all the butter has been incorporated into sauce and sauce is smooth. Whisk in cream and lemon juice. Microwave, uncovered, at Medium (50 percent) for 30 to 45 seconds more, until sauce is hot.

Tartare de pétoncle Fleurs de mer

Scallop flower appetizer

Chef Francine Roy learned to love scallops when she and her husband André ran a restaurant in Îles de la Madeleine in the Gulf of St. Lawrence. Now co-proprietors of La Camarine, she likes to marinate the fresh shellfish in lime juice, then arrange them to resemble the petals of flowers.

---

3 large fresh scallops
Juice of 1 lime
Salt
Chives
2 tiny sliced carrot rounds

Using only the freshest scallops, slice each horizontally into 3 or 4 slices. Marinate in lime juice with a little salt for about 15 minutes or until scallop slices have lost their transparent look.

On a plate of contrasting colour, arrange scallop slices as if they were the petals of 2 flowers. Use chives as flower stems and leaves and a carrot round as the centre of each flower. Serve cold. One serving. Recipe may be doubled or tripled, as desired.

PÂTÉ DE FOIE GRAS
À L'ANCIENNE

Old-fashioned calves' liver pâté

This pâté recipe can be traced back to the traditional cooking of Normandy. Use of the term *foie gras* for this blended preparation troubles classically trained French chefs, who reserve the words for specially fattened goose or duck liver. However, this particular recipe has been in the family of Kathleen Fiset Pineau of Quebec City for a century or more by this name. It is "not recommended for our cholesterol" she says of her special occasion dish.

1¼ to 1½ pounds (625 to 750 g) fresh pork fat*
¾ pound (375 g) calves' or goose liver
2 cloves garlic, crushed
2 tablespoons (25 mL) Cognac or brandy
½ teaspoon (2 mL) salt
Ground black pepper
Pinch ground nutmeg and dried rosemary
Truffles (optional)
2 or 3 bay leaves

　* Do not use salt pork.

Grind three-quarters of a pound (375 g) of the pork fat with the liver. Blend in garlic, Cognac, salt, pepper, nutmeg and rosemary, mixing well with a spoon or hands.

　Cut remaining pork fat into thin strips. Line 2 or 3 small moulds (2 to 3 cups/500 to 750 mL) with some of the strips of fat. Place a truffle, if desired, and a bay leaf in each mould. Add liver mixture and cover with more strips of the fat. Place moulds in a pan of hot water and oven-poach at 325°F (160°C) for 2 to 3 hours, depending on size of moulds. Cool, then chill. Serve cold as a spread on crackers or toast. Makes about 2 pounds (1 kg) pâté.

Les Poireaux

Strawberries, raspberries and small blue plums have long been the region's favourite fruits. But it's from the vegetables that the farmers originally acquired their nicknames. In the Beauport area north of Quebec City, the *habitants* were traditionally called *les oignons de Beauport*, while the farmers of Île d'Orléans are still teased with the name *les poireaux* because of their fondness for growing and eating leeks.

PÂTÉ AUX POIREAUX
Leek tart

This leek and cheese quiche from Île d'Orléans is related to the *Flamiche aux poireaux*, a savoury leek tart made in northern France and Flanders. The recipe can also be used to make small tarts.

---

6 tablespoons (75 mL) butter
4 to 5 leeks, finely chopped
½ cup (125 mL) water
2 tablespoons (25 mL) all-purpose flour
Salt and ground black pepper
1 egg
2 tablespoons (25 mL) light cream
1 cup (250 mL) mild white Cheddar cheese, grated
Pastry for a 9-inch (23 cm) tart shell

Heat 4 tablespoons (50 mL) of the butter in a heavy saucepan, add leeks and cook over low heat for 10 minutes. Add water, cover and simmer gently for 20 to 25 minutes or until tender.

In another saucepan, melt the remaining two tablespoons (25 mL) butter, blend in flour and cook over medium heat until bubbling. Blend in leek mixture, bring to a boil and season with salt and pepper. Remove from heat.

Beat egg and cream together, blend into leek mixture and pour into unbaked tart shell. Sprinkle top evenly with cheese. Bake in a preheated 400°F (200°C) oven for 25 to 30 minutes or until cheese begins to brown. Six servings.

SALADE DE CHOU

Cabbage salad

Traditional Quebec cooks often choose coleslaw as their favourite fresh salad. In the days before imported fresh vegetables, they made sauerkraut to last the winter. This recipe from an Île d'Orléans collection colours the salad with carrots and flavours it with mustard and celery seed.

¾ cup (175 mL) granulated sugar
¾ cup (175 mL) vegetable oil
1 cup (250 mL) white vinegar
2 teaspoons (10 mL) prepared mustard
2 teaspoons (10 mL) celery seed
1 teaspoon (5 mL) salt
1 large cabbage, chopped or shredded
2 carrots, peeled, grated
2 onions, finely chopped

In a medium saucepan, combine sugar, oil, vinegar, mustard, celery seed and salt. Bring to a boil, then cool slightly. In a large bowl, combine cabbage, carrots and onions. Pour warm sauce over vegetables, stirring to blend ingredients. Cover and refrigerate for several hours. Salad will keep in the refrigerator for a week or more. Sixteen servings.

MICROWAVE METHOD

Sauce: In a 4-cup (1 L) glass measure or casserole, combine sugar, oil, vinegar, mustard, celery seed and salt. Microwave, uncovered, at High (100 percent) for 4 to 5 minutes, just until sugar is dissolved and mixture comes to a boil, stirring twice. Let cool slightly. Continue with recipe as directed.

I welcome and I nourish

A sheaf of wheat, a grape vine and apples decorate the crest of the Île d'Orléans along with a map of the island county, six crosses which mark its six parishes, and the motto *J'accueille et je nourris.*

Ragoût de petites boulettes et de pattes de cochon

Meatball and pork hocks stew

Slow, careful cooking gives this time-honoured dish a rich flavour despite its humble ingredients. This dish is served frequently at L'Atre, the restaurant at St. Famille on Île d'Orléans which is located in a stone farmhouse dating back to 1680. Serve with miniature potato pancakes and pickled beets and cucumbers.

---

2 pork hocks (1½ pounds/750 g)
¼ cup (50 mL) all-purpose flour
Salt and ground black pepper
2 tablespoons (25 mL) butter
2 carrots
1 stalk celery
2 medium onions, quartered
1 bay leaf

Dredge pork hocks in flour seasoned with salt and pepper. In a large, heavy frying pan, brown pork in hot butter until it turns a deep, rich brown. Transfer to a large, heavy saucepan and cover with water. Add carrots, celery, onions and bay leaf. Season with salt and pepper to taste. Bring to a boil, skim off any foam that forms on top, and simmer until meat is tender, about 1½ to 2 hours.

Strain stock and return to saucepan. Remove meat from the bones, cut up and set aside. Return bones to stock and simmer very slowly for 2 more hours. Skim off fat, strain and reduce stock over medium heat to about 4 cups (1 L). Set aside.

Ragoût

The humble *ragoût de boulettes* (meatball stew) was once a festive dish on Île d'Orléans. Families would enjoy it only on Easter and New Year's Day. The original recipe called for lean ground pork plus a choice of beef, veal or chicken. Spiced and browned flour – the original gravy maker – gave flavour. In the 17th century, *ragoût aux oiseaux blancs* (pigeon stew) seasoned with onions and spices was a favourite dish.

Meatballs

---

1 pound (500 g) ground veal
2 pounds (1 kg) ground pork
¼ cup (50 mL) chopped fresh parsley
3 cloves garlic, minced
2 slices dry (or stale) bread, crumbled
¼ teaspoon (1 mL) ground cloves
Pinch ground allspice
Salt and ground black pepper
2 tablespoons (25 mL) butter
2 tablespoons (25 mL) sunflower or vegetable oil
¼ cup (50 mL) dry white wine

Combine ground veal and pork with parsley, garlic, crumbled bread, cloves, allspice, salt and pepper to taste. Shape into small balls, about 1 inch (2.5 cm) in diameter.

Heat butter and oil in a large, heavy frying pan and brown meatballs quickly on all sides. Transfer meatballs to a large, heavy flameproof casserole. Discard fat in frying pan and deglaze pan with wine. Add to meatballs in casserole along with reserved pork stock. Simmer gently, covered, for about 1 hour, adding reserved cooked pork after 30 minutes. Eight to ten servings.

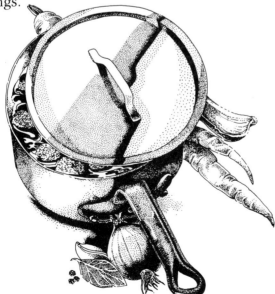

Tourtière de Québec
Quebec pork pie

This *tourtière* recipe is the region's traditional pork and vegetable pie. It belongs to Kathleen Fiset Pineau of Quebec City and was one of the winners of a 1984 *tourtière* contest conducted by *The Gazette* of Montreal. Mme Pineau originally obtained the recipe from an aunt who lived on the south shore of the St. Lawrence River. She considers it is the Quebec style; the use of rolled oats instead of potatoes to thicken the filling shows a Scottish influence.

1¼ pounds (625 g) ground pork
½ to ¾ cup (125 to 175 mL) cold water
½ cup (125 mL) finely chopped onion
¼ cup (50 mL) finely chopped celery
½ teaspoon (2 mL) ground black pepper
1 bay leaf
½ teaspoon (2 mL) dried savoury
¼ teaspoon (1 mL) dried rosemary
¼ teaspoon (1 mL) grated nutmeg
Pinch cinnamon
Salt
¼ cup (50 mL) old-fashioned rolled oats
Pastry for double-crust, 9-inch (23 cm) pie

In a large, heavy frying pan, combine pork with cold water and heat to boiling point. Add onion, celery, pepper, bay leaf, savoury, rosemary, nutmeg and cinnamon. Cook, covered, over medium-low heat for 1¼ hours, adding more water if mixture dries out. Halfway through cooking time, season with salt to taste. Stir in rolled oats and cook, stirring, for 1 to 2 minutes. Remove bay leaf.

Meanwhile, line a 9-inch (23 cm) pie plate with pastry. When meat mixture is lukewarm, spoon into pie shell and cover with remaining pastry. Trim

pastry, seal edges and cut steam vents in top crust.
Decorate as desired. Bake in preheated 425°F
(220°C) oven for 15 minutes, then reduce heat to
375°F (190°C) and bake another 25 minutes or until
crust is golden. Six servings.

Confiture aigre-douce
Fruit vegetable relish

This colourful chutney-type relish is served with the
tourtière at L'Atre, the restaurant in St. Famille on Île
d'Orléans. Proprietress Suzanne Howard Demers
makes a big batch at harvest time.

---

3 onions, chopped
1 stalk celery, chopped
2 green peppers, halved, seeded, coarsely chopped
6 tomatoes, peeled and chopped
6 peaches, or 1 can (19 ounces/540 mL), peeled and
   coarsely chopped
6 apples, cores removed, peeled, coarsely chopped
6 pears, cores removed, peeled, coarsely chopped
2 cups (500 mL) cider vinegar
1½ cups (375 mL) granulated sugar
3 tablespoons (45 mL) coarse salt
4 teaspoons (20 mL) pickling spices, tied in a
   cheesecloth bag

Combine onions, celery, peppers, tomatoes, peaches,
apples and pears in a large, heavy saucepan with
vinegar, sugar, salt and spice bag. Bring to a boil and
simmer, uncovered, for about 1 hour or until
thickened. Remove spice bag; ladle relish into
sterilized jars and seal. Makes about 3 to 4 one-pint
(500 mL) jars.

Tourtière

Culinary historians debate
whether this seasoned meat
pie was originally named
after the *tourte*, or *oiseau
blanc*, a white passenger
pigeon that was once
numerous on the south
coast of Île d'Orléans and a
one-time basic in pies and
stews, or for the French
cooking utensil *tourtière*,
used to cook the pie. Most
agree it was the dish that
determined the name.
Meats, potatoes and
seasonings vary, region by
region, but not its
popularity, particularly at
Christmas.

Angelica

Cakes baked in the 17th-century Ursuline convent in Quebec City regularly included angelica. Green stalks of this aromatic plant were candied and used as both a flavouring and decoration. It continues to be available in specialty shops.

LA PINTADINE DE L'ÎLE D'ORLÉANS AUX GROSEILLES

Île d'Orléans guinea hen with red currants

Miniature guinea hens, raised at a game bird farm near the island village of St. Laurent, are flavoured with red currants in this delicious dish from Chef Janet Duplain of Auberge La Goéliche in St. Pétronille. Rock Cornish hens or chicken breasts may be substituted for the tiny birds, but they will require slightly more cooking. Serve with fresh buttered noodles and vegetables in season.

---

2 guinea hens (1 pound/500 g each), or 2 Rock Cornish hens, or 2 large, skinless, boned chicken breasts
1 tablespoon (15 mL) vegetable oil
1 tablespoon (15 mL) butter
1 tablespoon (15 mL) red currant vinegar*
½ cup (125 mL) veal or chicken stock
1 tablespoon (15 mL) red currant jelly
¼ cup (50 mL) whipping cream
8 fresh or preserved red currants**

  * This vinegar is available in specialty shops. White vinegar sweetened with a little sugar may be substituted.
** A brand made in France called Bonne Maman is recommended.

Cut guinea hens in half lengthwise. Heat oil and butter in large, heavy frying pan and add guinea hens, skin side down. Brown quickly over medium heat, reduce heat to medium-low and cook, turning at intervals, for about 15 minutes, until juices run clear. Remove from pan and, while meat is still warm, remove and discard breast bones, leaving leg bones intact. (This should not be difficult because the meat is cooked.) Set meat aside and keep warm.

Make sauce by discarding drippings in pan and deglazing pan with vinegar. Add veal stock and jelly; stir briskly for 2 to 3 minutes until sauce is smooth. Stir in cream and red currants. Serve sauce over halved guinea hens. Two servings.

CRÊPES À NICOLE

Potato pancakes

The potato, Quebec's top vegetable, is grown in such large quantities around St. Ubalde, northwest of Quebec City, that the Club optimiste de St. Ubalde published a collection of over 200 recipes using the vegetable. Marie Claire Cauchon, who persuaded cooks of all ages to part with their favourites, says these crêpes are one of St. Ubalde's best-liked dishes.

---

2 cups (500 mL) peeled, grated raw potatoes
2 tablespoons (25 mL) minced onion
2 tablespoons (25 mL) all-purpose flour
½ teaspoon (2 mL) baking powder
½ teaspoon (2 mL) salt, or to taste
Pinch ground black pepper
2 eggs, lightly beaten
Oil for frying

In a bowl, combine potatoes, onion, flour, baking powder, salt and pepper. Blend in beaten eggs. Heat enough oil to coat the bottom of a crêpe pan or heavy frying pan. Drop batter by tablespoonfuls (15 mL) into hot oil and fry 2 minutes per side or until golden. Keep crêpes warm while cooking remaining batter. Serve hot. Four servings.

BOEUF À L'ANCIENNE AU VIN ROUGE

Old-fashioned beef in red wine

Suzanne Howard Demers, who owns the restaurant L'Atre on Île d'Orléans, found this recipe in *The Art of Cookery Made Easy*, an 1869 cookbook in the library of the Ursulines' convent in Quebec City. It's a rustic version of *Boeuf bourguignon*. She likes to marinate the meat for 24 hours before browning it, immersing the cubes of beef in the wine mixed with a little vegetable oil, the chopped shallots and carrots, and a sliced onion. The menu of her St. Famille restaurant records this tip from the old cookbook: "Note that you must take great care in doing your beef this way that your fire is low." At L'Atre, this dish is served with a salad, either tossed greens or sliced tomatoes with capers.

---

3 tablespoons (45 mL) butter
3 tablespoons (45 mL) vegetable oil
2 pounds (1 kg) lean boneless beef chuck or rump,
    cut in 2-inch (5 cm) cubes
Bouquet garni*
1 small carrot, finely chopped
2 dry shallots, finely chopped
2 tablespoons (25 mL) all-purpose flour
1 cup (250 mL) beef stock
1½ cups (375 mL) dry red wine
1 tablespoon (15 mL) tomato paste
2 cloves garlic, finely chopped
1 teaspoon (5 mL) dried savoury
½ teaspoon (2 mL) dried thyme
Salt and ground black pepper
20 small white onions, peeled
½ pound (250 g) fresh mushrooms

4 carrots, peeled, sliced
4 medium potatoes, peeled, cubed
2 tablespoons (25 mL) finely chopped fresh parsley

* Three parsley sprigs and a bay leaf tied in a cheesecloth
bag.

In a heavy frying pan, heat 1 tablespoon (15 mL) of the butter with the oil and brown beef cubes, a few at a time, on all sides. (If you have marinated the beef, drain and dry it before browning, reserving marinade to add in place of wine specified in recipe.) Use a slotted spoon to transfer beef to a casserole that has a cover. Bury the bouquet garni in the meat.

Sauté chopped carrot and shallots in the frying pan until golden. Sprinkle with flour, adding a little oil if mixture appears dry. Cook, stirring, until flour browns.

Pour in beef stock, stirring well. Blend in wine and tomato paste and bring to a boil, stirring constantly, until sauce thickens. Mix in garlic, savoury, thyme and salt and pepper to taste, and pour sauce over beef. The sauce should almost cover the meat; add more beef stock or wine if necessary. Cover casserole and bake in a 350°F (180°C) oven for 2 hours.

Half an hour before meat is cooked, heat remaining 2 tablespoons (25 mL) butter in frying pan and sauté small white onions. Remove from pan. If mushrooms are small, leave whole; if large, cut in quarters. Sauté mushrooms in frying pan. About 15 minutes before meat is cooked, add onions, carrots and potatoes to casserole. When vegetables are just tender, add mushrooms and continue cooking for another 5 minutes. To serve, remove bouquet garni and sprinkle with chopped parsley. Six to eight servings.

LA POIRE POCHÉE ET SON SABAYON AU MUSCAT

Poached pears with wine custard

A raspberry *coulis* or sauce is the final accent to this elegant fruit dessert. It's a specialty at La Camarine in Beaupré. Francine and André Roy, who ran a restaurant in Îles de la Madeleine, named La Camarine after the wild fruit found on the islands. Larger than a blueberry and bitter, it covers the grassy hills and sand dunes of the islands like a carpet each August.

---

4 pears, such as Bartlett or Anjou
4 cups (1 L) water
1⅓ cups (325 mL) granulated sugar
Juice of 1 lemon
Wine Custard (recipe follows)
Raspberry Coulis (recipe follows)
Mint leaves

Peel pears whole, keeping tip and stem intact, and scoop out cores. Combine water, sugar and lemon juice in a large saucepan. Bring to a boil, lower heat and simmer syrup for 5 minutes. Add pears and simmer in syrup for 10 to 15 minutes, just until tender. Using a slotted spoon, remove fruit from syrup and let cool slightly.

To serve, carefully slice poached pears lengthwise in thin slices, keeping the slices attached to the stem. Place on a baking sheet and fan out slices. Place under a preheated broiler until golden-brown.

Divide hot Wine Custard among 4 dessert plates. Carefully pour Raspberry Coulis around outside of custard sauce. Place broiled pears in centre of custard. Trim stems with mint leaves. Four servings.

Wine custard

---

4 egg yolks
¼ cup (50 mL) instant dissolving sugar
⅔ cup (150 mL) Muscadet white wine

Combine egg yolks, sugar and wine in the top of a
double boiler set over simmering water. Using an
electric mixer, beat mixture until custard thickens
enough to form a ribbon when dropped from a
spoon, about 5 to 7 minutes.

Raspberry coulis

---

2 cups (500 mL) fresh raspberries, or 1 package
   (300 g) frozen, unsweetened raspberries, thawed
½ to ⅔ cup (125 to 150 mL) granulated sugar
Juice of 1 lemon

Place raspberries, sugar and lemon juice in a food
processor or blender and purée until smooth. Strain
through a sieve to remove seeds.

MICROWAVE METHOD

Poached Pears: Place 2 cups (500 mL) water, ¾ cup
(175 mL) granulated sugar and the juice of 1 lemon
in deep casserole just large enough to hold the pears.
Microwave, uncovered, at High (100 percent) for 5 to
6 minutes or until liquid comes to a full boil and
sugar is dissolved, stirring once during cooking. Add
pears and microwave, covered, at High (100 percent)
for 7 to 8 minutes, just until tender, rearranging them
halfway through cooking. Remove from syrup using a
slotted spoon; let cool.

Wine Custard: In an 8-cup (2 L) bowl, beat egg yolks
and sugar with an electric mixer until thick and
lemon-coloured. Beat in Muscadet wine. Microwave,
uncovered, at Medium (50 percent) for 4 to 5
minutes, beating every minute with a wire whisk,
until custard is thick and creamy.

Pumpkins

These big, orange members
of the squash family were
grown in the Quebec City
region from the time of the
Iroquois Indians. French
explorer Jacques Cartier
thought they were melons.
Marie de l'Incarnation,
foundress of the Ursuline
convent, sent seeds of
citrouilles des Iroquois
(Iroquois pumpkins) back to
France in 1668 along with
tips on how to fry this food,
make it into a cream soup,
bake it in the oven like
apples or braise it like pears.

Strawberries

Traditional family cooks in the region make *beignes* (doughnuts) and stud them, while still hot, with fresh strawberries. And Canada's first strawberry shortcake was doubtless the firm-textured *galette* baked by the Ursulines and served with a layer of crushed fruit.

TARTE DU MANOIR AUX DATTES ET AUX NOIX
Country-style date nut pie

This rich, strongly flavoured dessert is one of the favourites on the menu at Restaurant Aux Anciens Canadiens in Quebec City. The tradition of cooking with dried fruit goes back to the earliest colonial times.

½ cup (125 mL) butter, at room temperature
1 cup (250 mL) packed light brown sugar
4 eggs
1 teaspoon (5 mL) cinnamon
½ teaspoon (2 mL) ground nutmeg
1 teaspoon (5 mL) vanilla
¾ cup (175 mL) whipping cream
½ cup (125 mL) chopped dates
½ cup (125 mL) raisins
½ cup (125 mL) chopped walnuts
1 unbaked, single-crust, 9-inch (23 cm) pie shell

In a bowl, cream butter with brown sugar until fluffy. Beat in eggs, 1 at a time, until incorporated. Blend in cinnamon, nutmeg, vanilla and cream, mixing well. Stir in dates, raisins and nuts. Pour filling into prepared pie shell. Bake in a preheated 350°F (180°C) oven for 45 minutes or until top is firm and lightly browned. Eight servings.

LES FRAISES VINAIGRETTE ET LEURS POUSSES VERTES

Strawberry spinach salad

Strawberries need not be confined to dessert, says Denis Pelletier, chef at Restaurant Le Moulin de St. Laurent on Île d'Orléans. The island is one of the province's lushest strawberry-growing areas. The chef suggests serving this colourful salad with a semi-soft cheese such as St. Nectaire.

½ cup (125 mL) raspberry vinegar
½ cup (125 mL) vegetable oil
1 cup (250 mL) water
3 dry shallots, finely chopped
Freshly ground black pepper
2 pint boxes (1 L) fresh strawberries, sliced
1 pound (500 g) trimmed fresh spinach

Make salad dressing by combining vinegar, oil and water. Add chopped shallots and pepper to taste. Arrange spinach leaves on a large platter. Arrange sliced strawberries in a spiral formation on the spinach and drizzle with the dressing. Six servings.

SAGUENAY-LAC ST. JEAN

 The nickname for a person from the Saguenay-Lac St. Jean region is *bleuet*, or blueberry, and its use is more likely to produce a smile than a frown. Residents of this remote, northeastern area of Quebec are proud of their reputation for harvesting more wild blueberries than anyone else in the province.

The most distinctive regional cuisine in Quebec is found in "the kingdom of the Saguenay," the name French explorer Jacques Cartier gave to the area in 1535. The *tourtière* here is different, a lavishly layered dish best made with the game that is so abundant in the forests north of Lac St. Jean. The favourite soup is made with the big, green, red-streaked bean known as the *gourgane*, which is just as popular here as in Charlevoix. And the kingdom has its own special fish, the land-locked salmon called *ouananiche*, now so rare that families consider themselves lucky to eat it once a year.

Despite the trend to two-career families, dining out and fast food, the people of this region continue to eat most of their meals at home. This means that, even though the pace of life has quickened, traditional recipes are in regular use. When I was living in Jonquière for three weeks as a student at the Centre Linguistique, I enjoyed such local specialties as the distinctive *soupe aux gourganes* and *tourtière du Saguenay* in private homes. The only restaurant examples I found were at the fairgrounds of the annual August blueberry festival at Mistassini. Mont Orford innkeeper Marcel Bouchard, for 10 years a restaurateur in his native Alma, explains: "Everyone who eats out wants something different from what they have so often at home."

"You often hear, 'This is my grandmother's recipe,' " says Mme Cécile Roland Bouchard, author of the 1971 book *Le pinereau: l'art culinaire au saguenay-lac-saint jean*. Her book, named for the camp kitchen of the early logging camps, was hailed by Quebec folklore historians as a model that other regions should follow.

Blueberry stories have been part of the folklore of this lush, food-producing region since the days of fur trapping and logging. Various Indian tribes had long enjoyed the fruit, sometimes combined with the dried meat called pemmican, sometimes blended with other fruits such as raspberries.

The first sight of a blueberry field is a surprising experience. It's as if a smoky, blue haze has settled over the land—the same blue of distant mountains that ring the fertile plain around Lac St. Jean. Skilled cultivators burn the *bleuetières*, or blueberry fields, each spring, fertilize the wild plants, add bees to help with pollination and get ready to welcome entire families of blueberry pickers each August. The result: both fresh and frozen fruit, and such modern blueberry products as an apéritif called Dubleuet, a wine and a syrup.

Blueberries that are truly wild can still be found in the area's forests. They're larger than the tiny, flavour-packed fruit that is produced on the farms. Some are reputed to grow as big as grapes. These big berries play a larger-than-life role for some, such as Chicoutimi's primitive painter Arthur Villeneuve. The elderly artist, who sells his *naif* scenes of regional life for thousands of dollars, won't part with his painting of a rustic scene of blueberry pickers beside a blueberry-blue river. When I visited his house, a modest clapboard which he has turned into a museum by painting murals on every wall, I asked the old gentleman why the blueberries in his painting were the size of apples. He grinned. "It takes only three to make a tart," he said, repeating a regional expression.

Salted herbs

Herbs preserved with vegetables and salt make a lively seasoning for soups—particularly pea soup—sauces, stews and omelettes. A commercial brand, Les Herbes Salées du bas du fleuve, is marketed by J.Y. Roy of St. Flavie and can be found in Montreal specialty stores. This recipe comes from the Métis district.

---

1 cup (250 mL) chopped
    fresh chives
1 cup (250 mL) chopped
    fresh savoury
1 cup (250 mL) chopped
    fresh parsley
1 cup (250 mL) chopped
    fresh chervil
1 cup (250 mL) grated carrots
1 cup (250 mL) chopped
    celery leaves
1 cup (250 mL) chopped
    green onions
¼ to ½ cup (50 to 125 mL)
    coarse salt

In a large bowl, combine herbs and vegetables. Layer 1 inch (2.5 cm) of herb mixture in the bottom of a crock or glass bowl and sprinkle with some of the salt. Repeat layers until all of herb mixture and salt is used.
    Cover and refrigerate for 2 weeks. Drain off accumulated liquid and pack herb mixture into sterilized jars. Refrigerate until ready to use. Makes about 5 to 6 cups (1.25 to 1.5 L).

SOUPE À L'IVROGNE

Drunkard's soup

Economical, easy-to-make and satisfying, this soup is thus named because it could sustain a drunkard's family when food money was short. Other theories are that it's a fast meal to make when you have a hangover or that it's a cure for a hangover. Micheline Mongrain-Dontigny included it in *150 Recettes pour Saguenay-Lac-St-Jean à cuisinier*, the cookbook she wrote to mark the 150th anniversary of settlement of the Saguenay-Lac St. Jean region.

---

2 tablespoons (25 mL) commercially prepared or
    homemade salted herbs (see margin note)
¼ pound (125 g) salt pork, cut into small cubes
3 large onions, chopped
6 slices white bread, cubed
8 cups (2 L) beef stock
Salt and ground black pepper

Soak herbs in cold water, then drain. Fry salt pork until crisp and brown in a large, heavy frying pan. Add onions and sauté until browned. Add bread cubes to the frying pan; toss to coat well. Place frying pan in a preheated 350°F (180°C) oven for 15 minutes to toast bread lightly.
    Transfer mixture to a large, heavy saucepan. Add beef stock and salted herbs. Simmer gently for 1 hour. Adjust seasoning with salt and pepper. Eight to ten servings.

Photo:
Saguenay meat pie (page 28)

SOUPE AUX GOURGANES
Bean soup

The big, meaty bean called *gourgane*, brought from France by the earliest settlers, has been grown in China since the 10th century BC. Each year Lac St. Jean growers dry and export millions of dollars worth of these beans to countries around the world. This recipe belongs to Jeannine Renouf, a talented Jonquière cook. When the beans mature each August, she shells and freezes a year's supply.

Saguenay-Lac St. Jean Menu

Bean soup
(page 27)

Saguenay meat pie
(page 28)

Relish and pickles

Green salad

Blueberry oat crumble
(page 38)

---

2 pounds (1 kg) fresh or frozen *gourgane* beans*
1 onion, finely chopped
1 carrot, finely chopped
¼ cup (50 mL) uncooked barley, rinsed
¼ pound (125 g) salt pork
Salt and ground black pepper
½ teaspoon (2 mL) dried savoury
2 tablespoons (25 mL) chopped fresh parsley
2 tablespoons (25 mL) chopped fresh chives

 * Or use 1 pound (500 g) dried fava beans that have been
   covered in water and soaked overnight, then drained.
   Proceed with recipe as directed.

If using fresh beans, shell and discard pods. (Some cooks believe that removing the tiny seed at the end of each bean prevents the soup from turning grey as it cooks. Others report that the practice has no effect.) In a large, heavy saucepan, combine beans with onion, carrot, barley and salt pork.

Cover with boiling water to a height of 2 inches (5 cm) above the ingredients. Simmer gently, covered, for 1½ to 2 hours or until beans are tender.

Season with salt, pepper, savoury, parsley and chives, continuing to cook gently until flavours blend, about 15 minutes more. (Salt port may be removed, cut into small pieces, and returned to soup.) Cool, chill and remove solidified fat. Reheat and serve. Six servings.

Photo:
Blueberry pie (page 37)

Tourtière du Saguenay

Saguenay meat pie

The most distinctive dish of the region is this combination of cubed meats, onions and potatoes, baked in layers in a deep, pastry-lined casserole. Marcelle Sénéchal of Jonquière assembles her pie in easy stages, then bakes it for 3 to 4 hours or, if it suits her, at a low temperature all day long. She and her husband Gérard consider this dish special occasion fare for family or friends.

---

1 pound (500 g) pork
3 pounds (1.5 kg) other meats*
1 large onion, chopped
Salt and ground black pepper
6 pounds (3 kg) potatoes
Ground cinnamon
Pastry for 2 double-crust, 9-inch (23 cm) pies

   * For example, one-third beef, one-third veal and one-third
     chicken, partridge or hare.

The day before, make pastry, wrap and refrigerate. Cut meat into small cubes and combine with onion in a large bowl. Season with salt and pepper to taste. Cover and refrigerate overnight.

Peel and cut potatoes into small cubes. (You will need 9-10 cups/2.5 L.) Place in another large bowl, add water to cover and refrigerate overnight.

The next day, roll out pastry so bottom layer is slightly more than ¼ inch (5 mm) thick, but the top layer is the usual thickness. Line a deep, heavy 14-inch (35 cm) oval or 12-inch (30 cm) round casserole dish. Drain potatoes.

Arrange alternate layers of meat and potatoes in the pastry-lined casserole, sprinkling each layer lightly with salt, pepper and a little cinnamon. Add just enough cold water to cover the mixture. Cover

Tourtière du Saguenay

This meat and vegetable pie is the most distinctive dish of the region. Unlike other *tourtières*, shallow tarts of ground meat and onions, this dish is composed of layers of cubed meat and potato in a pastry crust. It's often compared to the layered casserole called *cipaille* or *cipâte* in other regions. (In Saguenay, that name usually refers to a layered blueberry tart.) One theory is that the local *tourtière* was derived from the *pâté de famille* found in older, settled regions along the St. Lawrence River. This family meat pie is also made of cubed or thinly sliced meat and layered with sliced or minced onions and carrots. The closest relative to the usual *tourtière* in Saguenay-Lac St. Jean is *pâté à la viande*, a shallow pie made with ground meat, potatoes and spices.

with top pastry crust. Decorate with an extra border of pastry, if desired, and cut steam vents.

Bake in a preheated 425°F (220°C) oven for 1 hour. When pastry is golden, cover with casserole lid or double layer of aluminum foil, reduce temperature to 300°F (150°C) and cook slowly for 2 to 3 hours more. Or reduce temperature to 250°F (120°C) and cook for 6 to 7 hours more. Ten to twelve servings.

OUANANICHE FARCIE AU FOUR

Baked stuffed ouananiche

The celebrated *ouananiche*, fresh water ancestor of the salmon, once made Lac St. Jean a fisherman's paradise. But the dams and water pollution of the rivers that flow into the great northern lake have caused this fish to become more legend than habit. Older cooks remember feasting on *ouananiche*, stuffed with slices of lemon and hard-boiled eggs, then baked with a generous coating of butter. Another popular stuffing is made with bread crumbs, mushrooms and white wine.

---

1 whole *ouananiche*, salmon or trout (3 pounds/ 1.5 kg)
Salt and ground white pepper
2 tablespoons (25 mL) butter
¼ cup (50 mL) finely chopped onion
¼ cup (50 mL) finely chopped celery
1 small garlic clove, minced
1 cup (250 mL) sliced mushrooms
2 tablespoons (25 mL) chopped fresh parsley
1 cup (250 mL) fresh bread crumbs
Melted butter or oil
½ cup (125 mL) white wine

Regions within a region

Two terms are in regular use to describe cuisine in the kingdom of the Saguenay. *Cuisine jeannoise* refers to the cooking methods that are popular near Lac St. Jean. *Cuisine saguenéenne* refers to the culinary traditions along the Saguenay River, the great waterway that flows from Lac St. Jean southeast to Tadoussac on the St. Lawrence River.

Convent memories

Quebec's first domestic science school was opened by the Ursuline nuns in 1882 in Roberval on Lac St. Jean. Called L'École Ménagère de Roberval, it became famous throughout Quebec for publishing the cookbook *Cuisinière de la Reverende Mère Caron* in 1908.

Memories of the convent remain vivid for Mme Constance Garneau of Montreal, who was a student at the school from 1912 to 1914. The students, mostly daughters of farmers, were taught how to raise cows, pigs, sheep, hens and even bees, how to grow their own vegetables and fruits, and how to cook and preserve food. Lessons on making sausages and the blood pudding *boudin* involved scalding and scrubbing what Mme Garneau remembers as "yards and yards" of pig's intestines with soap and water, and seasoning great vats of blood with spices.

The bees would be brought into the convent to spend the winter in the basement under her dormitory. "We were often told to walk softly so as not to disturb the bees. We could hear them buzzing under the floor," she remembers.

Clean fish; rinse under cold running water. Remove head and tail. Pat dry with paper towels. Season cavity with salt and pepper.

Melt butter in frying pan and sauté onion, celery and garlic until soft. Add mushrooms and parsley; continue cooking for 1 minute longer.

Stir in bread crumbs; season with salt and pepper. Stuff fish with bread mixture, close the opening with skewers and lace up with string. Brush fish lightly with melted butter or oil. Arrange in a large buttered or oiled baking pan. Pour wine over fish and bake in a preheated 400°F (200°C) oven for 25 to 35 minutes, basting often, until fish flakes when tested with a fork. Six to eight servings.

MICROWAVE METHOD

Prepare fish as directed in recipe.

In a 4-cup (1 L) casserole, melt butter at High (100 percent) for 30 to 45 seconds or until melted. Add onion, celery and garlic; microwave, uncovered, at High (100 percent) for 3 to 4 minutes or until softened. Stir in mushrooms and parsley; microwave at High (100 percent) for 1 minute. Drain off any excess liquid and stir in bread crumbs; season with salt and pepper.

Fill cavity of fish with stuffing and close the opening with a wooden skewer. Place fish in a large microwave-safe serving dish. Cover with vented plastic wrap and microwave at High (100 percent) for 9 to 13 minutes or until fish flakes when tested with a fork near the backbone. Rotate dish twice during cooking. Let stand, covered, for five minutes.

PÂTÉ À LA VIANDE
Ground meat pie

There's a vigorous debate among cooks in Saguenay over the meats, vegetables and seasonings in this pie, a cousin of the *tourtière* of other parts of Quebec. Monique Girard-Solomita, a Montreal journalist from Roberval, calls it "heresy" to add potatoes. Some versions include beef, salt pork, cloves or dry mustard. Monique recommends serving her recipe with gherkins and pickled beets.

Vegetable oil
¾ pound (375 g) ground pork
¾ pound (375 g) ground veal
1 tablespoon (15 mL) butter
1 medium onion, chopped
1 teaspoon (5 mL) coarse salt
Ground black pepper
¼ teaspoon (1 mL) cinnamon
1 bay leaf
2 cups (500 mL) veal or beef stock*
Pastry for double-crust, 9-inch (23 cm) pie

* Beef consommé or chicken stock made from a concentrate may be used; reduce salt as these products tend to be salty.

Add a little oil to a large, heavy saucepan and fry pork and veal together until no longer pink. Remove meat, drain off fat and set aside. Heat butter in a saucepan and sauté onion until soft. Add cooked meat, salt, pepper, cinnamon, bay leaf and veal stock. Simmer gently, covered, for 2 to 2½ hours.

Line a 9-inch (23 cm) pie plate with pastry. Fill with meat mixture. Cover with top crust, trim, crimp edges to seal and cut steam vents. Bake in a preheated 400°F (200°C) oven for 15 minutes, then lower oven temperature to 350°F (180°C) and bake another 20 to 30 minutes or until top is lightly browned. Eight servings.

TOURTIÈRE
À LA OUANANICHE
Lac St. Jean Salmon pie

The prized *ouananiche* from Lac St. Jean makes a special *tourtière* when combined with vegetables and cream. Substitute salmon when making this dish, suggests cooking teacher Micheline Mongrain-Dontigny, who wrote a cookbook about the regional cuisine.

---

2 tablespoons (25 mL) butter
1 medium onion, thinly sliced
1 large potato, peeled, thinly sliced
1 pound (500 g) *ouananiche* or salmon, cut into
    small pieces
Salt and ground white pepper
¼ cup (50 mL) milk
2 tablespoons (25 mL) light cream
⅓ cup (75 mL) water (approximate)
1 egg, beaten with 1 tablespoon (15 mL) milk
Pastry for double-crust, 9-inch (23 cm) pie

Line a 9-inch (23 cm) pie plate with pastry. Heat butter in a frying pan and sauté onion until soft but not browned. Add potatoes, fish, salt, pepper, milk and cream; mix gently so as not to break up the pieces of fish. Arrange mixture evenly in the pastry shell. Gently stir in water; it should come halfway up the fish mixture. Cover with top crust, trim, crimping edge to seal. Cut a small hole in the centre. Brush pastry with the beaten egg and milk.

Bake in a preheated 375°F (190°C) oven for 45 to 50 minutes or until crust is browned. Six servings.

A festive place

Food is the centrepiece of community festivals throughout this region. Four different fish festivals, one for the *gourgane* bean, and another celebrating pheasant take place between June and September. The best festival is Mistassini's week-long blueberry party, *festival du bleuet*, held in early August just as the nearby *bleuetières*, or blueberry fields, are turning blue.

SOUFFLÉ DE CHOU-FLEUR

Cauliflower soufflé

The fertile plain around Lac St. Jean produces
excellent vegetables and supports thriving dairy
farms. A strong cheddar cheese, made at St. Prime on
the west side of the lake and aged up to four years, is
one of the region's finest cheeses. Adèle Copeman-
Langevin of St. Fulgence combines it with
cauliflower from her market garden in this soufflé.

---

1 medium cauliflower, cut into florets
2 tablespoons (25 mL) butter
2 tablespoons (25 mL) all-purpose flour
1 cup (250 mL) milk
Salt, ground black pepper, ground nutmeg
4 eggs, separated
1 cup (250 mL) grated strong Cheddar cheese

Cook cauliflower in boiling, salted water until
tender, drain well and mash. Melt butter in a medium
saucepan, blend in flour and cook, stirring over
medium heat until bubbly; do not let mixture brown.

Meanwhile, bring milk to a boil in another
saucepan. Add hot milk to butter-flour mixture and
cook, stirring over medium heat until sauce thickens
and is smooth. Season to taste with salt, pepper and
nutmeg. Remove from heat.

Lightly beat egg yolks and stir into sauce. Then stir
in cheese and cauliflower until smooth. In a large
bowl, beat egg whites until stiff but not dry. Fold
cauliflower mixture gently but thoroughly into
beaten egg whites. Pour into a buttered 2-quart (2 L)
soufflé dish. Bake in a preheated 350°F (180°C)
oven for 30 to 40 minutes, or until puffed, firm and
lightly browned. Serve at once. Four to six servings.

SALADE DE LA MER À LA VINAIGRETTE DE SAUMON FUMÉ DE LA RIVIÈRE STE. MARGUERITE

Fish salad with smoked salmon dressing

Fresh, local foods are the basis of the lively cuisine at Restaurant Le Chasseur, a winner in the 1989 Quebec restaurant competition, Ordre du mérite de la restauration. Run by co-owners Diane Tremblay, a Chicoutimi-born chef, and Joyce Caron, who comes from Sarnia, Ontario, the restaurant has been moved from Jonquière to Chicoutimi. The two women are the only Canadian members of the French women's organization Association des restauratrices-cuisinières de France. This dish of theirs uses fish from one of the region's large rivers, just east of the Saguenay.

---

1 cup (250 mL) oil
½ cup (125 mL) white wine
Juice of 2 lemons
1 garlic clove, finely chopped
Fresh rosemary, chopped
Salt and ground white pepper
4 fresh *doré* (walleye) fillets (about 1½ pounds/ 750 g), cut in small pieces
1 leek, white part only, finely chopped
4 ripe tomatoes, peeled, seeded, chopped
½ pound (250 g) fresh spinach leaves
2 dry shallots, finely chopped
½ cup (125 mL) chopped fresh mushrooms
1 ounce (30 g) smoked salmon, finely chopped

In a medium bowl, combine oil, wine, lemon juice, garlic, rosemary, salt and pepper to taste. Add fish pieces, turning to coat well with marinade. Cover and refrigerate for at least 24 hours, turning occasionally.

Place leek and tomatoes in a small saucepan and cook gently, over low heat, until vegetables are soft and their liquid has evaporated, about 10 minutes. Season with salt and pepper to taste; set aside and keep warm.

Lift fish pieces from marinade with slotted spoon and place in a large, shallow baking pan. (There is no need to grease the pan.) Bake in a preheated 400°F (200°C) oven for 5 to 7 minutes, or just until fish is opaque. Drain off any juices from fish. Transfer fish to hot platter and keep warm.

While fish is baking, pour marinade into medium saucepan, add spinach and cook gently over low heat, just until wilted. Remove pan from heat, lift spinach from liquid and set aside. Immediately add shallots, mushrooms and smoked salmon to hot marinade in saucepan.

To serve, divide spinach among 4 serving plates. Arrange an equal amount of freshly baked fish on spinach. Top with tomato-leek sauce. Spoon warm smoked salmon dressing over all. Four servings.

Auberge Le Presbytère

On the shores of the Saguenay River southeast of Chicoutimi, in a small and pretty village called St. Rose du Nord, a former priest's residence has recently been turned into a small inn. *Auberge Le Presbytère*'s location overlooking the great river attracts both artists who are interested in painting the Saguenay fiord and distant mountains, and nature lovers who enjoy hiking and fishing. Salmon and trout fishing are nearby and at Tadoussac, about an hour's drive downriver, it is possible to go whale-watching. Tennis and cross-country skiing are also available. Moderate rates. (Rooms: 6, bathroom on each floor; address: Route 172, 136 du Quai St., St. Rose du Nord, Québec, G0V 1T0; telephone: (418) 675-2503 or 1-800-463-9651.)

PÂTÉ ACCAÉ
Indian fish pie

Jocelyne Girard of Alma studied the cooking practices of the Indian tribes around Lac St. Jean and adapted this recipe for preparing the catch of the day, whether it be the treasured fresh water salmon (*ouananiche*), small trout, pike or walleye — all species available in the region. It's an easy meal-in-one.

4 medium potatoes, peeled and cubed
½ cup (125 mL) milk
Pinch dried savoury
Salt and ground white pepper
1 to 2 tablespoons (15 to 25 mL) butter
½ onion, finely chopped
6 to 8 fish fillets (about 1¼ pounds/625 g), cut into pieces
¼ cup (50 mL) white wine
Hot toast

Cook cubed potatoes in boiling water until tender; drain (do not mash) and add milk. Season with savoury and salt and pepper to taste. Set aside and keep warm.

Heat butter in a frying pan and sauté onion until soft. Add fish and continue to cook over medium heat until fish flakes with a fork, about 5 minutes. Moisten fish with wine and add to potatoes, stirring gently to combine. Simmer gently for about 5 minutes until hot. Serve hot on toast. Four servings.

MICROWAVE METHOD

Place cubed potatoes and ½ cup (125 mL) water in a 2-quart (2 L) casserole. Microwave, covered, at High (100 percent) for 10 to 14 minutes, stirring once during cooking, until potatoes are tender. Drain well. Add milk and savoury; season with salt and pepper to taste. Let stand, covered, while preparing fish.

In a large shallow baking dish, melt butter at High (100 percent) for 30 to 45 seconds. Add onion and microwave, uncovered, at High (100 percent) for 2 minutes or until soft. Arrange fish fillets in dish and pour wine over. Cover loosely with waxed paper and microwave at High (100 percent) for 4 to 6 minutes, rearranging halfway through cooking, until fish flakes when tested with a fork. Add to potatoes and gently stir to combine. Reheat, covered, at High (100 percent) for 1 to 2 minutes. Serve hot on toast.

TARTE AUX BLEUETS
Blueberry pie

The tiny wild blueberries of Lac St. Jean are called *fils du feu* because they grew in such vast quantities after a forest fire ravaged the region in 1870. Cécile Roland Bouchard of Chicoutimi believes in letting the fruit star in a simple pie, with no additional seasonings. She also makes this recipe with frozen wild fruit.

---

2 cups (500 mL) fresh blueberries, or 1 package
   (300 g) frozen, not thawed
2/3 cup (150 mL) granulated sugar
1 to 2 tablespoons (15 to 25 mL) butter
1 to 2 tablespoons (15 to 25 mL) all-purpose flour
1 egg yolk, beaten
Pastry for double-crust 8-inch (20 cm) pie

Line an 8-inch (20 cm) pie plate with pastry. In a bowl, combine blueberries and sugar; fill pastry shell. Roll out pastry for top crust and cut into 1/2-inch (1 cm) strips. Arrange strips on top of filling in a lattice design, pinching edges to seal.

Bake in a preheated 425°F (220°C) oven for 15 minutes, reduce temperature to 350°F (180°C) and bake for 20 minutes more or until top is lightly browned. Six servings.

Blue pearls

Blueberries or blue pearls, as the fruit is often called, are very popular in the kingdom of the Saguenay. The biggest blueberry dessert is the 500-plus serving pie sometimes baked as part of the August blueberry festival in Mistassini. Other blueberry treats include: an upside down cake that betrays its British connection with the name *pouding*; *grands-pères*, dumplings cooked in blueberry syrup; crêpes filled with the sweetened fruit; *parfaits* topped with stewed blueberries; and cantaloupe melon topped with blueberries soaked in liqueur and blueberry-flavoured whipped cream.

The brix factor

Lac St. Jean blueberries are tiny, under a quarter-inch (5 mm) in diameter, with a delicate sour taste that cuts their sweetness. A low-bush variety, they pack a far bigger flavour punch than the fat, pulpy, cultivated high-bush type and it's all because of the brix, the scientific term for the amount of natural sugar in the fruit. Deborah Buszard, plant scientist at McGill University in Montreal, explains that, for the high-bush variety, plant breeders took the wild fruit and developed a larger size for a more economical yield. The original amount of flavour is therefore diluted because it is spread through more fruit flesh. The term "wild" is loosely applied to Lac St. Jean blueberries, she adds. The fruit actually comes from managed wild stands.

CROUSTADE AUX BLEUETS
Blueberry oat crumble

This easy baked dessert comes from the recipe collection of Mme Guy Dupont of Arvida and was published in the Saguenay-Lac St. Jean cookbook *Le pinereau* by Cécile Roland Bouchard of Chicoutimi. It could be used with any fresh fruit in season.

---

4 cups (1 L) fresh blueberries, or 2 packages (300 g size) unsweetened, individually frozen
¾ cup (175 mL) granulated sugar
⅓ cup (75 mL) butter, softened
⅓ cup (75 mL) brown sugar
⅓ cup (75 mL) all-purpose flour
¾ cup (175 mL) rolled oats
Light cream

Butter an 8 or 9-inch (20 or 23 cm) square baking pan. Spread blueberries in an even layer in the pan and sprinkle with granulated sugar. In a bowl, cream butter with brown sugar, then blend in flour and rolled oats. Spread mixture evenly over fruit.

Bake in a preheated 350°F (180°C) oven for 30 to 35 minutes or until golden brown. Serve warm with cream. Six to eight servings.

MICROWAVE METHOD

Arrange blueberries in a 9-inch (23 cm) round or square baking dish or casserole. Sprinkle with granulated sugar. Microwave, uncovered, at High (100 percent) for 5 minutes, stirring twice during cooking, until berries are cooked. (If using frozen blueberries, increase cooking time to 8 minutes.) Let stand while preparing oat mixture.

Melt butter in a 9-inch (23 cm) glass pie plate. Microwave at High (100 percent) for 1 minute or until melted. Stir in brown sugar, flour and rolled oats. Microwave, uncovered, at High (100 percent) for 3 to 4 minutes, stirring every minute until lightly browned. Spoon the oat crumble over the warm blueberries and serve with cream.

MAINS À LA MÉLASSE
Molasses cookies

Traditionally these spicy cookies were shaped like hands. They used to be enjoyed with a glass of spruce beer, according to Mme Léopold Tremblay of Alma, the paper milling and aluminum smelting town near Lac St. Jean. Whatever their shape, they make a satisfying snack.

---

1 cup (250 mL) lard, softened
1 cup (250 mL) granulated sugar
1 egg
5 cups (1.25 L) all-purpose flour
1 tablespoon (15 mL) baking soda
2 teaspoons (10 mL) baking powder
1 teaspoon (5 mL) ground ginger
1 teaspoon (5 mL) cinnamon
1 cup (250 mL) molasses
½ cup (125 mL) hot tea

In a large bowl, cream lard with sugar until fluffy. Beat in egg. In another bowl, sift or mix flour with baking soda, baking powder, ginger and cinnamon. Add dry ingredients alternately with the mixture of the molasses and hot tea to creamed mixture, blending well.

On a lightly floured surface, roll out dough very thin. Using cookie cutters, cut cookies in desired shapes.

Arrange cookies on greased baking sheets and bake in a preheated 325°F (160°C) oven for about 10 minutes or until edges are crisp. Makes 8 to 9 dozen cookies.

POUDING DU CHÔMEUR DE SAGUENAY

Economy dessert, Saguenay style

This super-sweet baked dessert takes its name from *chômeur*—"unemployed person." Gilles Lemieux of Arvida was unemployed when he submitted wife Diane's recipe for inclusion in a little cookbook published in 1986. The book helped finance a strike by supermarket workers protesting the closure of several stores in the region. Gilles now works for the new store owners. Versions of the dessert turn up all over Quebec. In Saguenay-Lac St. Jean, the syrup is poured over the cake batter, rather than the reverse.

Base

---

1 cup (250 mL) all-purpose flour
1½ teaspoons (7 mL) baking powder
¼ teaspoon (1 mL) salt
⅓ cup (75 mL) butter or shortening, softened
⅔ cup (150 mL) granulated sugar
1 egg
1 teaspoon (5 mL) vanilla
⅓ cup (75 mL) milk

In a bowl, combine flour, baking powder and salt. In another bowl, cream butter with granulated sugar. Beat in egg and vanilla. Add dry ingredients alternately with milk to creamed mixture until combined. Spread batter evenly in a buttered 9-inch (23 cm) square baking pan.

Topping

1½ cups (375 mL) brown sugar
3 tablespoons (45 mL) all-purpose flour
2 tablespoons (25 mL) butter
2 cups (500 mL) water

In a saucepan, combine brown sugar, flour, butter and water. Bring to a boil, stirring until thickened slightly, and pour over mixture in the baking pan. Do not mix. Bake in preheated 350°F (180°C) oven for 50 to 60 minutes or until a tester inserted in the centre comes out clean. Eight servings.

POUDING RENVERSÉ DES BLEUETS

Blueberry upside-down pudding

Lemon-flavoured cake batter baked over fresh blueberries makes a perfect dessert. When I was immersed in French-language studies at Jonquière's Centre linguistique, Jeannine Renouf treated me to this recipe and also to a version she makes with wild raspberries. It was a delectable kind of immersion.

---

2 cups (500 mL) fresh blueberries, or 1 package
   (300 g) unsweetened, individually frozen
³/₄ cup (175 mL) granulated sugar
1 teaspoon (5 mL) grated lemon rind
1¼ cups (300 mL) all-purpose flour
1½ teaspoons (7 mL) baking powder
¼ teaspoon (1 mL) salt
¼ cup (50 mL) shortening
1 egg, beaten
1 teaspoon (5 mL) vanilla
²/₃ cup (150 mL) milk
Whipped or ice cream (optional)

Combine blueberries, ¼ cup (50 mL) of the sugar and lemon rind in a buttered 8-inch (20 cm) square baking pan.

In a bowl, combine flour, baking powder and salt.
In another bowl, cream shortening with remaining $\frac{1}{2}$
cup (125 mL) sugar until fluffy. Beat in egg and
vanilla. Add dry ingredients alternately with milk,
blending well after each addition and finishing with
dry ingredients.

Pour batter over fruit in pan and bake in a preheated 350°F (180°C) oven for about 40 minutes, or
until a tester inserted in centre comes out clean. Let
cool slightly; turn out onto serving plate. Cut in
squares and serve warm or at room temperature, with
whipped or ice cream, if desired. Six to eight
servings.

MICROWAVE METHOD

Combine blueberries with $\frac{1}{4}$ cup (50 mL) of the
sugar and lemon rind; spread in an ungreased 8-cup
(2 L) ring mould. If using frozen berries, microwave
at High (100 percent) for 2 minutes until defrosted.
Prepare batter as directed in recipe and spoon evenly
over blueberries.

Microwave, uncovered, at Medium (50 percent) for
5 minutes, rotating dish once. Microwave at High
(100 percent) for 3 to 4 minutes more or until top
has risen and a tester inserted in centre comes out
clean. Let stand on counter top for 5 minutes, then
run knife around edges to loosen and turn out onto
serving plate. Cut in wedges and serve either warm
or at room temperature, with whipped or ice cream,
if desired.

BEAUCE

Head south from Quebec City along the Chaudière River and you might expect to enter a forest of sugar maple trees. This is the Beauce, Pays de l'Erable or land of the maple, the region with the largest concentration of these trees in the province and about 4,000 *érablières* or maple syrup operations. Instead, the area is a pastoral valley of farms and small towns, their well-maintained ancestral homes occasionally interspersed with small businesses.

The maples are present, but up on the heights of land on either bank of the lazy-looking river. Each fall, the hills glow with the colour of their leaves. Down on the rolling flatlands, however, maple is a year-round presence at table.

Cooks in these parts slip the distinctively-flavoured syrup into just about everything. Stopping for a fast lunch in the railway town of Vallée Jonction, I found the roadside Restaurant Feuille d'Erable adding maple syrup to the coating on fried chicken and pouring it over freshly whipped cream on a parfait. It's used to glaze the region's favourite pork roast or meat stew such as *Ragoût de patte de cochon*. The best baked beans take a shot of it and so does the favourite pea soup. Crêpes and a host of baked desserts are usually rich with maple and the syrup adds character to pan-simmered eggs and cucumber pickles. I tasted my way through a range of maple-flavoured dishes and found that this habit does not result in a cloying sweetness.

As Cécile Grondin Gamache, St. Marie culinary historian and painter of scenes from pioneer life, explained, the maple syrup is as much a seasoning as a sweetener. The effect is to enrich the simplest foods.

Maple really stars at a spring sugaring-off party. The basic recipe is the egg and syrup dish *oeufs dans le sirop d'érable*. This combination is part of the lore of the original sugar shacks—cabins deep in the maple woods where the sap was boiled into syrup, maple taffy called *tire* and maple sugar. Back before any concern about calories or cholesterol, your only dilemma would be whether to have your eggs together with strips of fried pork known as *grillades*, or separately.

In days gone by, a regular treat at the *sucreries*—the other term for *érablières*—was the meat called *viande boucanée*. Slabs of salt pork would be rinsed of their brine, then hung in the rafters of the sugar shack where vapours from both the boiling sap and the maple log fire would gradually impregnate the meat. This delicacy would be enjoyed long after spring snows had melted.

Another favourite egg dish is called *omelette beauceronne* and has its roots in the cuisine of France's Loire River valley. The filling is usually potatoes, crisp-fried niblets of salt pork called *lardons*, tomatoes and the mild Cheddar cheese that is produced throughout the Beauce. Many regional dishes reflect this influence of northern and western France, homeland of so many of Quebec's first settlers. Pioneer Beaucerons, as residents are called, brought their recipes along when they moved south from older settlements in and around Quebec City and the Île d'Orléans.

The first settler to carve a farm out of the wilderness was Nicolas Comiré, who obtained land in 1737 on the Taschereau seigneury in St. Marie. A dozen other *habitants* also liked the looks of the river valley and its undulating hills and joined him.

The name Beauce came originally from fertile fields in France and it's aptly applied here. An economic backwater until recently, the Beauce has always had a do-it-yourself tradition of family businesses. Lately, it's become a model of entrepreneurial achievement, but I found that smokestacks and company billboards in no way obscured its charms.

Part of Beaucerons' family tradition is a respect for quality of life. "Young or old, in a hurry or not, we attach a great deal of importance to the values of days gone by," cookbook author Mariette Scully Bourque told me as she reminisced about best-liked dishes in her village of Notre Dame des Pins. "We take the time to prepare good meals and find pleasure in recipes that have been in our families for generations. And we are quite the *gourmands*," she admitted with a grin.

Today's Beaucerons use more vegetables and cheese in their cooking than was true in their parents' or grandparents' days, in Mme Bourque's opinion. Their liking for fresh fruit and vegetables is reflected in two superb green groceries, one in St. Marie and another in St. Georges, called Les Pères Nature.

SOUPE AUX POIS

BEAUCERONS

Pea soup, Beauce style

This hearty soup is a specialty at Auberge Benedict Arnold in St. Georges. It's the most requested dish of American visitors, says chef Rénaud Jacques, who was born in St. Elzéar. In summer, he flavours it with fresh herbs. The rest of the year he uses Quebec's favourite salted herbs (see recipe, page 26).

---

2 cups (500 mL or 450 g) dried white pea beans
2 tablespoons (25 mL) butter
½ cup (125 mL) chopped onion
¼ cup (50 mL) chopped leek, white part only
¼ cup (50 mL) smoked ham, plus ham bone
½ pound (250 g) salt pork
1 clove garlic
8 cups (2 L) cold water
2 tablespoons (25 mL) salted herbs, rinsed in cold
    water

Soak peas for at least 8 hours or overnight in water to cover; drain. Heat butter in a large, heavy pot and sauté onion and leek just until tender. Add peas, ham, salt pork (in one piece), garlic, water and salted herbs. Bring quickly to a boil, lower heat, partly cover, and cook gently for 2 to 3 hours or until peas are tender. Stir occasionally during cooking, adding more water if necessary. Remove salt pork, cut in small pieces, then return to soup. Eight servings. May be frozen.

Beauce Menu

Pea soup, Beauce style
(page 45)

Walleye in pastry with chive
butter sauce
(page 55)

Steamed spinach with
mushrooms

Apple maple pudding
(page 63)

POTAGE DU BLÉ

Corn soup

This fresh corn soup from Rénaud Jacques, chef at Auberge Benedict Arnold in St. Georges, is rich and creamy. It may be made with frozen or canned corn kernels, but it won't have the same delicate sweetness.

---

2 cups (500 mL) water
2 cups (500 mL) milk
4 cups (1 L) fresh corn kernels
1 teaspoon (5 mL) salt
2 tablespoons (25 mL) butter
⅓ cup (75 mL) chopped celery
¼ cup (50 mL) chopped onion
¼ cup (50 mL) chopped leek, white part only
2 tablespoons (25 mL) flour
½ cup (125 mL) whipping cream
Salt and ground black pepper

Bring water to a boil in a large saucepan. Add milk, corn and salt; cook just until corn is tender. Strain cooking liquid into a bowl and set corn aside. Heat butter in same saucepan and sauté celery, onion and leek until softened. Blend in flour; cook until bubbly. Stir in reserved corn cooking liquid. Bring to a boil, then partially cover and let simmer for 15 to 20 minutes.

Place corn and liquid in a food processor or blender and purée in batches until smooth. Return to saucepan and add cream. Adjust seasoning with salt and pepper to taste. Reheat until piping hot. Four to six servings.

MICROWAVE METHOD

In an 8-cup (2 L) casserole, microwave water at High (100 percent) for 5 minutes or until water boils. Add milk, corn and salt. Cover and microwave at High

(100 percent) for 8 to 10 minutes or until corn is tender. Strain cooking liquid into a bowl and set corn aside.

In the same casserole, melt butter at High (100 percent) for 30 to 45 seconds. Add celery, onion and leek; microwave, uncovered, at High (100 percent) for 3 minutes or until vegetables are softened. Blend in flour; stir in 2 cups (500 mL) of the reserved cooking liquid. Microwave, uncovered, at High (100 percent) for 5 minutes, stirring once during cooking.

In a food processor or blender, combine vegetable mixture, remaining cooking liquid and corn; purée in batches until smooth. Return to casserole. Stir in cream; adjust seasoning with salt and pepper to taste. Microwave, covered, at High (100 percent) for 5 to 7 minutes or until piping hot.

RAGOÛT DE PATTES DE LARD AUX GRANDS-PÈRES

Pork hocks stew with dumplings

This spicy dish, with the traditional combination of cinnamon and cloves, is always on the menu at special events in the Beauce, Christmas in particular.

2 pork hocks
2 upper pork hocks
2 tablespoons (25 mL) butter
3 medium onions, coarsely chopped
Salt and ground black pepper
1 bay leaf
2-inch (5 cm) chunk of salt pork (1/4 pound/125 g)
1/2 teaspoon (2 mL) cinnamon
1/4 teaspoon (1 mL) ground cloves
1/4 cup (50 mL) browned flour*
Dumplings (recipe follows)

* Heat flour in a heavy pan over medium heat, stirring occasionally, until it turns a light brown colour.

Seigneurial style

The first seigneury in the Beauce was granted in 1736 to the Taschereau family of Quebec City, who had originally emigrated from Touraine in west-central France. The family mansion, rebuilt and added to over many generations, has stood since 1809 on the northern outskirts of St. Marie overlooking the Chaudière River. A handsome neo-classical house, it's still occupied by descendants of the original family.

Tomato Béchamel Sauce

3 tablespoons (45 mL) butter
  or margarine
¼ cup (50 mL) finely
  chopped onion
3 tablespoons (45 mL) all-
  purpose flour
1½ cups (375 mL) milk
2 tomatoes, peeled, seeded
  and chopped OR
1 cup (250 mL) canned
  tomatoes, drained,
  chopped
Salt and ground white
  pepper

In a saucepan, melt the
butter and sauté the onion
over medium heat until
softened. Blend in the flour
and cook for 30 seconds;
stir in milk. Cook, stirring
constantly until sauce
thickens and is smooth. Add
tomatoes; cook for 1 to 2
minutes more, stirring
occasionally. Season sauce
with salt and pepper to
taste. Makes about 2½ cups
(625 mL).

Scrub pork hocks. Heat butter in a large, cast-iron
casserole or stock pot. Brown pork hocks on all
sides. Add cold water to cover, onions, salt and
pepper to taste, bay leaf and salt pork. Bring to a boil
and skim off any foam that rises to the surface. Lower
heat and slowly simmer, covered, for 3 hours.

Discard salt pork. Remove pork hocks, discard
bones and fat, cut meat into bite-size chunks. Strain
cooking liquid and return to casserole. Add chunks
of pork, cinnamon and cloves. Blend browned flour
with enough water to make a paste and blend into
stew. Bring to a simmer and season with salt and
pepper to taste.

Have Dumpling batter ready. With stew
simmering, add batter by tablespoonfuls (15 mL) and
cover tightly. Simmer for 10 minutes, then remove
cover and simmer for another 10 minutes. Six to
eight servings.

Dumplings

1 cup (250 mL) all-purpose flour
1 tablespoon (15 mL) baking powder
¼ teaspoon (1 mL) salt
3 tablespoons (45 mL) shortening
½ cup (125 mL) milk

Combine flour, baking powder and salt in a bowl.
Cut shortening into flour mixture with a pastry
blender or 2 knives until mixture resembles coarse
crumbs. Add milk and stir with fork to make a soft
dough.

ROULEAU DE BOEUF
Beef pastry roll

Leftover cooked beef is made into an attractive roll
with a tea biscuit dough in this recipe from an
elderly Beauceronne. She gave it to Cécile Grondin
Gamache of St. Marie to include in a collection of
traditional recipes from this region. Serve it sliced,
with either a tomato- or onion-flavoured *béchamel*
sauce or beef gravy.

---

2 cups (500 mL) ground leftover roast beef, or
    cooked ground beef
1 cup (250 mL) beef gravy
1 medium onion, finely chopped
2 cups (500 mL) all-purpose flour
4 teaspoons (20 mL) baking powder
½ teaspoon (2 mL) salt
¼ cup (50 mL) lard or shortening, chilled
⅔ cup (150 mL) milk

In a bowl, combine beef, beef gravy and chopped
onion. In another bowl, combine flour, baking
powder and salt. Cut in lard, using a pastry blender
or 2 knives, until mixture resembles coarse crumbs.
Work in milk with a fork until mixture forms a ball
around the fork.

Roll out dough on a floured surface into a
rectangle about ⅓ inch (1 cm) thick. Spread meat
mixture evenly over dough, leaving 1-inch (2.5 cm)
margin around edges. Roll up, jelly roll fashion, into
an evenly shaped sausage. Place, seam side down, in
a shallow, greased baking pan and bake in a
preheated 400°F (200°C) oven for about 30 minutes
or until pastry is golden-brown. Slice and serve hot
with a sauce (see margin note) or additional beef
gravy. Four to six servings.

FILET DE PORC À LA CRÈME LÉGÈRE DE CANNEBERGE

Pork tenderloin with cranberry cream sauce

Pork is a favourite in the Beauce. It is often combined with fresh fruit and vegetables at La Table du Père Nature in St. Georges, the fine restaurant attached to the fruit and vegetable store of the same name. Chef Laurent Moreau suggests a Beaujolais Village to accompany this dish.

---

2 pork fillets (1½ pounds/750 g)
2 tablespoons (25 mL) all-purpose flour
Salt and ground black pepper
1 tablespoon (15 mL) butter
1 tablespoon (15 mL) vegetable oil
Cranberry Cream Sauce (recipe follows)

Lightly dredge pork fillets in flour seasoned with salt and pepper to taste. Heat butter and oil in a large, heavy frying pan; brown pork quickly on all sides. Place fillets in a shallow baking dish. Roast in a preheated 350°F (180°C) oven for 15 minutes. Turn off heat, cover pork and leave in oven to keep warm while preparing sauce.

Cut pork into slices. Arrange on 4 heated serving plates and pour some of the Cranberry Cream Sauce over each serving. Four servings.

Cranberry Cream Sauce

½ cup (125 mL) fresh or frozen cranberries
¼ (50 mL) granulated sugar
1 beef bouillon cube dissolved in 2 tablespoons (25 mL) water
¼ cup (50 mL) whipping cream

Combine cranberries, sugar and dissolved bouillon in a small saucepan. Bring to a boil and cook until sugar has dissolved. With a slotted spoon, remove cranberries from syrup and set aside. Bring remaining liquid to a full boil and reduce until thickened, but not caramelized. Whip cream until stiff; fold into warm sauce, along with reserved cranberries. Season with salt and pepper to taste.

MICROWAVE METHOD

Pork Fillets: Brown pork fillets in hot butter and oil in a large, heavy frying pan as directed above. Arrange fillets on a microwave roasting rack or in a shallow casserole. Microwave, covered with a sheet of waxed paper, at Medium (50 percent) for 7 to 10 minutes or until pork is no longer pink in centre. Cover with foil and let stand while preparing sauce.

Sauce: In a bowl, combine cranberries with sugar and dissolved bouillon cube. Microwave, uncovered, at High (100 percent) for 3 minutes, stirring once during cooking. Using a slotted spoon, remove cranberries from syrup and set aside. Microwave syrup at High (100 percent) for 3 to 4 minutes, until reduced and thickened. Let stand for 1 minute. Whip cream until stiff and fold into syrup, along with the reserved cranberries. Cut pork into slices. Arrange on 4 heated serving plates and pour sauce over each serving.

Jarrets noirs

The moist and muddy banks of the Chaudière River helped give the Beaucerons the nickname *jarrets noirs*, which is used to this day. It's not that residents had black legs, oldtimers explain. The term refers to the black feet, or hocks, of the horses that pulled their owners' carts, or *charettes*, along the river to market in Quebec City, where their owners sold their wares and bought such essentials as salt, spices and molasses.

FÈVES AU LARD
Pork and beans

A basic of Beauceron cuisine, this traditional dish may be flavoured either with molasses and brown sugar or with maple syrup, says St. Marie culinary historian Cécile Grondin Gamache. When her region's favourite game bird, partridge, is available, she uses maple syrup in her beans and tucks the breasts of three partridges into the centre of the pot. A breast of chicken may be substituted for the partridge.

---

1 pound (500 g) dried white navy beans
½ cup (125 mL) molasses*
¼ cup (50 mL) brown sugar*
1 teaspoon (5 mL) salt
¼ teaspoon (1 mL) pepper
1 teaspoon (5 mL) dry mustard
2 medium onions, chopped
½ pound (250 g) salt pork**
3 breasts of partridge or 1 breast of chicken (optional)

 * The molasses and brown sugar may be replaced with ¾ cup (175 mL) maple syrup.
** Salt pork may be left whole and removed when beans are cooked, then chilled, sliced and served. Or it may be sliced before adding to the beans and incorporated into the dish.

Wash beans and place in a large saucepan or stock pot. Add cold water to cover and soak for at least 8 hours or overnight. Drain. Cover with 12 cups (3 L) fresh, cold water. Bring to a boil over medium heat. Reduce heat to low and simmer for about 1 hour or until beans have softened slightly.

Drain beans and reserve cooking liquid. In a heavy casserole with a cover, combine beans, 6 cups (1.5 L) cooking liquid, molasses, brown sugar, salt, pepper, mustard and onions. Tuck pork and partridge breasts

The American connection

Visitors from south of the border have been well received in the Beauce ever since 1775. That was the year General Benedict Arnold led an army north from Maine to try to entice the French, who had been defeated on the Plains of Abraham five years earlier, to join the American Revolution. After hacking their way through the forests of Maine, the soldiers were welcomed by settlers along the Chaudière River, who supplied the army with food in return for Yankee coin—an early sign of Beauceron economic sense. Arnold met eventual defeat at Quebec City, but the Auberge Benedict Arnold, a landmark hotel in St. Georges, commemorates his visit.

if desired, in centre of dish. Cover and bake at 250°F (120°C) for 6 to 8 hours. Remove cover for final hour of baking. Add more bean cooking liquid or water during baking if mixture appears to be drying out. To serve, arrange partridge breasts on heated platter; surround with beans. Six servings as a main course.

Oeufs dans le sirop d'érable

Eggs in maple syrup

This rich, sweet eggs and maple syrup recipe makes the ultimate brunch dish in the Beauce, particularly during the spring maple run. In the old days, if the thick maple taffy known as *tire* was cooking on the stove, a sugar shack cook might drop the eggs into this confection instead of using the usual bubbling hot syrup. In Beauce kitchens today, the eggs are often beaten before they are cooked, and sometimes a teaspoonful of butter is dropped into the syrup before the eggs. This recipe belongs to Mariette Scully Bourque of Notre Dame des Pins.

---

2 cups (500 mL) maple syrup
3 eggs
⅓ cup (75 mL) milk
Pinch salt

Bring syrup to a boil in a heavy saucepan and cook over medium heat just until syrup thickens. Meanwhile, beat eggs lightly with milk and salt.

When syrup has thickened, reduce heat to low. Using a wooden spoon, drop spoonfuls of the egg mixture into hot syrup. Cook for 2 to 3 minutes until eggs are set. Immediately remove saucepan from heat and place it in a larger pan of cold water to cool slightly. Spoon eggs into serving bowls and drizzle with syrup. Six servings.

FILETS DE POISSON HOSPITALITÉ DU MANOIR

Manor-style fish fillets

Lac Etchemin is a centre for year-round sports in what Chaudière River valley residents call "the other Beauce"—the eastern part of the Pays de L'Érable region. At Le Manoir Lac Etchemin, the large, comfortable inn on the north shore of the lake, Tunisian-born chef Mohamed Yahyaoui uses his choice of fish fillets in this quick, easy, but luxurious-tasting baked dish. It may be completely assembled in advance of baking and is good served with boiled parsleyed potatoes and a steamed green vegetable.

---

1 tablespoon (15 mL) butter
1 tablespoon (15 mL) vegetable oil
2 fresh fish fillets (6 to 7 ounces/170 to 200 g each), such as sole, haddock or trout
Salt and ground white pepper
2 tablespoons (25 mL) white wine
2 tablespoons (25 mL) whipping cream
3 green onions, chopped
1 tablespoon (15 mL) sliced or slivered almonds, toasted
½ to ¾ cup (125 to 175 mL) grated Gruyère or Mozzarella cheese
Juice of ½ lemon

Heat butter and oil together in a large frying pan and quickly brown fish fillets on both sides for no more than 30 to 60 seconds, depending on thickness.

Arrange fillets in a buttered, shallow baking dish, just large enough to hold the fillets in a single layer. Season fillets with salt and pepper to taste. Stir together the wine and cream; drizzle over fish. Sprinkle with green onions, almonds and cheese.

Bake fish in a preheated 350°F (180°C) oven for

about 15 minutes or until cheese mixture is bubbling hot and lightly browned. Drizzle fish with lemon juice. Two servings.

MICROWAVE METHOD

Omit butter and oil from recipe. Arrange fish fillets in a shallow baking dish large enough to hold the fillets in a single layer. Lightly season with salt and pepper to taste. Stir together wine, cream and green onions; pour over fish. Microwave, loosely covered with waxed paper, at High (100 percent) for 3 minutes or until fish just flakes when tested with a fork. Top fish fillets with cheese and microwave, uncovered, at Medium (50 percent) for 2 to 3 minutes or until cheese is melted. Sprinkle with almonds and drizzle with lemon juice before serving.

DORÉ DE LAC EN CROÛTE AU BEURRE BLANC DE CIBOULETTE

Walleye in pastry with chive butter sauce

One of Quebec's favourite fish is *doré*. Caught in Lac Mégantic, it's frequently served at La Table du Père Nature in St. Georges. French-born chef Laurent Moreau suggests a young Muscadet with this dish.

---

4 fresh walleye fillets (1½ pounds/750 g)
4 dry shallots, finely chopped
¼ cup (50 mL) dry white vermouth
Pinch dried thyme
Salt and ground white pepper
1 egg yolk
1 package (14 ounces/400 g) frozen puff pastry
Chive Butter Sauce (recipe follows)

Wild fare

Despite pollution, *doré* (walleye), pike, smelts and trout can still be caught in the lakes and streams of the Beauce. Deer is the principal game animal. Its nickname is *veau des bois*, veal of the woods, a name invented by poachers. The most plentiful game bird is the partridge. It turns up in recipes for soups, roasts and casseroles, where it's usually combined with cabbage or a combination of onions and herbs.

On a lightly floured surface, roll out puff pastry into a large rectangle ⅛ inch (3 mm) thick and approximately 12 × 16 inches (30 × 40 cm). Cut the pastry into 4 smaller rectangles, each 6 × 8 inches (15 × 20 cm). (The pastry should be large enough to totally enclose each fish fillet. If not, roll out pastry to make larger rectangles.)

Place a fish fillet in the centre of each rectangle, sprinkle with shallots and vermouth, season with thyme and salt and pepper to taste.

Enclose fish in pastry, pinching to seal edges. If desired, shape pastry in the form of a fish. Place seam side down on an ungreased baking sheet. Beat egg yolk with a little water and brush over pastry. Bake in a preheated 400°F (200°C) oven for 20 to 25 minutes or until pastry is golden. Serve with Chive Butter Sauce. Four servings.

Chive Butter Sauce

---

2 dry shallots, chopped
1 tablespoon (15 mL) butter
½ cup (125 mL) white wine
1 cup (250 mL) whipping cream
½ cup (125 mL) fresh chives, finely chopped
Salt and ground white pepper

In a medium saucepan, sauté shallots in butter until softened. Add wine, cook over high heat and reduce by half. Stir in cream and cook until sauce has reduced and thickened. Stir in chives and adjust seasoning with salt and pepper.

MARINADE
AUX CONCOMBRES
AU SIROP D'ÉRABLE

Maple-flavoured cucumber pickles

Maple syrup is preferred as a sweetener for pickles in the Beauce, although sugar or honey are also used. This recipe belongs to Cécile Grondin Gamache of St. Marie.

---

12 cucumbers, 8 inches (20 cm) in length
¼ cup (50 mL) coarse pickling salt
6 cups (1.5 L) white vinegar
1 cup (250 mL) maple syrup
2 tablespoons (25 mL) mixed pickling spices

Scrub cucumbers well and slice in half lengthwise; remove the seeds. Cut in half crosswise, then cut each quarter lengthwise into 6 strips. Spread cucumber pieces on a large baking sheet lined with paper towels. Sprinkle with salt. Let stand for 3 hours. Rinse in cold water and drain well. Pack cucumber strips into hot sterilized 1-pint (500 mL) jars.

Combine vinegar, maple syrup and pickling spices in a saucepan; bring to a boil. Simmer for 5 minutes, then strain. Pour hot vinegar mixture over cucumber pieces in jars and seal. Store for at least two weeks before using. Makes about 8 1-pint (500 mL) jars.

PAIN DE BLÉ ENTIER

Whole wheat bread

When farmers in the Chaudière River valley grew their own wheat and ground it into flour on a stone, they would make *pain de ménage*—"home-style bread"—much like this recipe.

1½ cups (375 mL) lukewarm water
2 teaspoons (10 mL) granulated sugar
2 packages (2 tablespoons/25 mL) active dry yeast
¾ cup (175 mL) milk
½ cup (125 mL) packed brown sugar
1 tablespoon (15 mL) salt
½ cup (125 mL) shortening
4 cups (1 L) whole wheat flour
2 cups (500 mL) all-purpose flour (approximate)

Pour lukewarm water into a bowl, stir in granulated sugar, then sprinkle with yeast. Let stand for about 10 minutes, until yeast is dissolved and foamy.

In a saucepan, scald milk, then stir in brown sugar, salt and shortening. Pour into a large mixing bowl and let stand until lukewarm. In another bowl, combine whole wheat and all-purpose flours.

Add yeast mixture to milk mixture, then stir in about half the flour mixture and beat well. Continue adding flour mixture until dough becomes stiff and leaves sides of bowl. Turn out onto floured surface and knead in as much of the remaining flour as needed to make a dough that is not sticky. Continue to knead dough for about 5 minutes or until dough becomes smooth and elastic. Place in a well-greased bowl, turn to coat dough with grease on all sides, cover with a dry tea towel and set in a warm place to rise until doubled in bulk, about 1½ hours.

Punch down the dough, divide in half and shape into 2 loaves. Place in 2 greased 8½ × 4½ inch (1.5 L) loaf pans. Cover with a dry tea towel and set

Photo:
Garlic-fried smelts (page 68)

in a warm place about 1 hour, until doubled in bulk.

Bake in a preheated 400°F (200°C) oven for 10 minutes, then reduce heat to 350°F (180°C) and bake for 25 to 30 minutes more or until loaves sound hollow when tapped on the top. Turn out on racks to cool. Makes 2 loaves.

SALADE D'HIVER

Wintertime salad

In days gone by, uncooked vegetables were salted and bottled in a vinegar-sugar mixture, then stored in a cold pantry. This "salad" provided a change from root vegetables from the cold storage bin, or pickles. Mariette Vachon of St. Marie contributed this family recipe to a collection published by the rural women's group Cercle de Fermières in her town.

---

8 pounds (4 kg) firm, ripe tomatoes, peeled and
   chopped
6 large onions, chopped
2 green peppers, cut in small cubes
1 red pepper, cut in small cubes
1 stalk celery, chopped
¼ cup (50 mL) coarse pickling salt
2 cups (500 mL) vinegar
2 cups (500 mL) granulated sugar
2 tablespoons (25 mL) mustard seeds

Place tomatoes, onions, peppers and celery in a large bowl; stir in salt. Cover bowl with a cloth and let stand overnight.

The next day, drain vegetables thoroughly. In a saucepan, heat together vinegar, sugar and mustard seeds just until sugar dissolves, then cool. Pour over drained vegetables and mix well. Ladle evenly into hot sterilized jars. Seal, cool and refrigerate, or store in very cool place, for at least 7 days before using. Makes 5 to 6 1-pint (500 mL) jars.

Photo:
Buckwheat pancakes (page 105)

Auberge Benedict Arnold

The best-known inn in the Beauce is a bustling social centre for Beaucerons, who come to dine in either the top-rated French restaurant or the cosy steakhouse, and for regular Quebec and American business visitors. Named after the American general who was welcomed in the region in 1775, it's run by the Lapierre family. Fresh, up-dated versions of traditional Quebec dishes are a specialty. Both the original white-painted inn and the modern motel wings are comfortable. Outdoor swimming pool; sauna. Moderate rates. (Rooms: 50, each with private bath; address: 18255 Kennedy Rd., St. Georges, Québec, G5Y 5C4; telephone: (418) 288-5558 or 1-800-361-6162.)

GÂTEAU JOS. LOUIS
Joe Louis Cakes

Home-made versions of this best-selling commercial snacking cake turn up in recipe collections throughout the Beauce. A product of the giant Vachon bakery at St. Marie, it was launched in 1928 by founder-bakers Arcade and Rose-Anna Vachon, who named it for their two eldest sons Joseph and Louis and not, as some believe, after the heavyweight boxing champion Joe Louis. Home recipes use a drop-cookie method and—sometimes—a marshmallow filling. The bakery cake is made automatically with a diameter of 3½ inches (9 cm). To achieve a symmetrical look and a light texture, I adapted a recipe belonging to Mariette Scully Bourque of Notre Dame des Pins to the muffin tin.

Cake

½ cup (125 mL) butter or margarine
½ cup (125 mL) granulated sugar
2 eggs, beaten
1 cup (250 mL) milk
1 tablespoon (15 mL) white vinegar
1 teaspoon (5 mL) baking soda
2 cups (500 mL) all-purpose flour
1 teaspoon (5 mL) baking powder
¼ cup (50 mL) unsweetened cocoa powder
½ teaspoon (2 mL) salt
1½ teaspoons (7 mL) vanilla

Grease 12 medium muffin tins or 24 small ones. In a large bowl, cream butter and sugar together until fluffy. Blend in beaten eggs. Measure milk into a 1-cup (250 mL) measure and stir in vinegar, then baking soda. In another bowl, sift or mix together flour, baking powder, cocoa powder and salt. Combine dry ingredients with butter mixture alternately with milk; stir in vanilla. Fill prepared muffin tins half full of batter. Bake in a preheated 350°F (180°C) oven for about 10 minutes or until a tester inserted in centre comes out clean. Cool for 10 minutes in pans. Turn out onto rack and cool completely.

Vanilla Filling

---

2 egg whites
½ cup (125 mL) granulated sugar
Pinch salt
2 tablespoons (25 mL) water
1 teaspoon (5 mL) vanilla

In the top of a double boiler set over boiling water, combine egg whites, granulated sugar, salt and water. With an electric mixer, beat until stiff and fluffy, about 3 to 4 minutes. Remove from heat and beat in vanilla.

Chocolate Icing

---

2 tablespoons (25 mL) soft butter or margarine
2 tablespoons (25 mL) unsweetened cocoa powder
2 to 3 tablespoons (25 to 45 mL) light cream
½ teaspoon (2 mL) vanilla
½ cup (125 mL) sifted icing sugar (approximate)

Cream soft butter with cocoa powder. Blend in cream and vanilla. Stir in sifted icing sugar until icing is of spreading consistency.

Slice cakes in half horizontally. Fill with Vanilla Filling and spread tops and sides with Chocolate Icing. Makes about 12 medium or 24 small muffin-sized cakes.

POITRINE DE POULET AU SIROP D'ÉRABLE

Maple-baked chicken breasts

Chicken and pork are often baked or braised in maple syrup in the Beauce. This easy recipe for chicken breasts can also be used with a whole cut-up broiler-fryer chicken. It's from the collection of Jeanne d'Arc Nadeau, long-time proprietor of Le Danube Bleu reception hall in St. Marie and a cookbook author.

---

4 single chicken breasts
¼ cup (50 mL) all-purpose flour
Salt and ground black pepper
2 tablespoons (25 mL) butter
½ cup (125 mL) maple syrup
1 teaspoon (5 mL) dried savoury
½ teaspoon (2 mL) dried thyme
¼ teaspoon (1 mL) dried sage
1 onion, sliced
½ cup (125 mL) water

Dredge chicken pieces in flour seasoned with salt and pepper to taste. In a heavy, flameproof casserole, heat butter until bubbling and brown chicken pieces quickly on both sides. Pour maple syrup over chicken. Sprinkle with savoury, thyme and sage. Arrange onion slices on top of chicken pieces. Pour water into the bottom of casserole. Bake, uncovered, in a 350°F (180°C) oven for 50 to 60 minutes or until tender, basting chicken occasionally with pan juices. Four servings.

MICROWAVE METHOD

Arrange chicken breasts, skins removed, in the bottom of a large, shallow baking dish. Combine ¼ cup (50 mL) maple syrup with ¼ teaspoon (1 mL) dried savoury and a pinch each of dried thyme and sage; season with salt and pepper to taste. Pour over chicken and cover with sliced onions. Microwave, covered with vented plastic wrap, at High (100 percent) for 12 to 14 minutes or until chicken is tender and juices run clear when meat is pierced. Remove chicken to a serving platter, cover and keep warm. Microwave remaining liquid in dish, uncovered, at High (100 percent) for 3 to 5 minutes or until reduced. Pour sauce over chicken breasts and serve.

POUDING AUX POMMES AU SIROP D'ÉRABLE
Apple Maple Pudding

Apples and maple syrup are natural partners in the Beauce. This easy recipe was obtained from an elderly family cook by St. Marie culinary historian Cécile Grondin Gamache.

---

3 large or 6 small cooking apples, peeled, cut into chunks
1 cup (250 mL) maple syrup
1 egg, beaten
1 tablespoon (15 mL) melted butter
2 teaspoons (10 mL) lemon juice
½ cup (125 mL) all-purpose flour
1 teaspoon (5 mL) baking powder
Pinch salt
½ cup (125 mL) raisins
Unsweetened whipped cream (optional)

Arrange apples in a greased 8-inch (20 cm) square baking pan. Pour ½ cup (125 mL) of the maple syrup over apples, stirring to coat well, and spread in an even layer.

Maple products

Until the 1950s, the average family in this sugar maple region consumed an estimated average of about 200 pounds (100 kg) of maple products a year, half of it maple sugar. Sugaring-off workers would use fresh maple sap instead of water to make tea. In the early days, woodsmen boiled the sap in cauldrons over an open air fire. Today most harvesting is done using plastic pipes, and the syrup is made in factory evaporators. Maple sugar is now a delicacy, to be snapped up in the spring at roadside stands and markets.

In a bowl, combine beaten egg, butter and lemon juice with remaining ½ cup (125 mL) maple syrup. In another bowl, combine flour, baking powder and salt. Stir the dry ingredients into the egg mixture. Fold in raisins.

Pour batter evenly over apple pieces. Bake in a preheated 375°F (190°C) oven for 30 to 35 minutes or until top is lightly browned. Serve warm with unsweetened whipped cream, if desired. Six servings.

MICROWAVE METHOD

Place apple pieces in an ungreased 9-inch (23 cm) round microwave-safe baking dish. Pour ½ cup (125 mL) maple syrup over apples, stirring to coat well. Microwave, uncovered, at High (100 percent) for 6 to 7 minutes or until apples are just tender, stirring slices once during cooking.

Prepare batter as directed in recipe, pour over cooked apple pieces and spread evenly. Microwave, uncovered, at High (100 percent) for 4 to 5 minutes or until top has risen and is no longer moist, rotating dish once. Let stand on counter top for 5 minutes. Serve warm with unsweetened whipped cream, if desired.

CHARLEVOIX

 The air of Charlevoix is fresh with the scent of salt water, and local residents refer to their tide-swept expanse of the St. Lawrence River as "the sea". Salt water also makes its presence felt at the table. Fishermen have caught two tiny fish—smelt and capelin—in the river from the days of the earliest French settlers. My mother, whose family came from Toronto to summer in Pointe au Pic in the years before the First World War, remembers when fishermen's children sold strings of little smelts door-to-door. "You'd see the children on the wharf with their bamboo fishing rods—the smelts would be fresh from the cold St. Lawrence. Dipped in flour and fried, they were delicious."

Herring and sardines were also plentiful in the time before water pollution. Rita Dufour Laurin of Île aux Coudres still likes these fish best marinated or salted, just as they were in the era before refrigeration. In those days, inland lakes and the streams that cascaded south to the river were also rich with salmon and speckled trout. My uncles would catch the trout at fishing camps. "Those fish were always the real delicacy of the summer," my mother remembers. "Just fried in butter or lard, nothing fancy."

In the inns that now flourish in the former summer houses of the rich, lamb, as well as fish, is a specialty. Over the years Charlevoix lamb has been compared to Brittany's *pre-salé* lamb because of the tang acquired from sea spray on meadow grasses. Auberge au Petit Berger in Pointe au Pic has at least eight lamb dishes on the menu; favourites are a braised shoulder stuffed with hare and mushrooms, and a roast leg seasoned with juniper berries and Cognac. Mint, almonds and maple syrup are some of the other seasonings applied to lamb by both family cooks and chefs, says Georgette Tremblay Rochette of Cap à l'Aigle. Lamb liver and kidneys are served with *chanterelle* mushrooms at the Tremblay family inn Auberge des Peupliers.

Local residents are expert hunters of three principal game meats—moose, hare and partridge. The land has also yielded plentiful wild fruits, in particular strawberries, raspberries, blueberries, apples and plums. Another of my mother's childhood recollections is of young berry pickers turning up at her door, swinging lard pails they had filled with freshly picked wild strawberries and blueberries. The perfect desserts in these parts continue to be very simple—fresh fruit in season, thick cream and a sprinkling of maple sugar.

When the weather turned cold, Rita Dufour Laurin remembers many combinations of dried fruit in a bread or rice pudding, or the year-round favourite—a slice of thickly cut fresh bread, drenched in cream, with maple or brown sugar sprinkled on top.

The time-honoured soups in this region contain roots—potatoes, onions, carrots and turnips—with seasonings to enliven them. "Soup needs a good piece of salt pork and some savoury," says Evariste Dufour, a retired Montreal chef who hails from Île aux Coudres. The best known regional soup is made with the locally grown *gourgane* bean, a large, green bean with red streaks. Horticulturalists trace it to the *fève des marais* grown around Paris. Quebec's first farmer-settler, Louis Hébert, is credited with bringing the *gourgane* to New France about 1618. Its flat, meaty seeds are simmered with other vegetables and barley to make a soup that is equally popular in Charlevoix and Saguenay-Lac St. Jean.

The favourite seasonings of this region—shallots, parsley, chives, savoury and mint—were grown in the earliest gardens. Nowadays Charlevoix is fortunate in having an exceptional market garden to supply the entire area. It's located just east of St. Joseph de la Rive, tucked into a verdant corner between the hillside and the riverbank. Even artichokes flourish in this protected spot.

Velouté de Gourganes
Cream-topped bean soup

The ingredients in this sophisticated version of the traditional Charlevoix *soupe aux gourganes* have changed little, but Chef Dominique Truchon of Auberge des Peupliers in Cap à l'Aigle blends all to a velvety smoothness. The *gourgane* is a large, green bean with rosy streaks and seeds that resembles fava beans.

---

1 pound (500 g) fresh or frozen *gourgane* beans*
1 onion
2 stalks celery
3 medium carrots, peeled
¼ pound (125 g) salt pork
2½ quarts (2.5 L) chicken stock
1 teaspoon (5 mL) commercially prepared or
  homemade salted herbs (see page 26)
Ground black pepper
Lightly whipped cream

  * Or use 1 pound (500 g) dried fava beans that have been
  soaked in water to cover overnight, then drained.
  Proceed with recipe as directed.

Shell beans, removing tiny tip of each seed, if desired, and discard pods. Chop onion, celery and carrots coarsely. Place vegetables and salt pork in a large, heavy pot. Add chicken stock. Partially cover and cook gently until beans are tender, about 1½ to 2 hours. Add salted herbs. Discard salt pork.

In a blender or food processor, purée soup until smooth, then strain through a sieve. Season with pepper to taste. Serve hot with a dollop of whipped cream on each bowlful. Six servings.

Charlevoix Menu

Garlic-fried smelts
(page 68)

Leg of lamb flavoured
with juniper berries
(page 72)

Buttered new potatoes

Green beans with bacon

Apple dumplings
(page 79)

Auberge des Peupliers

In a region with many outstanding country inns, this family-run enterprise is a leader. It has the friendly atmosphere of a home, and includes a charming, modern annex set into the hillside behind the original inn. The Tremblay family are at the helm, as they have been for generations, and local Charlevoix foods such as lamb, game meats, smelts, *gourgane* beans and berries are regularly prepared in sophisticated versions of early recipes. Quebec pine furniture and traditional Murray Bay weaving add warmth to the rooms. Expensive, but worth it for an exceptional experience. Tennis, swimming pool, sauna, nearby golf and skiing. (Rooms: 23, many with private bath; address: 381 St. Raphael St., Cap à l'Aigle, Québec, G0T 1B0; telephone: (418) 665-4423.)

FILETS D'ÉPERLANS À L'AIL
Garlic-fried smelts

Fried, breaded or plain, and served with parsley, lemon and a tartar sauce or mayonnaise, these little fish make either a first course or a whole meal in Murray Bay. This recipe is from the menu at Auberge des Peupliers in Cap à l'Aigle.

---

12 large smelts or 18 small smelts
⅓ cup (75 mL) butter
2 cloves garlic, chopped
½ cup (125 mL) fine, dry bread crumbs
½ cup (125 mL) freshly grated Parmesan cheese
2 tablespoons (25 mL) chopped fresh parsley
Lettuce leaves and finely sliced lemon

Split open smelts along belly, clean, remove backbones, fins and tails. Melt butter in a saucepan with garlic, then strain. Meanwhile, combine bread crumbs, cheese and parsley. Dip smelts in garlic-flavoured butter, then dredge in bread crumb mixture. Arrange on a lightly greased baking sheet.

Bake in a preheated 425°F (220°C) oven for about 5 minutes. Serve hot on lettuce and trim with lemon. Two servings.

MICROWAVE METHOD

Prepare smelts as directed in recipe. Arrange half the smelts on a microwave roasting rack, with small tapered ends of fillets pointing towards the centre. Microwave, uncovered, at High (100 percent) for 1½ to 2 minutes. Cover and let stand for 2 minutes. Repeat with remaining smelts. Serve as directed.

PÂTÉS CROCHES
Pork turnovers

A Charlevoix original, frequently served on Île aux
Coudres, this croissant-shaped turnover was
originally filled with game meats. Now it's made with
ground pork. Some recipes call for ground cloves
and sage, some for pre-cooking the meat mixture,
while others are baked with a raw meat filling. This
recipe belongs to Lise Dufour, who prepares it
regularly at the Hôtel La Roche Pleureuse. The word
croche refers to its ropelike border, achieved by
turning the edge of the pastry between the fingers to
make a row of small waves.

1½ pounds (750 g) ground pork
1 tablespoon (15 mL) butter or shortening
½ cup (125 mL) chopped onion
Salt and ground black pepper
2 tablespoons (25 mL) water
Pastry for double-crust, 9-inch (23 cm) pie

In a frying pan, cook pork briefly until it is no longer
pink, then drain off fat and set meat aside. Heat
butter in frying pan and sauté onion until soft. Stir in
meat and season with salt and pepper to taste.
Moisten filling with water.

   Roll out pastry into 6 circles, each measuring 8
inches (20 cm) in diameter. (Turnovers can be made
in a smaller size.) Divide meat filling evenly among
the circles, placing it to one side of the centre.
Moisten edges of pastry with water and fold over
filling to make a crescent shape. Pinch edge closed
with fingers to simulate a twisted cord and cut a
steam vent in the top of each turnover. Place
turnovers on a lightly greased baking sheet and bake
in a preheated 350°F (180°C) oven for about 50 to 60
minutes or until crisp and lightly browned. Six
servings.

A fare exchange

Guests at a tiny country inn
downriver from Murray Bay
used to be able to feast their
eyes on a handful of
paintings by Quebec's
noted figurative artist, Jean-
Paul Lemieux. Summering in
Port au Persil in the 1950s,
Lemieux would paint for his
supper at what's now called
Auberge La Petite
Madeleine. When his sales
improved, the artist built a
house on Île aux Coudres,
but his paintings remained
at the inn until it changed
hands in 1985 and the works
became the property of a
collector from Quebec City.

Casserole de lièvre et de perdrix parfumée à l'érable

Maple-flavoured hare and partridge casserole

Combinations of game meats are popular in Charlevoix. This dish is served at Auberge L'été in St. Joseph de la Rive.

---

2 hares or rabbits, 2½ pounds (1 kg) each
4 partridges
½ pound (250 g) salt pork
2 medium onions, thinly sliced
3 tablespoons (45 mL) maple sugar or ⅓ cup (75 mL) maple syrup
2 bay leaves
¾ cup (175 mL) water
Salt and ground black pepper
Fresh parsley

Cut hares and partridges into serving-size pieces. Cut 3 or 4 thin slices from salt pork and set aside; chop remainder.

In a large, heavy, flameproof casserole with a cover, sauté chopped salt pork until golden. Add onions and sauté until soft. Stir in maple sugar and cook gently until mixture caramelizes and turns golden-brown.

Arrange pieces of hare and partridge on onion mixture. Top with reserved slices of salt pork. Add bay leaves and water. Season with salt and pepper to taste. Cover and roast in a 425°F (220°C) oven for 1 hour. Lower oven temperature to 300°F (150°C) and remove cover. Turn meat, basting frequently to brown on all sides, and roast for about 1 more hour or until tender. Add more water if necessary.

Remove meat to a hot platter and keep warm. Drain off fat from pan. Remove bay leaves. Deglaze pan with a little water and season sauce with salt and pepper. To serve, pour sauce over meat and trim with parsley. Eight to ten servings.

PÂTÉ À L'ÉPERLAN
Smelt pie

When the tiny fish called smelts were plentiful in the waters around Île aux Coudres, this fish pie was frequently served. Now it has become a special occasion dish, says Rita Dufour Laurin, who was for many years owner-manager of Hôtel La Roche Pleureuse on the island.

---

1 egg white, beaten
1 pound (500 g) smelts
1 cup (250 mL) chopped green onions
Salt and ground black pepper
⅓ cup (75 mL) whipping cream
Pastry for double-crust, 9-inch (23 cm) pie

Line a 9-inch (23 cm) pie plate with pastry. Brush bottom and sides of pie shell with beaten egg white and let stand to dry for 15 minutes. Split open smelts along belly, clean and remove backbones, fins and tails. Arrange ⅓ of the fish fillets evenly in pie shell. Top with ⅓ of the onions. Repeat layers twice more. Season with salt and pepper to taste. Pour cream over filling. Cover with top pastry crust. Trim, crimp edges to seal and cut steam vents.

Bake in a preheated 350°F (180°C) oven for 45 to 60 minutes or until lightly browned. Serve hot. (This pie loses moisture and texture if cooled and reheated.) Six servings.

Not to be missed

Sights not to be missed by Charlevoix visitors: the Cabot garden at Cap à l'Aigle (open to the public on certain Saturdays in summer; call the local tourist office at (418) 665-4454 for dates); the old wharf at Port au Persil; whales downriver from Tadoussac; the original mills of Île aux Coudres; the art galleries of Baie St. Paul; the museum at La Malbaie; and the Manoir Richelieu at Pointe au Pic.

Favourite meat

Today's Murray Bay lamb is much more tender and delicately flavoured than the mutton of yesteryear. Now, because the lambs are often raised as carefully as calves, their meat is as tender as the finest veal. At a lamb farm in Cap à l'Aigle on the slopes of Mount Murray, the animals eat a special grain and milk diet and are marketed at no more than six months of age.

GIGOT D'AGNEAU AUX BAIES DE GENIÈVRE

Leg of lamb flavoured with juniper berries

This roast lamb recipe is the personal favourite of Chef Marthe Lemire, co-proprietor with husband Jacques, of the Pointe au Pic inn Auberge au Petit Berger. She likes to serve it with a *ratatouille niçoise*, green beans trimmed with bacon, and steamed potatoes. With the dish, Jacques suggests a red wine, either the Côtes de Bourg Château Les Heaumes or the Côtes du Rhone Hermitage.

---

1 fresh leg of lamb (4 pounds/2 kg)
2 tablespoons (25 mL) crushed dried juniper berries
2 tablespoons (25 mL) butter, softened
Salt and ground black pepper
3 tablespoons (45 mL) Cognac
1 small onion, chopped
1 clove garlic, chopped
2 tablespoons (25 mL) butter
1 cup (250 mL) lamb or chicken stock*

   * See recipe for lamb stock on page 119.

Cut a slit along the length of the lamb leg and insert 1 tablespoon (15 mL) of crushed juniper berries.

Combine softened butter, remaining juniper berries and salt and pepper to taste; spread over lamb. Insert meat thermometer in lamb and place in a shallow roasting pan. Roast in a preheated 375°F (190°C) oven for 1 to 1¼ hours or until medium-rare (internal temperature of 140°F/60°C). Transfer meat to a hot platter. Pour off fat from pan and reserve. Return meat to pan and flame with Cognac. Return meat to hot platter and keep warm.

In a small frying pan, sauté onion and garlic in

butter until soft. Add drippings and lamb stock and simmer until sauce is reduced and slightly thickened. Strain sauce and serve hot over sliced lamb. Six to eight servings.

POT AU FEU

Boiled beef and vegetable dinner

This comfortable meal-in-one dish has been part of Charlevoix family cooking for as long as Yvonne Cimon Desgagnés can remember. The proprietor of Auberge L'été in St. Joseph de la Rive likes to call it *Bouilli de boeuf et de légumes québecois.*

½ pound (250 g) salt pork
1 to 2 beef marrow bones
8 cups (2 L) cold water
4 pounds (2 kg) round roast of beef
Bouquet garni*
8 medium potatoes
3 to 4 medium onions
2 small rutabagas
8 medium carrots
1 leek
½ medium cabbage
1 stalk celery
1 pound (500 g) green or wax beans
Salt and ground pepper

* Savoury, chervil and parsley are recommended, preferably fresh.

Cut salt pork into ½-inch (1 cm) cubes and place in a large, heavy stock pot with marrow bones and cold water. Bring to a boil, skimming off any foam that forms on surface. Cut beef into 2-inch (5 cm) cubes and add with bouquet garni to stock pot. Cover and simmer gently for 2 to 3 hours.

Peel and quarter potatoes, onions, turnips and carrots. Cut leek, cabbage and celery into large slices or chunks. Tie beans in small bundles. About 45 minutes before end of cooking time, remove marrow bones, season stock with salt and pepper to taste and begin adding vegetables, timing each addition according to the amount of cooking needed to make them tender-crisp. Do not overcook. Adjust seasoning with salt and pepper. Eight to ten servings.

SAUTÉ DE LAPIN TANTE IRMA

Rabbit vegetable casserole

One of the inns in Charlevoix where traditional cuisine is celebrated is the Hôtel La Roche Pleureuse on the eastern tip of Île aux Coudres. Opened in 1934 by the Dufour family, its menu continues to include the dishes of the late Irma and Germaine Dufour and of Lise Dufour, who cooks under the direction of Chef Jeannot Desgagnés, also an island native. This rabbit recipe is a favourite with hotel guests.

½ pound (250 g) salt pork
2 rabbits (2½ pounds/1 kg each)
2 onions, coarsely chopped
¾ cup (175 mL) white wine
4 cups (1 L) veal or chicken stock
4 carrots, peeled, cut into long slices
½ teaspoon (2 mL) dried thyme
1 bay leaf
Salt and ground black pepper
2 cups (500 mL) whole, fresh mushrooms, quartered if large

Cut salt pork into thin strips and blanch in boiling water for 5 minutes. Drain and sauté in a large, heavy, flameproof casserole with a cover. When salt pork is crisp and brown, set aside.

Cut rabbits into 8 pieces each and brown on all sides in pork drippings. Set rabbit aside and add onions to pan; sauté until just beginning to turn golden, then set aside. Drain off fat from pan. Deglaze pan with wine. Simmer until it is reduced by half. Stir in veal stock, carrots, thyme, bay leaf and salt and pepper to taste. Add pork, rabbit and onions. Cover and bake in a 350°F (180°C) oven for 1 hour or until rabbit is tender. Add mushrooms for the final 15 minutes of cooking time. Eight servings.*

* Recipe can easily be halved to serve four.

PÂTÉ DE CHARLEVOIX

Charlevoix pastry

Thérèse Savard makes this rich biscuit pastry for both the *tourtière* and *cipâte* she serves at Auberge La Petite Madeleine in Port au Persil. She rolls it thickly for the *tourtière*, thinly for the *cipâte*.

4 cups (1 L) all-purpose flour
4 teaspoons (20 mL) baking powder
3/4 teaspoon (4 mL) salt
2 cups (500 mL) chilled vegetable shortening
2 cups (500 mL) cold milk

In a large bowl, sift or mix together flour, baking powder and salt. Using a pastry blender or 2 knives, cut in shortening until mixture resembles coarse crumbs. Make a well in centre of mixture and pour in cold milk. Mix gently with a fork until dough just comes together; do not overmix. Divide dough into 2 balls, cover or wrap, and refrigerate for at least 30 minutes. Makes enough for 2 double-crust, 9-inch (23 cm) pies.

A culinary blend

The cooking of Charlevoix represents a long, slow blending of traditions. The earliest French settlers, who had moved east from Quebec City, adopted some food habits from the Indians. Their cuisine altered again when British army officers settled in the region after the conquest of New France and planted oats and potatoes among the tree stumps of newly cleared land. In the 19th century, English-speaking Canadians from Montreal and Toronto contributed the use of cream in cooking and a liking for steamed puddings. When Americans arrived from New England and points west, they introduced such American tastes as cornbread.

TOURTIÈRE DE CHARLEVOIX

Charlevoix meat pie

This simple combination of meat, vegetables and seasonings varies from region to region. In Charlevoix, the custom is to include potatoes, cut in small cubes, and sometimes to cube the meat too. This recipe belongs to Thérèse Savard, who has been cooking it for many years for guests at Auberge La Petite Madeleine in Port au Persil.

---

1 pound (500 g) stewing beef
1 pound (500 g) pork cut from the leg
2 medium onions, finely chopped
Ground black pepper
4 to 5 medium potatoes, peeled, cut into ½-inch (1 cm) cubes
Salt
Pastry for double-crust, 9-inch (23 cm) or 10-inch (25 cm) pie (see page 75)

Cut beef and pork in ½-inch (1 cm) cubes. In casserole, combine meats, onions and pepper to taste (do not add salt) and let stand for at least 1 hour in the refrigerator.

Add potatoes to meat mixture, season with salt to taste and add water to cover. Cover casserole and bake in a 325°F (160°C) oven for 1½ hours. (Do not allow mixture to boil or meat will be toughened and cubes of potatoes may break up.)

Remove from oven and lower temperature to 275°F (130°C). Line a deep, 9-inch (23 cm) or 10-inch (25 cm) pie plate with pastry. Pour meat mixture into pastry-lined shell. Top with pastry, trim, crimp edges and cut steam vents. Return pie to oven and bake for another 1½ hours or until crust is golden. Six to eight servings.

Saga of resort life

Serious Charlevoix tourists travel about Pointe au Pic equipped with an illustrated French guide, a fascinating and scholarly history of the resort entitled *Deux cents ans de villégiature dans Charlevoix* by Philippe Dubé (Les Presses de l'Université Laval, Québec, 1986). The book traces the development of the settlement from before the British conquest in 1759 to modern times. By consulting the then-and-now photographs of the mansions built earlier in this century, visitors can identify those that are now comfortable inns as well as catch a glimpse, through well-tended gardens, of the large number that continue to shelter a luxurious summer lifestyle. The stone shell of the original Fraser seigneury, which burned during a filming session in 1975, can be seen from the highway just west of Cap à l'Aigle.

Cipâte

Layered meat pie

This sustaining meat pie is a dish of endless variety.
This version belongs to Thérèse Savard of Clermont.

---

4 to 5 pounds (2 to 2.5 kg) blade roast of beef
4 to 5 pounds (2 to 2.5 kg) pork butt or leg
5 medium onions, chopped
Salt and ground black pepper
Pastry for double-crust, 9-inch (23 cm) pie
  (see page 75)
10 (approximate) medium potatoes, peeled, cut into
  1-inch (2.5 cm) cubes

Trim fat, bones and gristle from beef and pork and
cut into ½-inch (1 cm) cubes. In a large (12 to 14
inches/30 to 35 cm wide), deep, heavy casserole
with a cover, combine meat, onions and salt and
pepper to taste; add enough water just to cover
ingredients. Cover and roast in a 300°F (150°C) oven
until mixture comes to a boil, then lower heat to
200°F (100°C) and continue to roast, covered, for a
total time of 2 hours.

Roll out pastry ¼-inch (5 mm) thick, large enough
to line casserole and make 3 crusts. Remove *cipâte*
from oven and raise temperature to 350°F (180°C).
Add potatoes to meat mixture, stirring to distribute
evenly. Line casserole with pastry and add one-third
of meat mixture. Cover with pastry; cut vent for steam
to escape. Repeat twice more, sealing top crust. Place
cover on casserole and return to oven. When mixture
is steaming hot, reduce oven temperature again to
200°F (100°C) and bake, still covered, for another 2
hours. Remove cover and bake another hour until
crust is light brown and crisp. Twelve to sixteen
servings.

BELLE CHASSE FORESTIÈRE

Game birds with mushroom and onion sauce

Poultry breeders are developing meatier versions of game birds. Chef Jeannot Desgagnés of Hôtel La Roche Pleureuse on Île aux Coudres uses a farm-raised game bird called a *belle chasse,* which is a cross between a pheasant and a guinea hen. A pheasant or a Rock Cornish hen may be substituted in this recipe.

---

2 *belle chasse* game birds (1 pound/500 g each)
3 carrots, peeled, coarsely chopped
2 onions, coarsely chopped
4 stalks celery, chopped
Vegetable oil
¼ teaspoon (1 mL) dried thyme
Salt and ground black pepper
2 cups (500 mL) game bird or chicken stock
1 cup (250 mL) white wine
½ cup (125 mL) chopped green onions
2 cups (500 mL) sliced mushrooms

Truss birds and arrange on a bed of carrots, onions and celery in a large, heavy, flameproof casserole. Oil birds lightly, then season with thyme and salt and pepper to taste. Add game bird stock and roast in a 350°F (180°C) oven for 1½ hours, basting with pan juices. Remove birds to hot platter and keep warm.

Strain pan juices through a sieve and skim off fat. Discard vegetables. Deglaze pan with wine. Add strained pan juices and reduce sauce over high heat. Adjust seasoning with salt and pepper. Add green onions and mushrooms; cook briefly, just until heated through. Pour sauce over birds and serve. Four servings.

CHAUSSONS AUX POMMES
Apple dumplings

This early Quebec recipe can be traced to Normandy, home of many of the province's first settlers. It's sometimes named *pommes en cage* because the fruit is baked whole in a container of pastry. Norman chefs call it *bourdelots* and use puff pastry; Quebecers make it with regular pie pastry. This recipe belongs to Rita Dufour Laurin, for many years owner-manager of Hôtel La Roche Pleureuse.

Juice from 1 lemon
6 apples, peeled, cored
½ cup (125 mL) brown sugar
Cinnamon
1 egg, beaten
Maple syrup
Whipped cream (optional)
Pastry for double-crust, 9-inch (23 cm) pie, or
   7 ounces (200 g) puff pastry

Drizzle lemon juice over prepared apples. Pack brown sugar into apple centres and sprinkle with cinnamon. Roll out pastry into a rectangle, 14 × 21 inches (35 cm × 53 cm), and cut into six 7-inch (18 cm) squares.

Place an apple in the centre of each pastry square and moisten the 4 corners with water. Lift up and join the corners of pastry together to enclose each apple completely. Pinch edges to seal and twist pastry at the top. Brush pastry with beaten egg. Place in a lightly greased, shallow baking pan. (Dessert may be prepared up to this point a few hours ahead and refrigerated until ready to bake.)

Bake apples in a preheated 400°F (200°C) oven for 30 to 35 minutes or until pastry is crisp and lightly browned. Serve warm with maple syrup and whipped cream, if desired. Six servings.

A glimpse of the past

The steep beautiful hillsides that rise from the St. Lawrence still show the boundaries of the original narrow farms. As recently as the 1950s, artists working in the hill country could observe farms and a way of life that were nearly self-sufficient. Montreal painter Jori Smith, who summered for 30 years near Petite Rivière St. François just west of Baie St. Paul, described the small farms: "It was like stepping into another age—the middle ages. Each family produced all its own food. They bought nothing but molasses, salt and pepper."

Charlevoix has long been a favourite resort for "pleasure seekers." The term was coined by my grandfather, the late University of Toronto historian George M. Wrong. A turn-of-the-century member of this breed, he used the term in his 1908 book *A Canadian Manor and Its Seigneurs,* which chronicles the Nairne seigneury of Pointe au Pic. Grandpapa, as we always called him, had married into a Toronto family who had summered in Murray Bay since the 1860s. Summer visitors came from as far away as Scotland and the American mid-west. The most famous American visitor was William Howard Taft, president of the United States just before the First World War. He summered in Pointe au Pic for more than 40 years.

Gâteau chaud à la farine de mais
Johnny Cake

An example of the influence of American visitors and their food tastes on Charlevoix cuisine, this dessert has been a favourite in the region since the early part of the century. It's sometimes flavoured with molasses, but is almost always referred to by its English name. This recipe was handed down by the late Ursule Duchenes Tremblay of Cap à l'Aigle to her daughter Georgette Tremblay Rochette.

---

1 cup (250 mL) all-purpose flour
1 cup (250 mL) yellow cornmeal
1 tablespoon (15 mL) baking powder
½ teaspoon (2 mL) salt
2 eggs
5 tablespoons (75 mL) granulated sugar
¼ cup (50 mL) butter, melted
1 cup (250 mL) milk
Maple syrup or sweetened whipped cream
  (optional)

In a bowl, combine flour, cornmeal, baking powder and salt. In another bowl, beat eggs, sugar and melted butter together. Add dry ingredients to egg mixture alternately with milk, about ⅓ at a time, stirring just until blended. Do not overbeat.

Pour into a buttered 9-inch (23 cm) square baking pan. Bake in a preheated 375°F (190°C) oven for 25 to 30 minutes or until tester inserted in centre comes out clean. Let cool for 10 minutes before serving, or turn out onto rack to cool completely. Serve with maple syrup or whipped cream, if desired. Eight servings.

MICROWAVE METHOD

Prepare batter as directed in recipe. Pour into a lightly greased 8-cup (2 L) microwave ring mould. Microwave, uncovered, at Medium (50 percent) for 5 minutes, rotating pan once. Microwave at High (100 percent) for 2 to 4 minutes or until tester inserted in centre comes out clean and cake is firm to the touch. Let stand on counter top for 10 minutes. Run a knife around the edges to loosen cake and turn out onto serving plate.

TARTE AU SUCRE DE TANTE LISE

Tante Lise's sugar pie

A fixture on the menu at Hôtel La Roche Pleureuse on Île aux Coudres, this dessert has links to northern France, homeland of many Quebec settlers. The recipe belongs to Lise Dufour, a member of the family that founded this inn in 1934. She is still a key figure in the hotel kitchen.

1½ cups (375 mL) brown sugar
¾ cup (175 mL) whipping cream
2½ tablespoons (35 mL) cornstarch
Pastry for single-crust, 8-inch (20 cm) pie

Line an 8-inch (20 cm) pie plate with pastry. In a bowl, mix brown sugar, cream and cornstarch. Pour into unbaked pie shell. Bake in a preheated 425°F (220°C) oven for 10 minutes, then lower temperature to 325°F (160°C) and continue baking for 25 to 30 minutes longer or until filling is set and golden. Serve warm or at room temperature. Six servings.

Bavarois aux framboises

Raspberry Bavarian cream

Raspberries are a favourite fruit in Charlevoix, a taste that dates back to the time when these berries grew wild throughout the region. At Auberge des Peupliers, the Tremblay family inn in Cap à l'Aigle, this classic recipe is often on the menu. Chef Dominique Truchon serves it plain or with creamy chocolate sauce.

1¼ cups (300 mL) milk
⅔ cup (150 g) granulated sugar
4 egg yolks
Pinch salt
1 envelope (1 tablespoon/15 mL) unflavoured gelatin
2 tablespoons (25 mL) water
1½ teaspoons (7 mL) vanilla
1 cup (250 mL) whipping cream
2 cups (500 mL) fresh raspberries, or 1 package
   (300 g) frozen unsweetened raspberries
Additional fresh raspberries or mint leaves

In a saucepan, combine milk with ⅓ cup (75 mL) of the sugar; heat until scalding. In a bowl, beat egg yolks with remaining sugar and salt. Slowly whisk hot milk into the egg mixture. Return to saucepan and cook over medium-low heat, whisking constantly, until custard thickens to the consistency of whipping cream and coats a wooden spoon. Do not let mixture come to a boil or it will curdle.

Sprinkle gelatin over water to soften; stir into hot custard and remove from heat. Add vanilla and strain sauce through a fine sieve. Cool custard by setting pan in a larger container filled with ice cubes. Stir occasionally until sauce starts to thicken and become syrupy.

Whip cream until stiff. Purée raspberries in food processor or blender, then strain through a sieve to remove seeds. Fold whipped cream into custard, then fold in puréed strained raspberries.

Rinse a 6-cup (1.5 L) mould with cold water. Pour in custard mixture and cover mould with plastic wrap. Refrigerate until firm, about 4 hours or overnight. To serve, dip mould briefly in warm water, dry off and place serving plate over top. Quickly invert and turn out onto serving plate. Trim with fresh raspberries or mint leaves. Six servings.

MICROWAVE METHOD

Custard: In a 2-cup (500 mL) glass measure, microwave milk and ⅓ cup (75 mL) of the sugar at High (100 percent) for 3 to 4 minutes, until mixture almost comes to a boil, stirring once.

In a 4-cup (1 L) glass measure, whisk together egg yolks, remaining sugar and salt. Slowly pour the hot milk into yolk mixture, whisking constantly. Microwave custard, uncovered, at Medium (50 percent) for 3 to 5 minutes, whisking every minute, until custard thickens slightly and coats a wooden spoon. Add softened gelatin; whisk until dissolved. Strain sauce through fine sieve and add vanilla. Continue with recipe as directed.

LAURENTIANS — OUTAOUAIS

Although the Laurentians are a popular holiday retreat today, the ancient hills of the Canadian Shield north of Montreal were settled slowly—the only welcome to this wilderness was the abundant wildlife in its forests, lakes and streams. Rabbit, partridge and trout continue to be prized on the better tables of this northwest corner of the province. Other gifts of nature—fiddleheads, morel mushrooms, maple products and honey—are still specialties in the region, just as they have been for centuries.

When I was travelling west along the Mille Îles River, through St. Eustache and Deux Montagnes, both evolved from 18th-century seigneuries, and then on up the Ottawa River, I found it easier to imagine colonizing these tranquil shores than the wilderness of the Laurentians.

For nearly two centuries, the riverbank has been lined with small but thriving farms, cleared originally by both English and French settlers, who brought—and adapted—their cuisine to an area made prosperous by lumbering on the Ottawa, Gatineau and Petite Nation rivers. Woodcutters and log drivers enjoyed the most sustaining dishes of Quebec's early cuisine—the thick soups, meaty stews, baked beans, pancakes and pies. Hefty dishes from days gone by continue to have special occasion status, according to members of the rural women's organization Cercles de Fermières.

Marie-Ange Rondeau of Buckingham, long-time member of the Cercles, gave examples from her family recipes: partridge baked with beans; *cipaille* layered with beef, pork, chicken and hare; *tourtière* filled with pork and maybe veal but never beef; ham braised with onions and beer; and desserts rich with molasses, pork or suet.

Some regional farms have now turned to producing domestic versions of game meats. One rabbit producer is Jean Marc Chaput, a conference speaker and author who runs a *lapinerie* at Fassett. "It's my way of promoting the natural aspects of life, the original foods from the land," he told me.

Chefs have lightened the early dishes. At Café Henry Burger in Hull, Chef Georges Laurier cooks a few of the dishes his grandmother prepared in the days when the restaurant was known as Madame Burger's. He uses red cabbage, Spanish onions and apples when braising partridge, then tops the dish with a brioche crust. Venison, marinated with red wine, is served with a sauce he flavours with cranberries and juniper berries.

Rabbit and duckling are among specialties at L'Orée du Bois, the Old Chelsea inn run by French-born chef-proprietor Guy Blain. He likes to combine these meats with wine or cider and local fruits such as blueberries.

At Papineauville, a bustling town on the Ottawa River halfway between Montreal and Hull, the restaurant La Table de Pierre DeLaHaye interprets the cuisine of Quebec's earliest Norman settlers. Chef DeLaHaye, born in Fécamp in Normandy, uses apples and cream, cider and Calvados with local foods. I so enjoyed his special dessert—honey-flavoured ice cream in a *madeleine* biscuit with a custard and raspberry sauce—that I went at once to his honey supplier, Jean Marc Peti. After a consultation at the honey shop on the northern outskirts of the town, I bought the extra-strong buckwheat honey the chef uses, plus a paler, milder version.

Even the bees must have had a harder time surviving in the less hospitable land north of St. Agathe. But, beginning in the 1870s, settlers were given a vision of a promised land. A persuasive priest called Antoine Labelle encouraged families to go in search of *les terres en bois debout*—free land with timber still standing.

In tiny valleys and ledges between rocky, forested slopes, the courageous settlers literally carved out homesteads in the wilds.

"My grandparents thought it would be good land. But often, nothing would grow," said Fleur-Ange Vanier Rochon, a descendant of two of St. Jovite's founding families. "They would dig and find only sand and rocks," said this distinguished great-grandmother, demonstrating with the width of her small hand the amount of arable land that was available to grow food. "And the further north they went, the worse it became," she said as we leafed through her hand-written recipes.

Scarcity forced this region's cooks to stretch every morsel of food. Nowhere in the province did I find so many economical recipes. Mme Rochon's daughter, Nicole Rochon Kretz of Val David, remembers that in their family of 14 even plentiful vegetables would be used to the fullest. Along with onions, chopped celery leaves were used to season a wide variety of dishes. "To this day, I feel guilty when I throw away celery leaves," said Nicole with a chuckle as we watched her mother demonstrate her *tourtière*. To this day, it's flavoured with celery leaves.

POTAGE AUX GOURGANES
Puréed bean soup

Leopold Handfield, of Restaurant La Table Enchantée at St. Jovite, serves this deluxe version of the traditional *gourgane* bean soup that is so popular in the Saguenay-Lac St. Jean and Charlevoix regions. Chef Handfield flavours his soup with a variety of vegetables and ham stock. A topping of whipped cream, browned under the broiler, is his final touch.

Laurentian Menu

Old-fashioned braised hare
(page 94)

Puff pastry with vegetables
in coriander sauce
(page 96)

Whipped potatoes

Green salad

Madeleines with honey
ice cream
(page 106)

1 tablespoon (15 mL) butter
1 carrot, cubed
1 onion, chopped
½ cup (125 mL) peeled, cubed potatoes
¼ cup (50 mL) cubed turnips
5 cups (1.25 L) ham cooking stock
2 cups (500 mL) shelled *gourgane* beans*
Salt and ground black pepper
⅔ cup (150 mL) whipping cream

   * Fresh *gourgane* beans are recommended, if in season. Frozen beans may be substituted, if available. Or you may use dried fava beans; soak the dried beans overnight, then drain and proceed with recipe.

In a large, heavy saucepan, heat butter and cook carrot, onion, potatoes and turnips gently for 10 minutes. Add ham cooking stock (or water and a ham bone) and bring to a boil. Add *gourgane* beans and simmer very slowly, partly covered, for about 2 hours or until beans are tender. (If you have used a ham bone, remove it at this point.)

Purée soup in a blender or food processor until smooth. Season with salt and pepper to taste. In a bowl, whip cream until stiff. Pour hot soup into 4 ovenproof bowls (the type used for onion soup). Add a generous spoonful of the whipped cream to each bowlful and place under a hot broiler just until cream is lightly browned. Serve at once. Four servings.

Salade de porc
et betteraves en gelée
Jellied pork aspic with beets

This meat and vegetable salad was traditionally served on New Year's Day in the Paquin family of Val David. The recipe belongs to Jeanine Forget Paquin and is a favourite with her son, Montreal chef Denis Paquin.

L'Eau à la Bouche

2 pounds (1 kg) boneless, cubed pork*
2 tablespoons (25 mL) vegetable oil
2 medium onions, halved
1 cup (250 mL) water
2 bay leaves
Salt and ground black pepper
1½ cups (375 mL) cubed pickled beets
1 cup (250 mL) chopped celery
½ cup (125 mL) finely chopped onion
1 envelope (1 tablespoon/15 mL) unflavoured gelatin
1¾ cups (425 mL) chicken stock

   * 2 cups (500 mL) chopped, cooked roast pork may be substituted.

In a heavy, flameproof casserole with a cover, brown meat well in the oil. Add halved onions, water, bay leaves and salt and pepper to taste. Cover and simmer at a low temperature or cook in a 250°F (100°C) oven until tender, about 2 hours. Cool, remove meat and cut in small cubes. Strain bouillon, chill and remove fat. Reserve for softening the gelatin.

In a bowl, combine cooked meat, pickled beets, celery and chopped onion. Season with salt and pepper to taste. Rinse 2-quart (2 L) mould with cold water. Add meat and vegetable mixture. Soften gelatin in chicken stock and bouillon, then heat until gelatin is dissolved. Let cool. Pour over meat mixture in mould and chill until set. To serve, unmould and cut into serving-size slices. Six to eight servings.

This inn has such a good reputation that it's now a member of the prestigious *Relais et Châteaux* group of hotels. The couple who own and run it are self-taught chef Anne Desjardins and her husband Pierre Audette, manager and sommelier. The latest contemporary cuisine is served in the small, elegantly rustic restaurant, at expensive prices. Comfort and decor in the spacious inn are outstanding in a region with many fine restaurants and hotels. The outdoor swimming pool is heated. Tennis, golf and skiing are near at hand. (Rooms: 26, each with private bath; address: Route 117, 3003 St. Adèle Blvd., St. Adèle, Québec J0R 1L0; telephone: (514) 229-2991.)

The Papineau manor

The elegant home of one of Quebec's last *seigneurs* can be seen by tourists who visit the Anglo-Norman manor house of Quebec political leader Louis-Joseph Papineau. Papineau, speaker in Lower Canada's House of Assembly, was a leader of the *Patriotes* in Lower Canada's rebellion of 1837. After the revolt was crushed, he lived in exile in the United States and France until an amnesty allowed him to return. He built this imposing stone residence on his family's seigneury of La Petite Nation between 1847 and 1850. The house, now on the grounds of Chateau Montebello (the former Seigneury Club), overlooks the Ottawa River and is furnished in Victorian style, as it would have been when Papineau and his family lived there. It is open to the public from May to October.

TOURTIÈRE DE FLEUR-ANGE

Fleur-Ange's pork pie

Marcel Kretz, prize-winning chef at Hôtel la Sapinière in Val David, and son-in-law of Fleur-Ange Vanier Rochon, says Mme Rochon's traditional pork pie is the best he has ever eaten. He looks forward to receiving two of them each Christmas to make up for the fact that he must often work on that day and miss the family dinner. Mme Rochon uses only pork and a careful hand with seasoning.

---

2 pounds (1 kg) lean ground pork
1 cup (250 mL) water
1 cup (250 mL) chopped celery
½ cup (125 mL) chopped celery leaves
2 large onions, chopped
2 cloves garlic, chopped
½ cup (125 mL) chopped fresh parsley
1 tablespoon (15 mL) fresh savoury chopped or
   1 teaspoon (5 mL) dried
Pinch each ground cinnamon and cloves
Salt and ground black pepper
Pastry for 2 double-crust, 8-inch (20 cm) pies
1 egg yolk combined with 1 tablespoon (15 mL) milk

In a large, heavy saucepan, simmer pork with water, celery and leaves, onions, garlic, parsley, savoury, cinnamon, cloves, and salt and pepper to taste. Cook, stirring occasionally, for 30 minutes, adding more water, if necessary, to prevent mixture from drying. Drain off fat. Adjust seasonings, if necessary. Let cool.

Line 2 9-inch (23 cm) pie plates with pastry and fill with cooled meat mixture. Roll out top crusts, cutting a generous vent in the centre of each. (Mme Rochon cuts her vents in the shape of an evergreen tree.) Cover each pie with top crust, trim pastry, crimp the edges to seal and cut small steam vents. Brush top of pastry with egg yolk and milk mixture. (At this point, pies may be refrigerated or frozen.)

Bake pies in a preheated 400°F (200°C) oven for 35 to 40 minutes or until crust is golden. Serve either hot or cold with pickles or relish. Twelve to sixteen servings.

PÂTÉ AUX PATATES
Potato pie

This potato pie makes a warming supper dish. It was a Friday favourite in the days when the meatless rule was observed in French Catholic families, says Nicole Kretz.

---

5 to 6 hot cooked potatoes
Milk
2 tablespoons (25 mL) butter
2 egg yolks
1 onion, finely chopped
¼ cup (50 mL) finely chopped celery and leaves
1 tablespoon (15 mL) chopped fresh parsley
Pinch dried savoury or chopped fresh chives
Salt and ground black pepper
Pastry for double-crust, 9-inch (23 cm) pie

Line a 9-inch (23 cm) pie plate with pastry. Mash potatoes with enough milk to make a smooth purée; add butter and 1 egg yolk. Combine potatoes with onion, celery, parsley and savoury; season with salt and pepper to taste.

Spread potato mixture in pie shell. Cover with top crust, trim and crimp edges to seal and cut steam vents. Brush top crust with remaining egg yolk. Bake pie in a preheated 400°F (200°C) oven for 30 to 40 minutes or until pastry is golden. Six to eight servings.

Le Boeuf Alphonsine dans le chaudron de fer de grand-mère

Grandmother's beef in a cast-iron pot

Served alongside *ragoût de boulettes* and *tourtière* at Christmas and New Year's suppers, this slow-cooked beef dish, though inexpensive, always meant a celebration, says Montreal chef Richard Bergeron, who comes from La Minerve north of Mont Tremblant. His grandmother, Alphonsine Lemieux Bergeron, would set the cast-iron casserole in the oven of her wood stove just before going to bed. The beef, tightly covered, would cook overnight as the fire was dying down and be ready to reheat when needed. Venison may be substituted; add a few juniper berries to the bag of seasonings if using game. Serve with mashed potatoes and root vegetables such as rutabaga.

---

1 onion
1 bay leaf
2 whole cloves
8 black peppercorns
3½ pounds (1.5 kg) shoulder of beef, cubed
1 tablespoon (15 mL) coarse salt
½ cup (125 mL) water

Cut a square of cheesecloth large enough to enclose the onion. Stud onion with bay leaf, cloves and peppercorns and tie closed in cheesecloth. Place onion and beef in a well-seasoned 2-quart (2 L) cast-iron pot with a tight-fitting lid or in a clay baker. (Enamelled cast iron may be used but does not give as good a result.) Sprinkle meat with salt. Pour water over. Cover and set in a preheated 400°F (200°C) oven for 15 minutes, then lower temperature to 250°F (120°C) and cook for about 4 to 5 hours without removing lid.

When ready to serve, carry the pot directly to the table before uncovering it and releasing the rich aroma. Remove seasoning bag and serve. Six to eight servings.

KETCHUP VERT

Green tomato ketchup

When an early frost halts the ripening of tomatoes in the Laurentians, cooks make a spicy green tomato ketchup to enjoy with *tourtière*, or *cipaille* or cold meats all year long. This is a favourite recipe of Montreal chef Denis Paquin, who remembers his mother Jeanine Forget Paquin making it when he was growing up in Val David.

---

6 pounds (24 medium or 2.5 kg) green tomatoes, chopped
3 pounds (15 medium or 1.5 kg) onions, chopped
½ cup (125 mL) coarse salt
3 cups (750 mL) white vinegar
2 cups (500 mL) granulated sugar
6 tablespoons (90 mL) mixed pickling spices, tied in a cheesecloth bag

---

In a large bowl, alternate layers of tomatoes and onions, sprinkling each layer with salt. Let stand for at least 8 hours or overnight. Rinse; drain well. Combine vegetables with vinegar, sugar and spice bag. In a large saucepan or stock pot, bring mixture to a boil, then simmer, uncovered, for about 30 to 45 minutes, stirring frequently until slightly thickened. Pour into hot sterilized jars and seal. Makes about 12 cups (3 L) ketchup.

Auberge Otter Lake Haus

This quiet, friendly inn run by the German-born Thiel family is located on trout-stocked Lac la Loutre northeast of Montebello. No power boats break the peaceful calm of a summer holiday, and in the winter you can cross-country ski from the door of this renovated farmhouse. High tea on the patio or a private beach picnic are summer treats. Winter appetites are satisfied at Sunday brunch with such favourites as scrambled eggs or sauerkraut with German sausages or apple pancakes with maple syrup. Home-raised lamb and chicken, the inn's garden vegetables and German-French cuisine combine to make eating a principal activity. Moderate rates. (Rooms: 21, some with private bath; address: P.O. Box 29, Huberdeau, Québec, J0T 1G0; telephone: (819) 687-2767.)

Highway to the west

Samuel de Champlain first paddled up the Ottawa River in 1613, one of many French explorers to travel what has been called the first Trans-Canada Highway. Explorers and soldiers who voyaged up the river included Dollard des Ormeaux, Radisson and Groseilliers, LaSalle and Iberville. Dams and power development have taken much of the rush and tumble out of these river waters, but the old river road (Route 148) is still a pretty one to travel. If it's spring or fall, glance overhead as you near the mouth of the Petite Nation River at Plaisance. You may see migrating ducks arriving or departing from the wildlife preserve maintained by the Quebec government on the shore.

PERDRIX À LA FAÇON DE MON GRAND-PÈRE RAOUL

Grandfather's partridge

When Georges Laurier was growing up in Hull, his grandmother often prepared the traditional Quebec dish of braised partridge and cabbage with birds that his grandfather caught in the Gatineau hills. Now chef at Café Henry Burger, the Hull restaurant that overlooks the new National Museum of Civilization, Laurier has created this refined version of the favourite family recipe. He serves it with cubed carrots, turnips and potatoes, and sliced zucchini, steaming the vegetables and then sautéing them briefly in a little butter. Recommended wine: an Alsatian white Gewerstraminer or a red Bordeaux Côte du Bourg.

---

2 partridges (about 1 pound/500 g each)
2 tablespoons (25 mL) white, unsalted pork fat, cut into thin strips
½ cup (125 mL) chicken stock
½ cup (125 mL) finely chopped lean salt pork or fat back
or 2 tablespoons (25 mL) vegetable oil
2 Spanish onions, minced
½ medium red cabbage, finely chopped
2 apples, peeled, coarsely chopped
1 teaspoon (5 mL) chopped, fresh thyme, or ¼ teaspoon (1 mL) dried
1 clove garlic, chopped
2 tablespoons (25 mL) brown sugar
Salt and ground black pepper
2 large pork sausages

To prevent partridge breasts from drying out, tiny slits may be cut in the meat and the strips of white, unsalted pork fat inserted in the slits with the tip of a knife. Or a butcher's larding needle may be used to do the job.

Truss birds. Place in a roasting pan with chicken stock. Roast, uncovered, in a 325°F (160°C) oven for 30 to 45 minutes until meat is half-cooked, basting 3 or 4 times with the chicken stock. Let meat cool sufficiently so that you can remove all the bones, keeping the larger pieces of meat intact. Refrigerate meat.

Place bones and pan drippings in a large heavy saucepan, add cold water to cover, and simmer for about 1 hour to make partridge stock. Strain and reserve. Cut lean salt pork or unsalted fat-back in strips about $1^1/_4 \times {}^1/_4$ inch (3 cm × 1 cm). Fry in a heavy, flameproof, 3-quart (3 L) casserole with a cover, until lightly browned. Add onions, cabbage and apples; sauté for 2 minutes, turning to coat ingredients in drippings.

Cover casserole and bake in a 300°F (150°C) oven for 1 hour, adding a little partridge stock if mixture dries out.

Add partridge meat, thyme, garlic, brown sugar, and salt and pepper to taste. Pour 1 cup (250 mL) of the partridge stock over all and continue baking, covered, for another hour. Add additional partridge stock if mixture begins to dry out. Remove cover for final 15 minutes of baking time. You may place casserole briefly under the broiler to give partridge a crisp skin.

Fry sausages until cooked and browned and slice horizontally. Put them in a ring around the edge of the casserole. Four servings.

The picnic tradition

The Indians, first inhabitants of Quebec, are believed to have taught the French settlers to cook and eat outdoors when the weather was fine, a custom unheard of at the time in France. The spring "sugaring off" maple syrup feast in the woods, the fish fry on the beach, and the late summer corn boil, *épluchette de blé d'inde*, are examples of their teaching.

The pleasure of eating corn was another Indian lesson. When Anne Desjardins, chef-proprietor of the St. Adèle restaurant L'Eau à la Bouche, served tender, buttered kernels of fresh corn to a group of chefs from France, she found her visitors puzzled. They left the corn on the plates because, she reasoned, in France this vegetable is considered fit only for animals.

LIÈVRE DE NOS ANCÊTRES
Old-fashioned braised hare

Growing up in St. Faustin, Luc Grand'Maison, chef at the St. Sauveur Inn Auberge St. Denis, remembers his mother making this family recipe for hare. The red wine marinade and the brown cubes of pork give the meat a rich flavour, which is accented with juniper berries. An apple pie flavoured with raisins and cinnamon could be dessert, he suggests.

---

1 hare or rabbit (3 to 4 pounds/1.5 to 2 kg), cut into
   serving-size pieces
3 medium onions, cut into sixths
1 carrot, peeled and sliced
1 sprig fresh thyme, or ¼ teaspoon (1 mL) dried
2 cups (500 mL) red wine
¼ cup (50 mL) vegetable oil
4 tablespoons (50 mL) butter
2 tablespoons (25 mL) all-purpose flour
1 tablespoon (15 mL) tomato paste
2 cloves garlic, finely chopped
Bouquet garni
Salt and ground black pepper
½ pound (250 g) mushrooms, quartered
¼ pound (125 g) smoked or salt pork, cubed
2 cups (500 mL) baby onions

Bouquet garni

Tie together in cheesecloth a small stalk of celery, several sprigs of fresh parsley, ½ bay leaf, 8 whole black peppercorns, 5 juniper berries and a sprig of fresh thyme.

Set pieces of hare in a large earthenware or glass bowl or pan. Add onions, carrot, thyme and red wine. Cover and marinate in the refrigerator for at least 24 hours, stirring occasionally.

Drain hare and vegetables and set marinade aside. Heat oil and 2 tablespoons (25 mL) of the butter in a large, heavy frying pan. Brown hare and vegetables briefly on all sides. Transfer to a flameproof, 3-quart (3 L) casserole with a cover and sprinkle lightly with flour. Cook and stir over medium heat until flour browns lightly. Add marinade, tomato paste, garlic, bouquet garni, and salt and pepper to taste. Cover and simmer over low heat for 2 hours or until hare is tender.

Meanwhile, sauté mushrooms lightly in 1 tablespoon (15 mL) of the butter. Blanch pork for 2 minutes in boiling water, drain and brown lightly. Blanch baby onions in boiling water for 1 minute, drain and peel. Brown baby onions in remaining butter.

When tender, remove hare and keep warm. Remove bouquet garni and reduce red wine sauce over high heat until thickened; adjust seasoning with salt and pepper. Return hare to sauce along with mushrooms, pork and onions. Simmer for 5 to 10 minutes more before serving. Four to six servings.

Séraphin's village

A miserly character known as Séraphin has been a legend in the Laurentians for generations. One of the most economical meals of earlier times was a buckwheat pancake named *Galette de sarrazin à Séraphin*. The story is that it was originally made only with flour, salt and water. The luxury version contained an egg and milk.

The character Séraphin Poudrier was immortalized, beginning in the 1940s, when writer Claude-Henri Grignon wrote a radio series about pioneer life entitled *Les belles histoires du pays d'en haut*. This series later was developed for television. Visitors to St. Adèle can tour a mock 19th-century village named for Séraphin. Built around an 1842 mansion, its series of buildings and a little train called *Le petit train du nord* carry out the theme of the Grignon story. The village is open to the public from May to October.

FEUILLETÉS DE PETITS LÉGUMES À LA CORIANDRE

Puff pastry with vegetables in coriander sauce

Guy Blain, chef-proprietor of L'Orée du Bois, a restaurant at Old Chelsea north of Hull, obtains many of his fresh vegetables from local gardeners; wild mushrooms come from Gatineau Park. The chef, who comes from Chateaudun in France's Loire district, grows herbs beside his comfortable, rustic restaurant.

Coriander Sauce

---

2 cups (500 mL) chicken stock
½ carrot, peeled
½ zucchini, peeled
1 small onion, cut into quarters
1 tablespoon (15 mL) coriander seeds, ground
¾ cup (175 mL) white wine
1 cup (250 mL) whipping cream

Combine chicken stock, carrot, zucchini, onion and ground coriander in a saucepan and cook until vegetables are tender, about 30 minutes. Purée in a food processor or blender until very smooth. Set aside.

   Add the wine to the saucepan and boil, uncovered, until reduced by half. Add reserved stock and cream. Bring to a boil and simmer, partially covered, until sauce thickens. Keep warm in covered saucepan over low heat.

Pastry

½ package (7 ounces/200 g) frozen puff pastry
1 egg yolk, lightly beaten

Roll out puff pastry to a 6 × 8-inch
(15 cm × 30 cm) rectangle and cut into 6 individual
rectangles, each 2 × 4 inches (5 cm × 10 cm) in size.
Place pastry on a baking sheet, brush tops with egg
yolk and bake in a preheated 400°F (200°C) oven for
12 to 15 minutes, until puffed and golden. Split each
pastry in half lengthwise and keep warm.

Vegetables

---

1 cup (250 mL) small cauliflower florets
1 small zucchini, cut into small julienne strips
1 red pepper, seeded and diced
1 small carrot, cut into thin julienne strips
1 small parsnip, cut into thin julienne strips
12 snow peas
6 Brussels sprouts, quartered
12 fiddleheads (optional)

In a pot of boiling, salted water, blanch each
vegetable separately until tender-crisp and refresh
under cold water. Drain well.

To serve, quickly heat the blanched vegetables in
the coriander sauce. Place a pastry bottom on each of
6 serving plates. Spoon some of the vegetables and
sauce into each of the pastries and arrange the pastry
halves on top. Serve immediately. Six servings.

MICROWAVE METHOD

Vegetables: In a large 10-inch (25 cm) pie plate or
quiche dish, arrange the julienne carrots and
Brussels sprouts around outside of dish. Next,
arrange the parsnips, cauliflower, zucchini, red
pepper and fiddleheads, if desired, in the middle.
Finish with snow peas in the centre. Sprinkle
vegetables with 2 tablespoons (25 mL) water. Cover
dish with vented plastic wrap. Microwave at High
(100 percent) for 4 to 5 minutes or until vegetables
are just tender-crisp. Continue with recipe as
directed.

FILET DE TRUITE, FAÇON COULIBIAC
Trout fillet, Coulibiac style

Lake trout is still plentiful in Quebec's north.
Montreal chef Richard Bergeron, who grew up in the
lake country north of Mont Tremblant, remembers
many a fine meal of trout. He likes this fish with the
classic *beurre blanc* sauce, but in this recipe, which
he developed along the lines of *cuisine renouvelée
du Québec* using phyllo dough, it could be served
with a beet *coulis* (sauce). Beets were regularly
grown in the Laurentians.

---

1 tablespoon (15 mL) commercially prepared or
  homemade salted herbs (see recipe, page 26)
1 cup (250 mL) cooked long-grain rice
½ cup (125 mL) cooked wild rice
2 hard-boiled eggs, chopped
Salt and ground black pepper
½ cup (125 mL) melted butter
16 sheets of phyllo dough (approximately ½ pound/
  250 g)
8 fresh trout fillets, boned, skinned
Beet Sauce (recipe follows)

Soak salted herbs in cold water, then drain. In a
bowl, combine herbs with long-grain and wild rice
and chopped eggs. Season with salt and pepper to
taste. Spread work surface with a sheet of plastic
wrap and brush lightly with some of the melted
butter. Lay a sheet of the phyllo on the plastic wrap.
Brush dough with butter and top with another sheet
of phyllo, brushing again with butter. Spread about 2
tablespoons (25 mL) of the rice mixture on the lower
third of the phyllo. Lay one trout fillet on the rice
mixture. Cover with another 2 tablespoons (25 mL)
of rice mixture.

Using the plastic wrap as a guide, roll up the trout fillet and rice mixture in the phyllo dough. Trim edges and fold ends under. Place phyllo-wrapped fish on a baking sheet. Brush lightly with butter. Repeat with the remaining 7 fillets.

Bake fish in a preheated 400°F (200°C) oven for 15 to 20 minutes, until pastry is crisp and golden. Just before serving, trim ends from each fish package. Serve with hot beet sauce. Eight servings.

Beet Sauce

---

4 medium beets, peeled, chopped
8 cups (2 L) fish stock
1 leek, white part only, chopped
1 onion, chopped
Salt and ground black pepper
½ cup (125 mL) whipping cream

In a saucepan, cook beets in fish stock with leek and onion until tender, about 40 minutes. Strain and purée in food processor or blender until smooth. Season with salt and pepper to taste. Add cream and blend sauce until smooth. Reheat over medium heat until very hot. Makes about 3 cups (750 mL) sauce.

Le roi du nord

A century ago the most important name in the Laurentians was that of Antoine Labelle, a St. Jérôme priest who was one of Quebec's earliest land developers. His presence continues as a place name throughout the region, beginning with a road in Laval, just north of Montreal, called Curé Labelle Blvd. You'll also find a town, lake and county named for this zealous colonizer, who dreamed of a francophone and Catholic land extending as far west as Winnipeg.

A statue of the huge churchman—he was said to be six feet tall and weigh 333 pounds—stands in his parish of St. Jérôme. His hand is flung out towards the north. Curé Labelle's nickname, *Le roi du nord*, was acquired after he had successfully pestered the Quebec government to build roads into a northland that geologists had described as primeval and uninviting. The priest, who became a Monsigneur, is credited with helping found some 20 northern communities.

FOIE DE PORC AU BACON SAUCE DE THÉ

Pork liver and bacon with tea sauce

In Quebec's early days, the pot of tea on the back of the stove came into play when gravy was being made. Montreal chef Richard Bergeron remembers both his mother and grandmother serving this dish at restaurants they ran in La Minerve, north of Mont Tremblant.

1½ cups (375 mL) strong tea
8 slices maple-smoked bacon
3 tablespoons (45 mL) all-purpose flour
Salt and ground black pepper
1 pound (500 g) pork liver,* cut into ½-inch (1 cm) slices
2 tablespoons (25 mL) browned flour**
Chopped fresh parsley

  * Calves' liver or beef liver may be substituted.
** Cook flour in a heavy saucepan, stirring, until lightly browned.

Make tea in advance and let cool. Fry bacon until crisp and keep warm. Strain bacon fat through a fine sieve and reserve. Season flour with salt and pepper to taste; coat liver slices with the flour, shaking to remove excess.

Heat bacon fat (or vegetable oil, if desired) in a large, heavy frying pan and sear liver on both sides. Lower heat and continue cooking to desired degree of doneness, keeping inside of slices pink. Transfer liver to a heated serving platter with bacon and keep warm. Sprinkle browned flour over pan drippings and cook, stirring to incorporate small particles. Add cold tea and simmer, stirring, until mixture turns a

rich, medium brown and sauce has reduced and
thickened. Season with salt and pepper to taste,
strain and serve hot over liver. Trim servings with
bacon and parsley. Four servings.

TARTE À LA FERLOUCHE
Molasses pie

This economical Quebec dessert was traditionally
made with molasses and whatever other ingredients
were on hand. Recipes sometimes include maple
syrup, cornstarch and spices. Marie-Ange Rondeau of
Buckingham, who taught cooking and ran a
restaurant in her area for many years, believes "if
you're making a recipe and you lack an ingredient,
find a substitute." Her recipe for one of Quebec's
favourite desserts may be made without the raisins or
with other dried fruit. It's included in *Les Recettes
des Fermières du Québec*, a collection of recipes
from members of the province's rural women's
group.

1 cup (250 mL) molasses
1 cup (250 mL) raisins
1 tablespoon (15 mL) melted butter
3 tablespoons (45 mL) soft bread crumbs
Juice of ½ lemon
1 egg, beaten
Pinch salt
1 single-crust, unbaked, 8-inch (20 cm) pie shell

In a bowl, combine molasses, raisins, melted butter,
bread crumbs, lemon juice, beaten egg and salt. Pour
into prepared pie shell. Bake in a preheated 350°F
(180°C) oven for 30 minutes or until filling is
bubbling hot and lightly browned. Serve warm or at
room temperature. Six servings.

GÂTEAU À LA CITROUILLE DE LOCHABER
Pumpkin cake

Pumpkins are a popular ingredient in cakes, cookies, pies, bread and even soup around Thurso, a lumbering town on the Ottawa River, which was originally settled by Scottish-Canadians. This recipe was named by its owner Florence Mongeon for her home district. It was published in a cookbook of recipes collected by the local women's group Les Fermières de Thurso and called *Cent ans de tradition culinaire québecoise.*

---

3 cups (750 mL) all-purpose flour
2 teaspoons (10 mL) baking soda
¼ teaspoon (1 mL) salt
2 teaspoons (10 mL) cinnamon
¾ teaspoon (4 mL) ground cloves
½ cup (125 mL) shortening or margarine
1¼ cups (300 mL) brown sugar
2 eggs, beaten
2 cups (500 mL) puréed pumpkin

In a bowl, sift or mix together flour, baking soda, salt, cinnamon and ground cloves. In another bowl, cream shortening with brown sugar until fluffy; beat in eggs. Add dry ingredients alternately with pumpkin to creamed mixture, a third of each at a time, beating well after each addition.

Spread batter evenly in 2 greased 8½ × 4½-inch (1.5 L) loaf pans. Bake in a preheated 325°F (160°C) oven for 50 to 60 minutes or until a tester inserted in centre comes out clean. Let cool in pans for 10 minutes, then turn out onto rack to cool completely. Makes 2 loaf cakes.

TARTE AU SUCRE

Fleur-Ange's sugar pie

Maple syrup has never been plentiful in the
Laurentians. More frequently, families served a pie
with a brown sugar filling. This recipe was given to
Nicole Kretz by her mother.

---

1 cup (250 mL) brown sugar
3 tablespoons (45 mL) all-purpose flour
1 cup (250 mL) whipping cream, light cream or half
    milk and half cream
1 teaspoon (5 mL) vanilla or pinch ground nutmeg
Pastry for double-crust, 8-inch (20 cm) pie

Line an 8-inch (20 cm) pie plate with pastry. In a
small saucepan, combine brown sugar, flour and
cream. Bring to a boil, stirring constantly until
thickened. Boil for 2 to 3 minutes more; remove
filling from heat and stir in vanilla or nutmeg. Let
cool.

Pour filling into prepared pie shell. Cover with top
pastry crust. Trim pastry, crimp edges and cut steam
vents. Bake in a preheated 375°F (190°C) oven for
40 to 45 minutes or until top crust is golden. Six
servings.

MICROWAVE METHOD

Filling: In a 2-quart (2 L) casserole, stir together
brown sugar, flour and cream. Microwave,
uncovered, at High (100 percent) for 4 to 6 minutes,
until mixture comes to a full boil and thickens,
stirring twice. Stir in vanilla or nutmeg and let filling
cool. Continue with recipe as directed.

Tire à la mélasse de Grand-Mère

Grandmother's molasses taffy

Quebec's sweet tooth is often satisfied by this old-fashioned candy made from molasses and sugar. This recipe belongs to Marguerite Legault, a member of Les Fermières de Thurso, a rural women's group in the town on the Ottawa River.

---

1 cup (250 mL) molasses
½ cup (125 mL) granulated sugar
½ cup (125 mL) brown sugar
⅓ cup (75 mL) water
2 tablespoons (25 mL) butter
¼ teaspoon (1 mL) baking soda
Pinch salt

In a medium, heavy saucepan, combine molasses, granulated and brown sugars and water. Heat to boiling and stir to dissolve sugars. Let mixture boil, without stirring, until syrup reaches the hard ball stage (260°F/125°C) on a candy thermometer. Remove from heat, stir in butter, baking soda and salt. Immediately pour onto a buttered marble slab or baking sheet.

When cool enough to handle, butter hands and gather taffy into a ball. Pull taffy between hands and continually stretch and fold, then stretch again until taffy turns lighter in colour (this can take from 5 to 15 minutes).

Stretch and twist taffy into a rope about 1 inch (2.5 cm) thick and cut into pieces using buttered scissors. Wrap each piece in waxed paper. Makes about 48 pieces.

MICROWAVE METHOD

In a 2-quart (2 L) glass measure, combine molasses,

River with a past

Travel up the Ottawa River and you'll notice the variety of architecture in the old farmhouses that line the highway. Beginning in the early 19th century, both French and English settlers cleared the forest and started small farms. Their stone and clapboard houses, 150 years old and more, are on lots laid out either in the long strips of the French seigneuries or the wider lots of the English township style. Most settlers had two careers—farming and working in either the fur or the lumber business. Many of the woodsmen were of Irish background and many a confrontation took place between Irish and French when the lumbering business was active on the river in the 1830s and 1840s.

granulated and brown sugars and water. Microwave, uncovered, at High (100 percent) for 4 to 5 minutes, until mixture comes to a boil, stirring once to dissolve sugars. Continue to microwave at High (100 percent) for 6 to 8 minutes more until syrup reaches the hard ball stage (260°F/125°C) on a candy thermometer. Stir in butter, baking soda and salt; immediately pour onto buttered marble slab or baking sheet. Follow directions for pulling taffy as outlined in recipe.

GALETTE DE SARRAZIN À SERAPHIN

Buckwheat pancakes

This economical recipe is named for a legendary St. Adèle character who kept close guard over his money. Fleur-Ange Vanier Rochon of St. Jovite recommends making these pancakes with coarsely ground buckwheat and serving them with butter and molasses or maple syrup as a supper dish.

---

1 cup (250 mL) buckwheat flour
1 teaspoon (5 mL) baking powder
½ teaspoon (2 mL) salt
1¾ cups (175 mL) milk
2 eggs, beaten
Melted butter

In a bowl, combine flour, baking powder and salt. Stir in milk and eggs; beat well to make a smooth batter.

Heat a large, 10-inch (25 cm) pancake or heavy frying pan until very hot. Brush with melted butter and pour in ¼ cup (50 mL) of batter. When pancake is lightly browned, flip over and briefly cook the other side. Transfer to a warmed serving platter. Makes 12 large pancakes.

LA MADELEINE GLACÉE AU MIEL "PAPINEAU"

Madeleines with honey ice cream

Chef Pierre DeLaHaye of Papineauville on the Ottawa River fills the classic small French cakes, shaped in the form of sea shells, with strongly flavoured honey ice cream and sets this confection in a pool of rum-flavoured custard. He decorates the dessert with fresh mint leaves and a sauce made from fresh fruit in season.

12 Madeleines, either homemade or store bought*
Honey Ice Cream (recipe follows)
Custard Sauce (recipe follows)
Fruit Sauce (recipe follows)
Additional fresh fruit in season
Mint leaves (optional)

    * Lady fingers may be substituted.

Honey Ice Cream

2 cups (500 mL) milk
¾ cup (175 mL) strong, dark honey, such as buckwheat
4 egg yolks
1 cup (250 mL) whipping cream

In a heavy saucepan, combine milk and honey. Heat, stirring often, until bubbles form around edge of pan. In a bowl, beat egg yolks with an electric mixer until lemon-coloured. Pour in cream and continue to beat until mixture thickens. Stir in ¼ of the hot milk mixture into the beaten yolks, then pour yolk mixture into remaining milk in saucepan. Cook over low heat, whisking constantly, until custard thickens enough to coat a wooden spoon; do not let mixture come to a boil. Remove from heat, and strain through a fine sieve.

Let custard cool to room temperature, then chill thoroughly. Freeze in ice cream maker, according to manufacturer's instructions. Makes about 1 quart (1 L) ice cream.

Custard Sauce

1½ cups (375 mL) milk
4 egg yolks
⅓ cup (75 mL) granulated sugar
2 teaspoons (10 mL) vanilla
1 tablespoon (15 mL) dark rum

In a medium saucepan, bring milk almost to a boil. In a mixing bowl, beat together egg yolks and sugar with a wire whisk until well blended. Pour hot milk, little by little, into egg yolk mixture, beating continuously with wire whisk.

Pour mixture into a saucepan and cook over medium heat, stirring continuously with a wooden spoon, until custard thickens sufficiently to coat spoon. Immediately remove from heat; do not permit to boil or custard will curdle. Strain through sieve into a bowl.

Cool slightly, then blend in vanilla and rum. Let cool, then refrigerate, covered, for up to 3 days. Makes 1½ cups (375 mL) sauce.

Fruit Sauce

---

2 cups (500 mL) fresh fruit in season
Instant dissolving sugar

In a food processor or blender, purée fruit until smooth. Strain, if necessary, to remove seeds. Sweeten lightly with sugar to taste. Makes about 1¼ cups (300 mL).

To serve: Divide custard sauce among 6 large dessert plates. Arrange a madeleine on the sauce, top with a scoop of ice cream and another madeleine. If using ladyfingers, arrange on each side of ice cream. Drizzle with fruit sauce and trim each plate with additional fresh fruit and mint leaves, if desired. Six servings.

MICROWAVE METHOD

Honey Ice Cream: Place milk and honey in a 2-quart (2 L) casserole or glass measure. Microwave at High (100 percent) for 6 to 8 minutes or until almost boiling.

In a bowl, beat yolks with an electric mixer until lemon-coloured. Pour in cream and continue to beat until mixture thickens. Stir ¼ of the hot milk into the beaten yolks, then pour yolk mixture into remaining milk in casserole. Microwave, uncovered, at Medium (50 percent) for 4 to 6 minutes, whisking well every minute, until custard thickens enough to coat a wooden spoon. Strain custard through a fine sieve and let cool to room temperature, then refrigerate until chilled. Freeze in ice cream maker according to manufacturer's directions.

Custard Sauce: Place milk in a 4-cup (1 L) glass measure and microwave at High (100 percent) for 3 to 4 minutes or until almost boiling (bubbles appear around edge). In a bowl, whisk egg yolks and sugar together. Stir the hot milk into yolk mixture, stirring constantly. Return mixture to glass measure; microwave at Medium (50 percent) for 3 to 4 minutes, whisking every minute, until custard thickens slightly. Strain through a sieve. Add vanilla and rum; let cool.

CÔTE DU SUD

 If you travel along the southern bank of the St. Lawrence River, northeast of the Île d'Orléans and it's summertime, you'll probably see sheep grazing in lush green fields. Nearing Rivière du Loup, you may catch a whiff of salty air as the great waterway widens on its way to the sea. But you would be wrong to assume, as I did, that lamb and fish are the traditional foods in this gently rolling, sometimes forested, stretch of riverbank and farmland called the Côte du Sud.

The original settlers raised sheep for wool, not meat. Although fish, ranging from smelt to whale, were part of the original cuisine, and sturgeon and eel were once local specialties, pork and game meats have always been the favourite foods.

It is the newcomers and chefs who have recently made lamb a specialty meat in these parts—and with delicious results. I dined in inns along this lower St. Lawrence shore and ate exceptional lamb from both St. Mathieu, east of Trois Pistoles, and Trinité des Monts on the Rimouski River, where a vast sheep farm is located and locals hold an annual lamb fair.

Salty mists flavour the meadow grasses here, as they do in Charlevoix, and I found that the meat here can resemble the *pre-salé* or naturally salted lamb of Brittany just as it does on the north shore of the river. Lamb has become a food for experimentation with examples like an herb-seasoned *ragoût* at Auberge St. Simon, in the village of St. Simon east of Trois Pistoles, and tender *medaillons* with pepper sauce at Au Coin de la Baie in Métis sur Mer.

Fish has always been a favoured food here—with the huge river washing by, and lakes and streams in the highlands yielding freshwater varieties. Montreal home economist Suzanne Paré Leclerc, who was born and raised in Trois Pistoles, remembers eating fish three or four times a week in summer and almost as often in winter.

Still, the dishes that bring the happiest smiles to the faces of family cooks in this region are based on pork and game meats—the same foundation of traditional Quebec cuisine elsewhere in the province. And their *cipâte* and *tourtière, ragoût* and *bouilli, fèves au lard* and *cretons* and the staple pea or cabbage soups are made the same way as they were two centuries ago.

Game such as moose and deer, hare, partridge, wild goose and duck turns up in the simplest family recipes. In earlier times, the highlands ran with wild animals, while the many islands along the shore between Montmagny and Trois Pistoles harboured lavish flocks of wild birds. Ducks and snow geese continue to be prize catches for hunters—and a menu specialty at Manoir des Érables in Montmagny.

Soeur Monique Chevrier—chef, gastronome and director of a leading Montreal cooking school—has an explanation for why the Côte du Sud has such carefully maintained cooking habits. Food traditions, she told me, can be traced to Quebec's top domestic science school, which was started in 1905 in St. Pascal de Kamouraska. Her order, Congrégation de Notre Dame, sent her there to teach cooking from 1947 to 1955. By then the school was called École Normal Classico-Menagère and had become part of the Institution Chanoine-Beaudet. It was attracting girls from as far away as Lac St. Jean and Gaspé for a four-year course that was designed to teach the basics of traditional Quebec cuisine. "Technique was not a grand affair," the nun told me, recalling that at first, students, who came mostly from farms, were accustomed to wood stoves. "We taught on wood," said Soeur Monique.

Food preservation techniques were a big part of the course. She would teach how to store root vegetables in sand for the winter and how to wrap green tomatoes in paper and keep them in a cool, humid cellar. "You could be eating fresh, ripe tomatoes into February with this method," she said.

Even more wide-reaching as a culinary influence was the order's basic cookbook, *La Cuisine Raisonnée*, published in 1919. Now in its 11th edition (1984), the book has sold over a million copies. Published since 1967 by Éditions Fides of Montreal, the book is also available in a metric edition (1985). The role of this book cannot be overestimated, in Soeur Monique's opinion. "It was the cookbook that influenced every woman in the province. To this day, it represents Quebec family cooking."

The use of local vegetables has increased as chefs return to tradition— vegetables such as the Indians' prized fronds of young ferns known as fiddleheads and herbs such as *herbe St. Jean* (ground ivy or Creeping Charlie), as well as the region's many wild fruits—strawberries, raspberries, blueberries, cranberries, blackberries and gooseberries.

In earlier times, these fruits would be made into jam and jelly, then used to make winter tarts. "They were made in the French manner," Edith Martin of Trois Pistoles told me. "Just the plain fruit in a pastry shell with none of the American touches such as custard or meringue." Mme Martin has traced many of her region's dishes to French country cooking. Besides the links with the cuisine of northwestern France, she has identified ties with Alsace. Cakes made with dried fruit such as raisins and prunes, and nuts, in particular hazelnuts, are an example, she told me.

SALADE DE SAUMON FUMÉ AUX ENDIVES ET COURGETTES

Smoked salmon with endives and zucchini

Slivers of vegetables tossed with a peppery dressing and topped with smoked salmon make a first course or light lunch dish at Auberge Manoir de Tilly in St. Antoine de Tilly just west of Lévis.

Côte du Sud Menu

Scallop soup
(page 112)

Layered meat pie
(page 120)

Green salad

Apple cream
(page 127)

---

2 endives
1 small zucchini
2 tablespoons (25 mL) Vinaigrette (recipe follows)
4 ounces (125 g) smoked salmon, thinly sliced
Fresh parsley

Cut endives in half lengthwise and remove core. Cut into very fine julienne strips. Cut zucchini in half lengthwise and cut in the same manner.

Place in a bowl and toss with Vinaigrette. Divide between 2 salad plates, mounding salad in the centre. Arrange slices of smoked salmon spoke-fashion around the salad to give the shape of a star. Trim with parsley. Two servings.

Vinaigrette

⅓ cup (75 mL) olive oil
1 tablespoon (15 mL) each red wine vinegar and
  lemon juice
1 teaspoon (5 mL) Dijon mustard
Salt and ground black pepper

In a jar, combine oil, vinegar, lemon juice, mustard and salt and pepper to taste. Shake vigorously before using. Makes about ½ cup (125 mL) Vinaigrette.

LES PÉTONCLES À LA NAGE

Scallop soup

Claude Cyr, chef-proprietor of Au coin de la baie in Métis sur Mer, makes a simple soup from scallops and vegetables.

---

1 cup (250 mL) dry white wine
1 cup (250 mL) fish stock
¼ cup (50 mL) each fine julienne strips of carrots, turnips and leeks
Salt and ground white pepper
12 large fresh scallops

In a medium saucepan, bring wine, fish stock and vegetables to a boil; season with salt and pepper to taste. Reduce heat and simmer for 5 minutes or until vegetables are tender-crisp. Place 6 scallops in each of 2 heated bowls. Divide the very hot stock among the bowls, stir briefly and serve at once. Two servings.

MICROWAVE METHOD

In a 4-cup (1 L) casserole, combine wine, stock and vegetables; season with salt and pepper to taste. Cover and microwave at High (100 percent) for 7 to 8 minutes or until vegetables are tender-crisp. Continue with recipe as directed.

ESTURGEON EN RAGOÛT BLANC

Sturgeon in cream sauce

This once-plentiful fish was popular along the St. Lawrence River and is still regarded as a delicacy. The recipe comes from Rivière Ouelle in

Fish Stock

---

2 pounds (1 kg) fish heads, bones and trimmings*
8 cups (2 L) water**
1 onion, sliced
1 carrot, chopped
1 celery stalk, chopped
3 parsley stems
1 bay leaf
Pinch salt and ground white pepper

  * Bones from mild-flavoured varieties such as halibut, sole and cod are recommended.
 ** Or use 1 cup (250 mL) white wine for 1 cup (250 mL) of the water.

Place fish trimmings in a large saucepan or stock pot and cover with water. Add onion, carrot, celery, parsley and bay leaf; season with salt and pepper to taste. Bring to a boil and skim, then simmer, partially covered for 20 minutes. Strain through a fine sieve, let stock cool slightly and refrigerate. Makes about 6 cups (1.5 L)

Kamouraska county and is adapted from one of the first regional cookbooks to be published in the area, *Recettes typiques de la côte-du-sud* by the late Mme Charles Gagné of La Pocatière. Serve the fish with fresh whole wheat bread.

---

1 sturgeon, salmon or swordfish (2½ to 3 pounds/ 1 to 1.5 kg)
¼ cup (50 mL) white vinegar
1 onion, chopped
1 stalk celery, chopped
1 cup (250 mL) peeled, cubed potatoes
¼ pound (125 g) salt pork, slivered
1 tablespoon (15 mL) chopped fresh parsley
1 tablespoon (15 mL) chopped fresh chervil, or 1½ teaspoons (7 mL) chopped fresh savoury
2 tablespoons (25 mL) chopped fresh chives
1 bay leaf
Salt and ground white pepper
3 tablespoons (45 mL) all-purpose flour
1 cup (250 mL) hot milk

Marinate fish in vinegar and enough water to cover for 1 hour. Drain, fillet fish, remove skin and cut into serving-size pieces.

In a large saucepan, combine onion, celery, potatoes, salt pork, parsley, chervil, chives and bay leaf; season with salt and pepper to taste. Top with fish pieces and add enough water to cover. Bring to a boil and simmer over medium heat just until fish flakes when tested with a fork, about 10 to 15 minutes.

Using a slotted spoon, lift fish out onto a warmed platter. In a bowl, blend flour with milk to make a paste and stir into remaining liquid and vegetables in pan. Cook, stirring often, until sauce thickens and vegetables are tender, about 10 minutes. Adjust seasoning with salt and pepper; remove bay leaf. Return fish to sauce and cook just until heated through. Eight servings.

Not to be missed

In the Côte du Sud, tourist attractions include: Maison Lamontagne, built between 1744 and 1810, on the east side of Rimouski; Moulin Paradis at Kamouraska, a flour mill dating from 1804; and in the same town, a museum displays antiques in a one-time convent. At St. Roch des Aulnaies, visitors can see the oldest seigneury on the Côte du Sud, which includes an operating flour mill. Beaumont has 20 historic houses and a mill which can be toured in the summer.

CANARD SAUVAGE AUX FEUILLES D'AIL

Wild duck with garlic leaves

From the Manoir des Érables at Montmagny comes this recipe for wild duck. Chef-proprietor Renaud Cyr says it can also be used with farm-raised ducks.

---

2 whole duck breasts (½ pound/250 g each)
2 tablespoons (25 mL) olive oil
½ teaspoon (2 mL) dried thyme
Salt and ground black pepper
½ cup (125 mL) red wine
1 tablespoon (15 mL) butter
¼ cup (50 mL) stock from game, beef or veal
½ cup (125 mL) whipping cream
2 tablespoons (25 mL) Calvabec liqueur
1 teaspoon (5 mL) butter
1 teaspoon (5 mL) chopped wild garlic leaves, or a combination of chopped garlic clove and spinach leaves

---

Using poultry shears, debone breasts of duck by cutting down centre and along one side of wishbone, trimming away bits of bone, skin and fat.

Heat oil in a heavy frying pan and sauté breasts on all sides, seasoning with thyme and salt and pepper to taste during cooking. When browned and tender, transfer meat to a hot plate and keep warm.

Drain off fat from pan and deglaze with wine. Cook over high heat and reduce by half, then add 1 tablespoon (15 mL) butter, stock and cream. Simmer, stirring until sauce is smooth and slightly thickened. Stir in Calvabec liqueur and serve sauce over duck breasts.

Blend 1 teaspoon (5 mL) butter with garlic leaves and spread over the top of each breast. Two servings.

Game Bird Stock

4 to 6 cups (1 to 1.5 L) bones of quail, guinea hen, duck, chicken or turkey
2 tablespoons (25 mL) unsalted butter
1 medium onion, coarsely chopped
1 carrot, finely chopped
½ cup (125 mL) finely chopped leek
½ cup (125 mL) chopped celery
3 cloves garlic, unpeeled
Pinch fresh or dried thyme
1 bay leaf
Salt and ground black pepper

Place bones in a roasting pan and roast in a preheated 450°F (230°C) oven until lightly browned, about 20 to 30 minutes.

Meanwhile, heat butter in a large, heavy saucepan or stock pot and sauté onion, carrot, leek and celery until softened; do not brown. Add bones, garlic, thyme, bay leaf, salt and pepper, enough cold water to cover. Simmer over low heat, partially covered, for about 2 hours or until liquid has reduced by half. Strain. Makes about 1 quart (1 L).

SUPRÊME DE PINTADE
AU THYM ET MIEL

Breast of guinea hen with thyme and honey

At Auberge Manoir de Tilly, a country inn in a 1786 manor house at St. Antoine de Tilly just west of Lévis, game birds are regularly prepared by Chef Carlos Angulo.

---

3 tablespoons (45 mL) unsalted butter
2 breasts of guinea hens, Rock Cornish game hens or chicken
2 tablespoons (25 mL) chopped dry shallots
¼ cup (50 mL) white wine
½ cup (125 mL) Game Bird Stock (see margin note)
1½ teaspoons (7 mL) chopped fresh thyme, or ½ teaspoon (2 mL) dried
3 tablespoons (45 mL) honey
1 tablespoon (15 mL) white wine vinegar

Heat 1 tablespoon (15 mL) of the butter in a large, heavy frying pan, and brown breasts quickly on all sides. Transfer meat to a shallow roasting pan and roast in preheated 400°F (200°C) oven for 10 to 12 minutes to complete cooking.

Drain off fat from frying pan. Add 1 tablespoon (15 mL) of the butter and sauté shallots until softened. Deglaze pan with wine, add Game Bird Stock and thyme. Cook over high heat until reduced by two-thirds. Add remaining tablespoon (15 mL) of butter, honey and wine vinegar; stir until sauce is hot and smooth. Serve over guinea hen breasts. Two servings.

A celebration of food

The Côte du Sud's fondness for food is demonstrated in the number of annual, food-inspired festivals. In the town of Cabano on the shores of Lac Temiscouata, southeast of Rivière du Loup, a *touladi* or grey trout tournament is staged each June. A lamb fair, including a *méchoui* or barbecue of a whole lamb on a spit, takes place in mid-July at Trinité des Monts. There's a corn festival each August at Rivière Bleue south of Rivière du Loup. In August, St. Lazare stages a buckwheat pancake festival and, in October, the fall migration of the snow goose is celebrated with a festival at Montmagny.

LIÈVRE AU VIN ROUGE AVEC SAUCE AUX MORILLES

Hare in red wine with morel sauce

Alain Choinière, chef-proprietor of Auberge St. Simon in St. Simon, accents the flavour of hare with a marinade of rosemary and red wine. He trims the finished dish with morsels of crisp salt pork and serves it with vegetables such as whole baby carrots, broccoli spears and boiled potatoes.

---

1 hare* (about 4 pounds/2 kg), cut into serving-size
   pieces
2 cups (500 mL) red wine
1 large sprig fresh rosemary, chopped, or 1 teaspoon
   (5 mL) dried, crumbled
6 dried juniper berries
6 green peppercorns
½ cup (125 mL) dried morels
¼ pound (125 g) salt pork, cut into small cubes
Beurre manié** (optional)
Salt and ground black pepper

  * Rabbit may be substituted for hare, but it will not have
    the same flavour.
** Beurre manié is a paste made of equal amounts of
    softened butter and flour.

Place hare in a large bowl. Pour wine over and sprinkle with rosemary, juniper berries and peppercorns. Cover and marinate in the refrigerator for at least 8 hours or overnight.

Soak dried mushrooms in cold water to cover for 30 minutes, then set aside.

Fry salt pork in a large, heavy, flameproof casserole until crisp and set aside; reserve drippings.

Drain marinade and reserve. Dry hare with paper towels and fry in pork drippings in casserole over

Mushrooms celebrated

St. Simon innkeeper Alain Choinière cooks as many as seven different wild mushroom dishes for the annual October dinner of a gastonomic society named L'Anneau, after the upper part of the stem of the mushroom. Members, mostly from nearby Rimouski, help collect the fungi for the event. Morels are on the menu at his charming inn, Auberge St. Simon, as often as Choinière can find them in the woods nearby.

high heat until browned on all sides. Add marinade, stirring to incorporate bits from the bottom of casserole. Stir in mushrooms and soaking liquid. Cover and place pan in a preheated 325°F (160°C) oven for 2 to 2½ hours, until hare is tender.

Remove meat to a heated plate and keep warm. Boil remaining liquid in casserole until reduced by half. Thicken sauce, if desired, with beurre manié. Adjust seasoning with salt and pepper to taste. Strain sauce and pour over meat; sprinkle with reserved crisply-fried diced pork. Four servings.

The Kamouraska roof

The pretty clapboard farmhouses of the Kamouraska region, which can be seen from Montmagny to St. Fabien along the lower St. Lawrence, have a distinctive roof. It has a pronounced concave curve, starting just under the edge of the eave and dipping down to join the wall of the house. The shape is reminiscent of the side of a boat. The building style is explained by the fact that carpenters hereabouts were as accustomed to building boats as they were to building houses.

A fine example of this unusual type of architecture is the 1842 Maison du Notaire, or notary's house, in Trois Pistoles. Restored and furnished with antiques, it's now an arts and crafts centre open daily to the public in the summer, and Thursday through Saturday, afternoons only, during the rest of the year.

Ragoût d'agneau à l'herbe St. Jean

Lamb meatballs in herb-flavoured sauce

Fresh ground lamb is made into meatballs and flavoured with mustard and a fresh herb called *herbe de St. Jean* or Creeping Charlie. Fresh mint may be substituted for the herb, says Alain Choinière, who serves this dish with boiled parsleyed potatoes and vegetables in season at Auberge St. Simon at St. Simon, just east of Trois Pistoles.

---

1 pound (500 g) freshly ground lamb
1 medium onion, finely chopped
1 teaspoon (5 mL) Dijon mustard
1 egg, beaten
1 tablespoon (15 mL) finely chopped Creeping Charlie or fresh mint
Salt and ground black pepper
2 tablespoons (25 mL) olive oil
1½ cups (375 mL) Lamb Stock (recipe follows)
2 tablespoons (25 mL) browned flour*
½ teaspoon (2 mL) commercially prepared or homemade salted herbs (see recipe, page 26)

* Place flour in a dry frying pan and cook over medium heat, turning occasionally, until light brown. A 350°F (180°C) oven may be used instead.

In a bowl, combine ground lamb, onion, mustard, beaten egg and chopped herb; season with salt and pepper to taste. Shape into 1¼-inch (3 cm) balls.

In a large, heavy frying pan, heat oil and brown meatballs on all sides. Set meatballs aside, drain off fat and deglaze pan with 1 cup (250 mL) Lamb Stock. In a bowl, combine browned flour with remaining stock to form a paste and stir into sauce; cook until thickened. Return meatballs to the sauce and let simmer for 10 minutes or until cooked through. Rinse salted herbs in cold water; drain and add to sauce. Four servings.

Lamb Stock

---

1 lamb leg bone
1 medium onion, quartered
1 tablespoon (15 mL) each chopped fresh thyme and
   rosemary, or 1 teaspoon (5 mL) each dried
Salt and ground black pepper

Place the lamb bone with water to cover in a large saucepan or stock pot and add onion, thyme, rosemary, and salt and pepper to taste. Bring to a boil and simmer, partially covered, for 2 hours. Cool and strain. Refrigerate stock; remove chilled fat layer before using. Makes about 6 cups (1.5 L).

In search of whales

For whale-watchers, it's a toss-up whether you take a boat trip down the St. Lawrence River from Trois Pistoles or Tadoussac. Chances of seeing these gentle, sociable creatures of the sea are good from early August to mid-October. You can also sometimes catch a glimpse of whales from the ferry boats that link Trois Pistoles with Les Escoumins.

The earliest European visitors to the Côte du Sud knew it as a gathering place for whales. Fishermen from France's Basque country came to the river a century before the arrival of 16th-century explorer Jacques Cartier. They hunted the big sea mammals and landed on Île aux Basques just off Trois Pistoles to melt whale fat in furnaces they constructed there. Vestiges of three of these furnaces can still be found.

CIPAILLE
Layered meat pie

This traditional layered pie is best made with game, say cooks in the region. Failing a supply of venison or pheasant, you can make *cipaille* or *cipâte*, as it's often called, with a mixture of meats and poultry. This recipe belongs to Gisèle Beaulieu of Trinité des Monts on the Rimouski River.

---

2 pounds (1 kg) boneless chicken meat
2 pounds (1 kg) lean beef
2 pounds (1 kg) lean pork
4 medium onions, coarsely chopped
¼ pound (125 g) salt pork, thinly sliced
2 cups (500 mL) peeled, cubed potatoes
1 teaspoon (5 mL) salt
½ teaspoon (2 mL) ground black pepper
¼ teaspoon (1 mL) mixed spices*
2 cups (500 mL) chicken stock (approximate)
Pastry for double-crust, 9-inch (23 cm) pie

* Ground cloves, nutmeg, cinnamon and allspice.

Cut chicken, beef and pork into 1-inch (2.5 cm) cubes and place in a large bowl. Combine with onions; cover and refrigerate for at least 12 hours or overnight.

Arrange salt pork evenly in the bottom of a 3-quart (3 L) casserole, preferably cast iron with a cover. Layer with ⅓ of the meat mixture and ⅓ of the potatoes; season with ⅓ of salt, pepper and spices. Roll out half of the pastry slightly thicker than for a normal pie and arrange on the potato layer, cutting a small hole in the centre. Repeat with 2 more layers of meat and potatoes seasoned with salt, pepper and spices. Cover with the remaining pastry, cutting a small hole in the centre.

Slowly add enough chicken stock through the hole until liquid appears. Cover dish and bake in a pre-

Island smokehouses

The island called L'Isle Verte in the St. Lawrence River off Cacouna provides the region with much of its smoked food, such as salmon and bacon. Given its name by French explorer Jacques Cartier in 1535, it has the oldest lighthouse in Quebec, located at Notre Dame des Sept Douleurs on the western tip of the island. The island was always a refuge for birds and is a bird sanctuary and interpretation centre.

heated 400°F (200°C) oven for 45 minutes or until liquid simmers. Reduce temperature to 250°F (120°C) and continue to bake, covered, for 5 to 6 hours more or until top crust is a rich golden brown. Eight to ten servings.

CONFITURE AUX MÛRES
Blackberry jam

Blackberries have become scarce throughout Quebec, but enough of these raspberry look-alikes grow down the river to make jam. Here is a family recipe from Suzette Couillard of L'Îslet sur Mer. It could also be used with raspberries.

---

1 pound (500 g) fresh blackberries or raspberries
¾ pound (375 g) brown sugar

In a heavy saucepan, crush fruit lightly, then stir in brown sugar. Over low heat, stir with wooden spoon until sugar dissolves. Bring to a full, rolling boil over high heat and cook, uncovered, until jam thickens and reaches gel stage. Remove from heat and skim off foam. Pour into hot, sterilized jars and seal. Recipe may be doubled. Makes about 2 cups (500 mL).

An exceptional garden

One of North America's greatest gardens is at Grand Métis, just east of St. Flavie. Now named the Jardins de Métis, it was known for almost half a century as Mrs. Reford's garden. Horticulturalists are fascinated by the 500 or more species that grow in this imaginatively landscaped British-style garden.

Visitors with an interest in history also enjoy wandering its walkways and wooded paths, admiring the view of the St. Lawrence River and imagining the luxury of holidays at this summer mansion in days gone by. It was built in 1886 by the Canadian Pacific Railway baron Lord Mount Stephen, who enjoyed the superb salmon fishing available nearby. He gave the estate to his niece, Elsie Stephen Meighan Reford. The spacious house contains many of the Reford possessions—furniture, clothing, fishing equipment, gardening diaries—which are displayed almost as if the family were still in residence. Well-kept by the Quebec government, the garden and house are open to tourists from mid-June to mid-September.

LANGUE DE BOEUF BRAISÉE AUX LEGUMES

Braised beef tongue with vegetables

This recipe comes from Rivière Bleue on the Maine border. It was included in a collection of recipes from the Côte du Sud compiled by Mme Charles Gagné. It may be served hot with vegetables and mustard or horseradish, or jellied and served cold.

---

1 beef tongue (3 to 4 pounds/1.5 to 2 kg)*
¼ cup (50 mL) white vinegar
4 cups (1 L) hot water
1 large onion, chopped
1 clove garlic, chopped
1 bay leaf
Salt and ground black pepper
3 carrots, peeled and diced
1 cup (250 mL) diced rutabaga or turnip
3 potatoes, peeled and diced
1 envelope (1 tablespoon/15 mL) unflavoured gelatin (optional)
3 tablespoons (45 mL) cold water (optional)
Fresh parsley (optional)

  * Two small beef tongues may be substituted for one large
    one; reduce cooking times by about one-quarter.

Place tongue in a large, heavy saucepan. Add vinegar and enough cold water to cover. Let stand for 2 to 3 hours, then drain.

Cover with hot water and bring to a boil. Reduce heat, cover and simmer very slowly for about 2 hours. Add onion, garlic, bay leaf, and salt and pepper to taste. Return to the boil, then simmer, partially covered, for another hour. Add diced carrots, rutabaga and potatoes, and continue to cook for another 30 to 40 minutes or until meat and vegetables are tender.

If serving meat hot, remove from stock, reserving the latter for soup. Remove roots of the tongue, the skin, bones and gristle. Slice meat thinly on the diagonal and serve hot. Eight servings.

To serve cold and jellied, remove meat from stock, reserving the latter; measure 1 cup (250 mL) of the stock, strain and set aside. Trim and slice tongue as described above and arrange in a shallow pan or mould that has been rinsed with cold water. In a small saucepan, soak 1 envelope unflavoured gelatin in 3 tablespoons (45 mL) cold water, then add the reserved 1 cup (250 mL) stock and heat until dissolved. Pour mixture over sliced meat and chill until jellied, about 4 hours. Unmould and trim with fresh parsley. Eight servings.

CHIARD DE GOÉLETTE

Fishermen's hash

This comfortable supper dish was invented by fishermen's wives for their husbands to take out in the *goélette*, or fishing boat. This recipe belongs to Marie-Jeanne Levesque of St. Jean Port Joli, who recommends that the dish be served with her *Biscuits matelots*, fishermen's biscuits. The secret to a good *chiard*, says Mme Levesque, is salt pork with a pink colour. If the meat has a greyish cast, it has lost moisture and will not give the best flavour. If you wish to reduce the salt in the meat, soak it overnight in cold water or blanch in boiling water for five minutes, then drain. Fat can be reduced by frying the sliced pork first, then discarding fat.

½ pound (250 g) salt pork
8 cups (2 L) peeled potatoes, cut in ½-inch (1 cm) slices
1 cup (250 mL) chopped onions
Ground black pepper
Fishermen's Biscuits (recipe follows)

A fishy name

The word *chiard* usually means an economical hash made of potatoes, onions and leftover meat. Along the south shore of the St. Lawrence River, fishermen's wives would make *chiard* for their husbands to take out in the boat. However, in their version, the only meat used was salt pork, in order that, as Marie-Jeanne Levesque of St. Jean Port Joli explains, the meal would keep properly during the fishing trip. This sustaining dish was usually known as *chiards blancs*, or white hash. Other names are *chiard de goélette* (the name used on the menu at La Coureuse des Grèves, a restaurant in St. Jean Port Joli; the *goélette* is a fishing boat) and *chiard du pêcheur* (fisherman's hash). Some recipes call for a touch of brown sugar or savoury. Others suggest a sprinkling of chopped parsley and green tomato ketchup on the side.

Trim rind from salt pork; slice thinly, then chop finely. In a 2-quart (2 L) flameproof casserole, arrange a layer of potatoes on the botton. Spread with a layer of salt pork and sprinkle with onions and pepper (salt is probably not required because the meat is salty). Continue layering ingredients until all are used. Add cold water, carefully so as not to disturb layers, just until water is almost level with top layer.

Heat mixture almost to boiling point, then lower heat and slowly simmer, uncovered, until potatoes are cooked and liquid has reduced, about 30 to 40 minutes. Serve with Fishermen's Biscuits, if desired. Arrange the biscuits on the surface of the casserole and partially cover for the final 10 minutes of cooking so that biscuits become moist. Six servings.

Fishermen's biscuits

---

2 cups (500 mL) all-purpose flour
3½ teaspoons (17 mL) baking powder
½ teaspoon (2 mL) baking soda
½ teaspoon (2 mL) salt
2 tablespoons (25 mL) butter, shortening or lard
¾ cup (175 mL) ice water

Combine flour, baking powder, baking soda and salt in a bowl. Using a pastry blender or 2 knives, cut in butter until mixture resembles coarse crumbs. Add water, little by little, mixing in gently with a fork until dough forms a ball. Wrap and chill for 30 minutes.

On a lightly-floured surface, roll out dough to a thickness slightly less than ¾ inch (2 cm). Use a 2-inch (5 cm) cookie cutter or glass to cut into rounds. Arrange on a greased baking sheet. Prick biscuits all over with a fork. Bake in a preheated 375°F (190°C) oven for 15 to 20 minutes or until firm and very lightly coloured. Makes about 2 dozen.

TARTE AU SIROP D'ÉRABLE

Maple syrup tart

Rich and simple, this delectable pie recipe belongs to Rose-Aimé Dumais, who runs a maple syrup operation, Érablière Dumais, at St. Alexandre near Rivière du Loup.

1½ cups (375 mL) maple syrup
1 cup (250 mL) whipping cream
¼ cup (50 mL) cornstarch
¼ cup (50 mL) cold water
1 baked, single, 9-inch (23 cm) pie crust

In a saucepan, combine maple syrup and cream. Blend cornstarch and water together until smooth and stir into cream mixture. Bring filling to a boil over medium heat and cook for 2 minutes, stirring constantly until thickened.

Pour filling into baked pie shell and let cool until set. Six to eight servings.

MICROWAVE METHOD

Filling: In an 8-cup (2 L) casserole or glass measure, combine maple syrup and cream. Blend cornstarch and water together until smooth and stir into cream mixture. Microwave, uncovered, at High (100 percent) for 6 to 8 minutes or until filling comes to a full boil and thickens, stirring twice. Pour filling into baked pie shell and let cool until set.

The Tatin sisters' tart

An apple dessert that is baked and served upside down was brought from France by early settlers and is served at tables on the Côte du Sud. Called *tarte des Demoiselles Tatin*, or simply *tarte Tatin*, it was originally served by two sisters at an inn at Lamotte-Beuvron just south of Orléans in the Loire River valley. The French original calls for browning white sugar in a heavy frying pan, then adding sliced apples to braise before a pastry crust is laid on top. Brown sugar, maple sugar or syrup, nuts or fruit other than apples have been added to this dessert in the centuries that it has been enjoyed in Quebec.

POUDING AUX POMMES ET À L'ÉRABLE

Apple maple upside-down tart

This recipe is adapted from a Métis regional cookbook called *L'Ordinaire 2* by Thérèse Beaulieu-Roy, published in Mont Joli in 1979. It's a local version of the French upside-down dessert, *Tarte Tatin*.

---

4 tart, firm cooking apples, such as Cortland or Spy
1 tablespoon (15 mL) butter
¾ cup (175 mL) maple syrup
Pastry for single-crust, 9-inch (23 cm) pie

Peel and cut apples into ¾-inch (2 cm) wedges, measuring at the thickest part. In a heavy, 9-inch (23 cm) frying pan, melt butter and tilt pan to coat the bottom evenly. Remove from heat. Arrange apple wedges in concentric circles in pan and pour maple syrup over.

Roll out pastry into a circle slightly larger than the size of the frying pan and arrange on top of apple slices, tucking edges under. Cut steam vents in pastry.

Cook over medium heat until syrup bubbles vigorously, about 5 minutes. Place frying pan in a preheated 375°F (190°C) oven and bake the tart for 30 to 35 minutes or until pastry is lightly browned. Let cool for 15 minutes. Run a knife around the edge to loosen and invert tart onto serving plate. Serve either warm or at room temperature. Six to eight servings.

CRÈME AUX POMMES
Apple cream

This light and foamy combination of beaten egg whites and applesauce is sometimes called *pommes en neige*, apples in the snow. Although best made with grated maple sugar, it can be sweetened with brown sugar or granulated sugar. It takes on a luxurious look if served in tall glasses. Cookbook authors Suzette Couillard and Roseline Normand included this recipe from L'Îslet sur Mer in their collection entitled *Les meilleures recettes québecoises d'autrefois* (Best Quebec Recipes of Bygone Days).

---

2 egg whites, at room temperature
½ cup (125 mL) grated maple sugar or brown or
   granulated sugar
1 cup (250 mL) unsweetened applesauce, chilled
Grated rind of 1 lemon or orange

No more than an hour before serving, in a bowl, beat egg whites until stiff, then beat in sugar, a spoonful at a time, to make a stiff meringue. Gently fold in applesauce and grated rind until well combined. Spoon into individual dessert dishes and refrigerate until serving time. Four to six servings.

Manoir des érables

Tourists have long appreciated the cuisine of this landmark inn's chef-proprietor Renaud Cyr, an early advocate of the movement to serve regional foods in top restaurants. His specialties are fish, game birds and rabbit. Built in 1814 by a descendant of the first *seigneur* of the region, Louis Couillard de l'Espinay, the inn has turn-of-the-century decor and is surrounded by handsome maple trees. A member of the prestigious Relais et Châteaux group of hotels, it is expensive. Outdoor swimming pool, golf handy. (Rooms: 16, all with bath; address: 220 du Manoir St., Montmagny, Québec, G5V 1G5; telephone: (418) 248-0100.)

GASPÉ

Gaspésians speak of living "on the coast," and even inland, away from the seas that surround their mountainous promontory, there's an ever-present sense of the ocean. I sniffed its moist, salt air as I drove southeast along the Matapédia River, nourished for my trip by a mixed fish *bouillabaisse* from the salmon fishing town of Causapscal. But no amount of advance warning prepared me for the spectacular shoreline and breathtaking wildness of a region the Micmac Indians named *Gespeg*—the end of the earth. The rock at Percé turned out to be only one of many memorable sights.

The sea and its bounty formed the character of this beautiful region, determined its settlement and still distinguish its cuisine. I chose to eat little but fish for my entire visit, never remember it so fresh and good, never the same twice, and never so simply prepared.

Gaspésians have been called *mangeurs de morue*—cod-eaters. It's a nickname that can bring a defensive look to the faces of these people, who are the friendliest of Quebecers. It's only since the Second World War that prosperity has varied their dependence on cod, whether fresh, salted or dried.

Cooks here are experts with fish. I learned a new appreciation for the trusty cod—meaty yet tender, slightly sweet yet endlessly variable. Cod is the most popular, followed by herring (particularly when pickled), mackerel, halibut, salmon and trout.

Tender chunks of cod surface in *bouillabaisse*, made in a fashion more closely tied to Brittany than the Mediterranean. Tiny cod tongues or cheeks make a delicacy when sautéed. Cod liver is blended into a delicately flavoured *pâté* or *terrine* to enjoy with fresh lemon and parsley. And all other parts of the fish are simmered into a *fumet*, the stock for making soups and sauces or poaching other foods of the sea.

In earlier times, families would end a week of dining on fish with a meal of pork, beef or chicken. But many Gaspésians, such as the late merchant Percy Hyman, were loyal to fish, even at Christmas. His wife, Mable Reynolds Hyman, remembers him saying, "I'd rather have codfish than turkey."

Salt is an essential part of Gaspé flavour. More than most Quebecers, Gaspésians have always been accustomed to well-salted food, a taste than can be traced to early fish-preserving methods.

When the first fishermen landed to preserve their catch, they would clean the fish, then layer them in barrels with generous amounts of coarse salt. The brine that formed would keep the fish for months. The other method of preserving fish, by drying it outdoors, included salt to slow down decomposition. Legend was that it took 10 suns, meaning 10 separate, bright days, to do the drying job properly.

Salted herbs, Quebec's traditional winter seasoning, are used year-round in fish, meat and vegetable dishes. Rogers Fournier told me spicing is generous too, when I stayed at his Auberge La Martre at Rivière La Martre on the northeast coast. Spices, rum and sugar were regularly obtained in exchange for fish in such regions as the West Indies.

Fast food is fast fish along the coastal Route 132, dispensed from independent family establishments. At a mundane road stop in New Carlisle, I had chowder followed by fish and chips worthy of gastronomic stars. West of Rivière du Loup, a roadside trailer sold fried shrimp to go. They were crisp and sweet, the ideal snack to munch while admiring the late afternoon sun on the St. Lawrence. Another delicious fast food is the *guadielle*, buttery chunks of fresh-cooked lobster in a toasted hot dog roll.

All along the Gaspé coast but particularly on the northern stretch, small bays are sandwiched between tree-clad canyons. The terrain makes for spectacular tourist views, but it must have been arduous work to clear the small and hilly fields, mere fingers of land for growing food. Early settlers relied on four root vegetables—potatoes, onions, carrots and turnips—to combine with the fish of the day.

Tender, leafy vegetables were also grown or harvested wild. Fiddleheads, lambs' quarters and dandelion greens were used in early recipes. Mrs. Hyman, now retired to Montreal after living more than half a century in Gaspé, savours memories of the sweet garden peas she would pick to cook with fresh-caught salmon and scalloped potatoes. "We'd plant peas on Good Friday and they'd be ready in time for the salmon season in June," she told me.

Bubble and Squeak was an alternative. The English dish of mashed potatoes and cabbage, which is named from the sound it makes while being fried into a flat cake, was traced to Jersey by the late Ethel Renouf of Percé. She included her recipe in *The Black Whale Cook Book*, which she published in 1948. It calls for green beans, cubed new potatoes and fried salt pork. Sliced cucumbers with vinegar, salt and pepper would be served on the side.

Sugar, and plenty of it, alternating with molasses or maple syrup, has always been lavishly used in desserts. Puddings, often based on rice or cubed stale bread, pies, cakes including Johnny cake, and molasses cookies wind up traditional meals here.

Cod

Cod, available in vast numbers off the Gaspé coast, attracted fishermen from Europe as early as the 16th century. After Jacques Cartier landed at what is now the town of Gaspé in 1534, fellow Frenchmen from Normandy, Brittany and the southwest, Spaniards from the Basque coast, British and Anglo-Normans from the Channel Islands, and even Scandinavians would land to preserve their catch, either by salting or drying, then sail back across the Atlantic Ocean to sell it. All along the coast, you can still see the remnants of abandoned cod-drying racks or trellises, called "flakes."

LANGUES DE MORUE AUX AMANDES

Cod tongues with almonds

Cod tongues are usually dipped in batter or heavily floured, then deep-fried. At the Hôtel Baie Bleue in Carleton on the Bay of Chaleurs, chef Étienne Dubé created this lighter version. He adds lemon juice and almonds to a recipe that came originally from a family cook in Cloridorme on the north Gaspé coast.

1¼ pounds (625 g) fresh or frozen cod tongues
1 cup (250 mL) all-purpose flour
½ cup (125 mL) fine, dry bread crumbs
Salt, ground black pepper and paprika
⅓ cup (75 mL) vegetable oil
2 tablespoons (25 mL) clarified butter
2 tablespoons (25 mL) fresh lemon juice
¼ cup (50 mL) toasted, sliced almonds
Lemon wedges and parsley sprigs
Tartar sauce

Wash cod tongues and dry well with paper towels. In a bowl, combine flour and bread crumbs; season with salt, pepper and paprika to taste. Dredge cod tongues in coating mixture.

Heat oil and butter together in a large frying pan. Brown tongues lightly on all sides.

To serve, arrange cod tongues on 4 individual serving plates; sprinkle with lemon juice and toasted almonds. Trim each serving with a lemon wedge, parsley sprig and accompany with tartar sauce. Four servings.

Tourtière Leboutillier

Aunt Gertie's meat pie

"That pie is real Gaspé," says Mable Reynolds Hyman, lifelong friend of the late Gertrude Leboutillier. Aunt Gertie was a member of a long-time fish marketing family, which came originally from the Anglo-Norman island of Jersey. She was considered a "fabulous" cook, says her niece, Kay Leboutillier McCarthy of Montreal. Her recipe for a spiced beef and pork pie may be frozen unbaked or baked.

---

2 pounds (1 kg) lean ground beef
1 pound (500 g) lean ground pork
2 medium onions, chopped
Salt and ground black pepper
3/4 teaspoon (4 mL) ground allspice
1/2 teaspoon (2 mL) dried savoury
3/4 cup (175 mL) water
Pastry for 2 double-crust, 9-inch (23 cm) pies

In a large saucepan, combine beef and pork, stirring to blend. Cook until no longer pink. Stir in onions, salt and pepper to taste, allspice, savoury and water. Lower heat, partially cover, and simmer very gently so that mixture is just bubbling, for 1 to 2 hours, stirring occasionally.

To remove fat, strain meat mixture using a sieve; refrigerate both meat and liquid. Remove hardened fat from the jellied meat stock and discard.

Divide meat and jellied meat stock between 2 pastry-lined, 9-inch (23 cm) pie plates. Cover with top crust, trim, crimp edges to seal and cut steam vents. Bake for 10 minutes in a preheated 425°F (220°C) oven, then reduce temperature to 350°F (180°C) and bake another 20 to 25 minutes or until golden. Twelve to sixteen servings.

Gaspé Menu

Garlic-flavored fiddleheads
(page 137)

Cap Chat bouillabaisse
(page 132)

Crusty bread

Lemon pudding
(page 145)

Matane shrimp

Shrimp from the St. Lawrence River town of Matane sell far and wide. Recipes for this shellfish include a *fondue mongolaise*, bubbling hot fish stock in which you cook shrimp, scallops, thin slices of beef and vegetables; a *raclette gaspésienne* based on the melted Swiss cheese dish and including both shrimp and pickled herring; a *croque Matane*, the open-face sandwich made with shrimp, tomatoes and cheese; a shrimp bisque; a shrimp omelette; and a shrimp salad topped with Cognac-seasoned mayonnaise and finely chopped fresh parsley.

BOUILLABAISSE À LA CAP CHAT

Cap Chat bouillabaisse

This unusual main course soup is flavoured with *pastis*, the liqueur Pernod. It's the invention of Cap Chat chef-proprietors Yvan Belzile and Nicole Raymond, who run the restaurant Le Cabillaud.

---

2 tablespoons (25 mL) olive oil
1 medium onion, chopped
1 clove garlic, chopped
4 cups (1 L) fish stock
1 can (19 ounces/540 mL) tomatoes, drained and chopped
1/4 cup (50 mL) Pernod liqueur
1 tablespoon (15 mL) chopped fresh parsley
1/2 teaspoon (2 mL) grated orange rind
Pinch each fresh or dried thyme, savoury, marjoram and oregano
2 pinches saffron
1/2 pound (250 g) cod
1/2 pound (250 g) Greenland halibut or Atlantic turbot
Salt and ground white pepper
30 Matane shrimp, cooked and peeled, or 1/2 pound (250 g) medium shrimp, cooked, peeled, deveined
Chopped fresh parsley or chives

In a large, heavy saucepan, heat 1 tablespoon (15 mL) of the oil and sauté onion and garlic until softened. Add fish stock, tomatoes, 2 tablespoons (25 mL) of the Pernod, parsley, orange rind, thyme, savoury, marjoram, oregano and a pinch of saffron. Bring just to a boil, then partially cover and let simmer for 15 minutes.

Cut cod and halibut into 1-inch (2.5 cm) pieces and combine with remaining oil, Pernod and second pinch of saffron, tossing to blend.

Five minutes before serving time, add fish mixture to soup; cook gently for 5 minutes or until fish flakes with a fork. Adjust seasoning with salt and pepper to taste. Ladle soup into 6 heated soup bowls. Divide the shrimp among the bowls and top with chopped parsley. Six servings.

MICROWAVE METHOD

In a large, 3-quart (3 L) casserole, microwave 1 tablespoon (15 mL) of oil, onion and garlic at High (100 percent) for 3 to 4 minutes or until softened. Add fish stock, tomatoes, 2 tablespoons (25 mL) of the Pernod, parsley, orange rind, thyme, savoury, marjoram, oregano and a pinch of saffron. Cover and microwave at High (100 percent) for 10 to 12 minutes. Combine cod and halibut with remaining oil, Pernod and second pinch of saffron, tossing to blend.

Add fish to casserole just before serving, cover and microwave at High (100 percent) for 4 to 6 minutes more or until soup is piping hot. Adjust seasoning with salt and pepper to taste.

Ladle soup into 6 heated soup bowls. Divide shrimp among the bowls and top with parsley.

A head-to-tail dish

Quebecers, so economical that they have been reputed to use every part of the pig but the squeal, also developed the head-to-tail cod dish *cambuse* or *combuse*. Some recipes call for the whole codfish, plus extra heads and livers. The basic recipe usually starts with sautéing *lardons*, or little strips of salt pork, in a deep, cast-iron casserole. A layer of sliced onions and cubed—but not peeled—potatoes are then added. Finally comes the cod, laid whole on this bed. The fish is cleaned but with head, tongue, tail, liver and skin intact. Salt and pepper are sprinkled over all, water is added just to cover, and the dish is simmered gently for up to an hour and three-quarters, or until tender. The dish is a particular favourite in Acadian settlements along the south coast around Bonaventure and Paspébiac.

Crème de bourgot de Gaspé

Gaspé whelk soup

The large member of the periwinkle family, sometimes called a whelk or sea snail, is referred to as a *bourgot* in the Gaspé and a *buccin* in France. It is used to make this soup at Le Cabillaud, a restaurant in Cap Chat on the north coast. The seafood is popular in northern Europe. Well-stocked fish shops handle whelks and periwinkles, sometimes selling them cooked and frozen. Do not use *bourgots* packed in vinegar, warns chef Yvan Belzile. Squid may be substituted, however.

---

2 cups (500 mL) large whelks, either fresh or shelled, 2 inches (5 cm) in size
2 tablespoons (25 mL) butter
1 medium onion, sliced
1 large clove garlic, chopped
2 tablespoons (25 mL) all-purpose flour
4 cups (1 L) fish stock
½ cup (125 mL) white wine
6 large leaves of leaf or Boston lettuce, chopped
1 tablespoon (15 mL) chopped fresh sorrel or juice of ½ lemon
1 teaspoon (5 mL) grated orange rind
Pinch fresh chervil
Salt and ground white pepper
1 cup (250 mL) milk
⅓ cup (75 mL) whipping cream

If *bourgots* are fresh and still in the shell, cook them in boiling, salted water for 20 minutes, then remove meat from shells. Trim off the curled intestine and cut into pieces.

In a large saucepan, melt butter and sauté onion and garlic until softened. Blend in flour, then stir in fish stock, wine, whelks, lettuce, sorrel, orange rind, chervil and salt and pepper to taste. Simmer soup, partially covered, for 30 minutes. Purée soup in batches, first in a food processor, then in a blender until very smooth.

Return soup to saucepan. Add milk and cream; adjust seasoning, if necessary, with salt and pepper. Heat soup until piping hot, but not boiling. Six to eight servings.

MICROWAVE METHOD

In a 3-quart (3 L) casserole, melt butter at High (100 percent) for 30 seconds or until melted. Add onion and garlic; microwave, uncovered, at High (100 percent) for 3 minutes or until softened. Blend in flour, then stir in stock, wine, whelks, lettuce, sorrel, orange rind, chervil and salt and pepper to taste. Microwave, covered, at High (100 percent) for 15 to 18 minutes, stirring twice during cooking.

Purée soup in batches, first in a food processor, then in a blender, until very smooth.

Return soup to casserole. Stir in milk and cream; adjust seasoning, if necessary, with salt and pepper. Reheat, covered, at High (100 percent) for 5 to 6 minutes or until piping hot.

Auberge du Gargantua

The mountaintop Auberge du Gargantua serves some of the finest fish and seafood in the gastronomy-minded community of Percé. Pierre Péresse, who came here from his native Brittany in 1951, runs this inn, which is so high in the hills you often climb through clouds to reach it. Péresse has observed Gaspésian food tastes changing over his years here. "There was a time when Gaspé people did not eat many types of fish from these waters, fish popular in France and other countries such as *lotte* (monkfish), crab, or *bigorneaux* (sea snails, winkles or whelks). Now they enjoy these varieties," he says. His *bouillabaisse* contains six types of fish, including fresh cooked lobster claws. Drive up to the inn by the Coin du Banc side of the point and descend on the Percé side for the best views. And note his two carefully cultivated vegetable gardens too. (Rooms: 11 in motel; address: 222 Route des Failles, Percé, Québec, G0C 2L0; telephone: (418) 782-2852.)

BOUILLABAISE LA COULÉE DOUCE

Coulée Douce bouillabaisse

In the salmon and trout fishing town of Causapscal in the Matapedia River valley, this Breton-style *bouillabaisse* soup is regularly served at the Auberge La Coulée Douce. Contents depend on the catch of the day, say innkeepers Suzanne Cousineau and Vianney Morin, but the soup is always served in shallow bowls surrounded by hot garlic toast.

½ pound (250 g) salmon steak
½ pound (250 g) halibut steak
½ pound (250 g) cod fillet
½ pound (250 g) scallops, halved if large
¾ pound (375 g) shucked clams
1 pound (500 g) shelled and deveined raw shrimp
¼ cup (50 mL) olive oil
2 medium onions, chopped
2 cloves garlic, finely chopped
4 ripe tomatoes, peeled, seeded and coarsely
  chopped
½ teaspoon (2 mL) ground coriander
1 tablespoon (15 mL) chopped fresh parsley
1 tablespoon (15 mL) chopped fresh herbs, such as
  marjoram, oregano, basil and chives
Salt and ground white pepper
8 cups (2 L) fish stock
½ cup (125 mL) white wine
Hot garlic toast as accompaniment

Cut salmon, halibut and cod into large chunks. Combine with scallops, clams and shrimp; set aside.

Heat oil in a large saucepan or stock pot over medium heat and sauté onions and garlic until softened. Add tomatoes, coriander, parsley and herbs; season with salt and pepper to taste.

Gift from the sea

Along the Bay of Chaleurs shore off Miguasha, a flat, forked seaweed washes up on the beach. Gaspésians know how to turn it into a light and refreshing dessert, a jelly or a soup. It's called *mousse d'Irlande* or Irish moss and Peter Bujold, whose family are landowners along this shore, compares it to a frayed sponge, curled up at the edges. Green or reddish brown when fresh, it dries to a creamy white. To cook it, heat it in a pan of milk until it thickens, much like cream of wheat cereal. The only addition, and it's optional, is a dash of vanilla. The delicate flavour resembles tapioca. The cooked mixture is chilled and served in individual dishes. A dried version is sometimes available in health food shops under the name carageenan.

Add fish stock and wine; bring to a boil. Let simmer for 10 minutes. Add prepared fish, scallops, clams and shrimp all at once. Return to the boil, then lower heat and let soup simmer for 8 to 10 minutes more or just until fish flakes when tested with a fork. Serve in large heated bowls accompanied with garlic toast. Eight servings.

TÊTES DE VIOLON À L'AIL
Garlic-flavoured fiddleheads

The tiny, curled fronds of ferns, which have gained a reputation as one of Canada's national foods, come in large part from the Matapedia River valley. At Auberge La Coulée Douce in Causapscal, Suzanne Cousineau likes to steam fiddleheads, then season them with a garlic sauce.

---

1 pound (500 g) fresh fiddleheads, or 1 package (300 g) frozen
¼ cup (50 mL) butter
6 cloves garlic, finely chopped
2 dry shallots, finely chopped
1 tablespoon (15 mL) soya sauce
1 teaspoon (5 mL) granulated sugar
3 tablespoons (45 mL) white wine

Shake fresh fiddleheads in a paper bag until brown skins come off; discard skins. Steam fresh or frozen, unthawed, fiddleheads just until tender. Meanwhile, heat butter in a heavy frying pan and sauté garlic and shallots until softened. Blend in soya sauce, sugar and wine. Add steamed fiddleheads, turning to coat them well in the sauce. Serve at once. Four servings.

Dry Shallots Explained

A green onion is a scallion or an *échalote* but not a shallot, according to Quebec's Office de la langue française. But the habit of referring to green onions as shallots persists and creates some confusion for cooks in the regions. Recipes in this book use the term "dry shallot" to define the small reddish-skinned onion that seasons so many French sauces.

PERDRIX AU CHOU
Partridge and cabbage

Braising partridge with salt pork in a bed of chopped cabbage is traditional in Norman and Breton cooking. Mable Reynolds Hyman's addition of apples is a Norman touch to a recipe which dates back to the Gaspé's earliest French settlers. Partridge are now obtainable from specialty farms.

---

2 partridges* (1½ to 2 pounds/750 g to 1 kg each)
2 tablespoons (25 mL) butter
¼ pound (125 g) salt pork, cubed
1 medium cabbage, coarsely chopped
2 medium onions, finely chopped
1 clove garlic, finely chopped
2 medium cooking apples, unpeeled and grated
¼ teaspoon (1 mL) dried thyme
Salt and ground black pepper
½ cup (125 mL) water
Large slices of hot, buttered toast

* Farm-raised partridges should require no more than an hour's cooking; wild mature birds may take up to 2 hours to tenderize. Rabbit may be substituted for the partridges called for in this recipe.

Truss partridges. In a large, deep, flameproof casserole or Dutch oven, heat butter and brown partridges on all sides. Set birds aside. Add salt pork to casserole and fry until crisp and brown. Drain off excess fat, if desired. Add cabbage, onions, garlic, apples and thyme; season with salt and pepper to taste. Sauté over medium heat, stirring for 5 minutes. Bury partridges in cabbage mixture. Add water, cover and cook over low heat for 1½ to 2 hours or until meat is tender. Or cook in a pressure cooker for 30 minutes.

To serve, cut partridges into serving-size portions and arrange on toast, surrounded by the cabbage mixture. Six to eight servings.

CIPÂTE AU SAUMON
Layered salmon pie

This traditional salmon dish comes from Auberge La Martre, an inn on the north coast near St. Anne des Monts. Proprietors Rogers Fournier and Marie-France Crevier specialize in fish and game dishes.

¼ pound (125 g) salt pork
1 pound (500 g) salmon steaks or fillets, skinned and
   cut into pieces*
2 tablespoons (25 mL) all-purpose flour
¼ cup (50 mL) finely chopped celery
1 tablespoon (15 mL) finely chopped onion
1 medium potato, peeled and sliced
Salt and ground white pepper
Pastry for double-crust, 9-inch (23 cm) pie

  * Cod or other fish may be used.

Cut salt pork into thin strips and spread evenly in the bottom of a 2-quart (2 L) casserole. Dredge salmon lightly with flour. Arrange half of fish on the salt pork. Sprinkle with half of the celery, onion and potato slices; season with salt and pepper to taste.

Roll out half of the pastry, slightly thicker than normal, to fit the size of the casserole. Cover potato layer with the pastry, cutting 2 large vents. Pour in water through vents until level with pastry. Layer with the remaining fish, celery, onion and potato slices in the same way; season with salt and pepper to taste. Cover with top pastry crust and again cut out 2 vents. Pour water in vents until level with pastry.

Bake pie in a preheated 350°F (180°C) oven for 1½ hours or until crust is golden-brown. Four to six servings.

Salmon country

Whether from Gaspé's famous salmon-fishing rivers or from a new salmon "farm" on the Bay of Chaleurs, this superior fish, although scarce, is as popular as ever. On Gaspé tables, it's best when grilled or poached and topped with a lemon cream sauce that sometimes includes sliced hard-boiled eggs, or a trimming of butter-sautéed mushrooms and chives. The whole fish makes a feast when baked with an herb-flavoured bread crumb stuffing or grilled with bacon or salt pork. And then there's salmon pie, croquettes or a soufflé to consider.

A tip on improving a generously proportioned salmon, one weighing 15 to 25 pounds (7 to 11 kg), is offered by Carleton restaurateur Pierre Landry, who runs the easygoing beach restaurant Café de l'Indépendant'e: "Pack the fish in plenty of ice and store it in the refrigerator for four to five days. This adds to the flavour and tenderness."

POT-EN-POT "TANTE YVONNE" AUX FRUITS DE MER

Seafood pie

In Îles de la Madeleine, family cooks are expert at preparing foods from the deep. This mixed seafood casserole belonging to Yvonne Bouffard of Étang du Nord on the west coast of Île du Cap aux Meules won first prize in a province-wide regional cooking contest sponsored by the Quebec agriculture department in 1983.

Pastry

---

4 cups (1 L) all-purpose flour
8 teaspoons (40 mL) baking powder
1 teaspoon (5 mL) salt
2 teaspoons (10 mL) dry mustard
2 tablespoons (25 mL) chopped fresh parsley
⅔ cup (150 mL) lard
1¾ cups (425 mL) milk

In a bowl, sift together flour, baking powder, salt and dry mustard. Stir in parsley. Cut in lard with pastry blender or 2 knives until mixture is the texture of coarse crumbs. Using a fork, stir in milk, a little at a time, to make a soft dough. Shape into a ball, wrap and refrigerate for at least 30 minutes.

Divide dough into 2, ⅔ of the amount in 1 ball. Roll out larger ball just less then ¼ inch (5 mm) thick and line bottom and sides of a deep, 3-quart (3 L) casserole (8 × 15 × 3 inches or 20 × 38 × 7 cm is recommended). Roll out the remaining pastry to fit the top.

Filling

---

1 cup (250 mL) water
2 cups (500 mL) finely cubed potatoes
1 pound (500 g) scallops, cut in small pieces
1 pound (500 g) lobster meat, cut in small pieces
1 pound (500 g) shrimp, shelled and deveined
1 cup (250 mL) finely chopped celery
1 cup (250 mL) finely chopped onion
1 medium carrot, coarsely shredded
¼ cup (50 mL) chopped green onions
1 teaspoon (5 mL) dried *fines herbes**
Salt and ground white pepper
½ cup (125 mL) butter
1½ cups (375 mL) light cream, or 1 can (14 oz./
   385 mL) evaporated milk
¼ cup (50 mL) cornstarch
¼ cup (50 mL) water
Milk
Olives

* Tarragon, chives and parsley are suggested.

In a large saucepan, combine water, potatoes, scallops, lobster, shrimp, celery, onion, carrot, green onion and *fines herbes*; season with salt and pepper to taste. Bring to a boil and simmer for 10 minutes. Remove from heat. Stir in butter and cream. In a small bowl, blend cornstarch with water, stir into seafood mixture and return to medium heat, stirring just until mixture thickens.

Pour into pastry-lined casserole dish. Brush border of pastry with milk. Add top crust and seal edges with a fork. Decorate crust with 3 pastry cut-outs in the shape of fish. Make steam vents in the shape of waves. Pieces of olives can be used to make the eyes of the fish. Bake in a preheated 375°F (190°C) oven for 35 to 45 minutes or until pie crust is golden brown. Eight servings.

The phantom ship

If the Bay of Chaleurs is brewing up a storm, scan its waters for a glimpse of the phantom ship, a pirates' vessel that once was chased up the bay from Percé by a warship until it caught fire and all on board died. She's said to be a square-rigged ship and those who have sighted her over the years say she moves very fast. As rigging, masts and hull burn, you may see sailors climbing the rigging and a beautiful woman calmly issuing commands as the deck turns into an inferno.

MAQUEREAU FARCI
Stuffed baked mackerel

Mackerel is in fashion now that research has shown it to be rich in Omega-3, a polyunsaturated fat that is beneficial to the heart. Long popular in the Gaspé and neighbouring Îles de la Madeleine, this meaty, pink fish was traditionally sliced, floured and browned with salt pork, then braised with onions. Another popular recipe is to stuff it with bread crumbs or rice, plus chopped vegetables or mushrooms. This dish is from a collection published by the Cercles de fermières of Îles de la Madeleine.

---

2 mackerels (about 1 pound/500 g each)
2 tablespoons (25 mL) butter or vegetable oil
1 small onion, chopped
¼ cup (50 mL) chopped celery
1½ cups (375 mL) fresh bread cubes
1 small egg, beaten
Salt and ground white pepper
Additional melted butter or oil

Clean fish, remove heads, tails and fins. Debone, being careful to keep the fish intact. Sprinkle interior lightly with salt.

Melt butter in a frying pan and sauté onion and celery until softened. In a bowl, combine bread cubes, beaten egg and sautéed vegetables. Season with salt and pepper to taste.

Stuff fish with bread mixture and close using toothpicks or skewers. Arrange fish in a shallow, greased baking pan and brush with melted butter or oil. Bake in a preheated 450°F (230°C) oven, allowing 10 minutes per inch (2.5 cm) measuring at thickest point, or until fresh flakes when tested with a fork. Four servings.

MICROWAVE METHOD

Prepare fish as directed in recipe. To make stuffing, combine butter, onion and celery in a 4-cup (1 L) measure; microwave, uncovered, at High (100 percent) for 3 to 4 minutes or until softened. Add bread cubes and egg; season with salt and pepper.

Stuff fish as directed and place in a shallow baking dish. Cover with vented plastic wrap. Microwave at High (100 percent) for 4 to 6 minutes or until fish flakes when tested with a fork. Let stand, covered, for 2 minutes.

MORUE À LA GASPÉSIENNE

Gaspé-style cod

At the comfortable inn Auberge Le Coin du Banc in Percé, chef Fernand Rehel, who comes from neighbouring Bridgeville, prepares the traditional Gaspé fish dish of poached cod topped with crisp-fried *lardons*—morsels of salt pork—and onions.

3 cups (750 mL) water
1 cup (250 mL) white wine
1 small carrot, finely chopped
1 stalk celery, including leaves, chopped
¼ cup (50 mL) chopped chives
Few sprigs fresh parsley
1 small bay leaf
Salt and black peppercorns
¼ pound (125 g) salt pork, cut into ½-inch (1 cm) cubes
1 Spanish onion, sliced
1¼ pounds (600 g) cod fillets*

* Fresh or salt cod may be used. Salt cod must be soaked for 4 hours in cold water, then rinsed. Or it may be covered with cold water, brought slowly to a boil, then rinsed.

Island bird sanctuary

The offshore island called Bonaventure is home to North America's largest colony of gannets. About 50,000 of these water-loving members of the goose family crowd onto the island's tall, red cliffs or swoop and swirl over the waters nearby. Half-a-dozen other species, including seagulls, cormorants and puffins, congregate here, all clearly visible from one of the excursion boats that operate during the summer from the dock at Percé.

Where to stay

If you want to savour the true tastes of Gaspé cooking, prepare for your trip by obtaining a brochure of independent inns, joined in an association called La Barouche. Founded in 1980 by Alain Choinière, chef-proprietor of Auberge St. Simon just east of Trois Pistoles, it's made up of seven inns or restaurants where the owner is on the spot to receive you and probably cook for you too, using local foods and recipes. If you visit each inn, you can make a complete tour of the Gaspé, down the Matapedia River valley to the Bay of Chaleurs, around the peninsula and back along the St. Lawrence River by way of Matane. The organization has become successful enough to import its own white wine, labelled Cuvée Barouche and available at all member establishments. Some Quebec tourist offices have this brochure, or you can write to P.O. Box 1226, St. Anne des Monts, Québec, G0E 2G0 to request it. Telephone for reservations; these places are small and not all are open year-round.

Make a court bouillon by combining water, wine, carrot, celery, chives, parsley, bay leaf, salt and peppercorns in a saucepan. Simmer, partially covered, for 30 minutes. Strain.

In a frying pan, sauté salt pork cubes until golden and crisp. Drain on paper towels. Use pan drippings to sauté onion over medium heat until lightly browned and softened.

Place fish in a large saucepan. Pour court bouillon over fish and heat just until liquid is about to simmer. Cook fish very gently, without letting liquid simmer, for about 7 to 10 minutes or just until fillets flake when tested with a fork.

Using a slotted spoon, transfer fish to a heated serving platter. Top fish with crisp, cooked salt pork and fried onions. Four servings.

MICROWAVE METHOD

It is not necessary to make court bouillon.

Cook salt pork and onion as directed in recipe.

Arrange fish fillets in the bottom of a shallow baking dish just large enough to hold the fillets. Pour $1/4$ cup (50 mL) wine over fillets. Cover with lid or vented plastic wrap. Microwave at High (100 percent) for 4 to 5 minutes or just until fish flakes when tested with a fork. Let stand, covered, for 3 minutes.

Using a slotted spoon, transfer fillets to a heated serving platter and top with crisp, cooked salt pork and fried onions.

Lemon pudding

British cooking is part of the culinary mix in the Gaspé, as this baked lemon dessert from a Percé recipe collection indicates. It's a favorite with Mable Reynolds Hyman, a long-time Gaspé resident, and her daughter Barbara Maclaren of Montreal.

---

2 tablespoons (25 mL) butter, softened
3/4 cup (175 mL) granulated sugar
Juice and grated rind of 1 lemon
3 tablespoons (45 mL) all-purpose flour
2 eggs, separated
1 cup (250 mL) milk
Pinch salt

In a bowl, cream butter and sugar together. Stir in lemon juice and rind, flour and beaten egg yolks. Stir in milk and salt. In another bowl, beat egg whites stiffly and fold in. Pour into a buttered 1 1/2-quart (1.5 L) baking dish. Oven-poach in a pan of hot water in a preheated 350°F (180°C) oven for 45 minutes or until firm and lightly browned on top. Serve either warm or cold. Six servings.

MICROWAVE METHOD

Prepare batter as directed in recipe and pour into baking dish. (It is not necessary to use water bath.) Microwave, uncovered, at Medium (50 percent) for 6 to 8 minutes or until cake layer is just set, rotating dish twice during cooking. Six servings.

Auberge Le Coin du Banc

There are fancier inns in the tourist centre of Percé, but this long-established retreat has the genuine flavour of the region. It's been there, hunkered down on a long beach just north of the famous rock, since 1860. It emphasizes warmth of welcome, superb local cuisine and a decor with lots of character. Irishman Sidney Maloney has run the inn, which resembles a Cape Cod house, for years, much of the time with the assistance of Quebecer Lise De Guire as manager. Local specialties should be sampled—cod, cod and more cod, from tongue, cheeks and liver to fillets and the whole fish. Lobster and shrimp, beef steak and lamb chops are also well prepared. Tea or cocktails on the terrace overlooking the ocean is relaxing. (Rooms: 12, a few with private bath; address: Route 132, Coin du Banc, Percé, Québec, G0C 2L0; telephone: (418) 645-2907.)

Pouding du chômeur de Matane

Economy pudding, Matane style

The recipe for this traditional Quebec dessert comes from a collection published by a woman's service group called Le Club Lionnes de Matane, active since 1980 in the St. Lawrence River town. Batter is dropped by spoonfuls to bake, dumpling style, in a hot brown sugar syrup. Other versions of this dish call for the syrup to be poured over the batter before baking.

Syrup

2 cups (500 mL) brown sugar
2 tablespoons (25 mL) all-purpose flour
3 cups (750 mL) water
1 tablespoon (15 mL) butter

In a saucepan, blend brown sugar with flour; add water and butter. Heat just until sugar dissolves and butter melts. Pour into a 9 × 13-inch (3.5 L) baking pan.

Batter

2 cups (500 mL) all-purpose flour
⅓ cup (75 mL) granulated sugar
1 tablespoon (15 mL) baking powder
Pinch salt
2 tablespoons (25 mL) butter, melted
¾ cup (175 mL) milk
1 egg, beaten

In a bowl, combine flour, sugar, baking powder and salt. Stir in melted butter, milk and beaten egg. Drop large spoonfuls of batter into syrup and bake in a preheated 375°F (190°C) oven for 35 minutes or until dumplings are lightly browned. Serve warm. Eight servings.

MICROWAVE METHOD

In a 9 × 13-inch (3.5 L) baking dish, blend brown sugar and flour together. Reduce water to 2 cups (500 mL), pour in pan and add butter. Microwave, uncovered, at High (100 percent) for 8 to 10 minutes, until syrup comes to a full boil, stirring twice during cooking.

Prepare batter as directed and drop large spoonfuls into hot syrup. Microwave, uncovered, at High (100 percent) for 5 to 6 minutes or until dumplings have risen and are dry to the touch, rotating dish once. Let stand on counter top for 5 minutes. Serve warm.

Not to be missed

Gaspé historical sights include: the wreck of a French ship in the museum marking the 1760 battle at Pointe à la Croix near Restigouche; fossils from the shore of the Bay of Chaleurs that date back millions of years on display in a museum at Miguasha; a museum about Acadian life at Bonaventure; and the 1852 mansion of lawyer John Hamilton at New Carlisle. There are fisheries museums at the old Robin and Leboutillier plants at Paspébiac and Le Havre on the north coast of Forillon National Park; the Jacques Cartier monument and the Musée de la Gaspésie are at Gaspé; and the tiny house and barn of the Blanchette family and Hyman's general store have been reconstructed on the south shore of Forillon National Park. Manoir Leboutillier, the 1840 house of fish merchant John Leboutillier at Anse au Griffon, is open for visitors, as is the Anglo-Norman Chateau Lamontagne, built in 1873 at St. Anne des Monts by millionaire Théodore Lamontagne.

TARTE AU SUCRE GASPÉSIENNE

Sugar pie, Gaspé style

This dessert, in which brown sugar is combined with rolled oats and evaporated milk in a lattice-topped pie shell, was acquired by the Hyman family of Gaspé from Mme Olympe Boulanger, the late proprietor of one of Percé's oldest inns, the Hôtel Bleu Blanc Rouge. The addition of rolled oats is typical of the blend of Anglo-Saxon and French cuisines found in this region. A small serving should satisfy even the sweetest tooth.

---

2 cups (500 mL) packed brown sugar
½ cup (125 mL) old-fashioned rolled oats
1 small can (160 mL) or ⅔ cup (150 mL) evaporated milk
Pastry for double-crust, 8-inch (20 cm) pie shell

Line a 8-inch (20 cm) pie plate with pastry. Mix brown sugar and oats together and spread evenly in pie shell. Roll out pastry for top crust and cut into ½-inch (1 cm) strips. Arrange strips on top of filling, in a lattice design, pinching edges to seal. Just before baking, pour evaporated milk carefully through each gap in the lattice topping.

Bake in a preheated 350°F (180°C) oven for 30 to 35 minutes or until bubbling hot and lightly browned. Serve warm or at room temperature. Eight to ten servings.

MONTÉRÉGIE

 Fanning out to the south of Montreal is her food basket, a huge and intensively cultivated region of farms and orchards with a culinary history dating back to seigneurial times. Beginning at the mouth of the Richelieu River at Sorel—home of a certain fish and vegetable stew called *gibelotte*—and extending west through apple and dairy farm country to the Ontario border, is a wide crescent-shaped area called Montérégie.

Those who live there, and we who come to visit, tend to think more of the smaller divisions of this "garden of the province" as the region has long been named. When I cross the St. Lawrence River to pick strawberries at Jacques Wera's farm near the old village of Chambly, I'm on the South Shore. When I head southeast to pick apples around Mont St. Hilaire, I'm in the Richelieu River valley. And when I travel southwest to Ormstown's annual June fair, I'm in the Chateauguay River valley.

Directly south of Montreal is the biggest market gardening area in the province. On verdant fields around Sherrington and St. Remi is the rich, black *terre noire* where so many of western Quebec's leafy and root vegetables are grown. The English word for it, "muckland", isn't as pretty as the sight of a lush field of spinach or green onions or tomatoes. Here you find the carrot headquarters of the province. So many superb carrots are grown around Sherrington that producers regularly export the vegetable to other parts of Canada, the United States and abroad.

Some of the best and most expensive restaurants in the province are in Montérégie, profiting by the proximity of such specialties as white asparagus from St. Damase, oyster (*pleurotte*) mushrooms from Carignan, artichokes from St. Hyacinthe and Belgian endive from St. Clet. Chefs from Au Tournant de la Rivière at Carignan and the Hostellerie Les Trois Tilleuls at St. Marc can obtain farm-raised game birds, rabbits and milk-fed veal from nearby sources.

The St. Marc inn was started in 1974 by Thérèse Daigle. Restoring an old stone farmhouse on the banks of the Richelieu, this talented cook and descendant of one of the valley's original farming families served local foods in dishes of Norman and Breton origin.

Mme Daigle, who then went on to teach cooking in Montreal and write cookbooks that sell all over the province, has vivid memories of the cuisine

149

of her grandparents' day and the region's prevailing fondness for pork. Her father, who ran a butcher and grocery store, would make such pork favourites as *boudin* (blood pudding), *saucisses en coiffe* (hand-made sausages), and *tête fromagée* (spiced pâté made from a pig's head), and take those foods to sell in Montreal's Bonsecours Market. (The old market building, which now houses municipal offices, is still one of the landmarks of Old Montreal.) "We still produce the pig that our colonists lived on and we still enjoy every part, from snout to tail," said Mme Daigle.

Apples are the region's favourite fruit. Much of Quebec's apple processing is done in the Rougemont area—apple juice and cider, applesauce and pie filling. "I can remember my grandmother, Rose Anna Marcotte, making a wonderful apple dessert like a *pouding du chômeur*, and *pommettes par la queue*, small crab apples dipped in a sweet, jellied syrup," said Mme Daigle.

Spices, dried fruits and nuts are often added to apples in pies and cakes, puddings and preserves—a habit that can be traced to northern France. Carol Petch of Hemmingford, who collected early recipes from her village to mark its 100th anniversary in 1977, uncovered this custom among families of Anglo-Saxon background too. The nuts would be harvested before the first frost, then dried and shelled as needed. Many a winter evening was spent shelling the nuts by the open fire.

Carol's family operates a large apple orchard and "you-pick" apple business. Her husband Robert and his brother Charles are both plant scientists and maintain a few of what are now called "antique" apple varieties among their 15,000 trees.

Each August, Carol and her family make apple jelly and applesauce from Duchess apples, a yellow and green variety with red stripes that was a popular cooking apple a century ago. The sweet, yellow Tolman Sweet, brought north by United Empire Loyalists, cooks well and makes exceptional pickles, in her opinion. The *Fameuse* (Snow is its name outside Quebec), round and red, and white inside, is the top Hallowe'en snack.

Since few of the early varieties travel well, the Petches now grow mainly McIntosh, Cortland and Lobo apples. But they are increasing their early season trees, planting Jersey Mac, a relative of the McIntosh, and Empire, a cross between a McIntosh and a Delicious.

"Wealthy apples make wonderful applesauce," says Carol. "You don't need much sugar in it. And I love making apple jelly with early apples because there's no colour in it and lots of pectin, and I can colour it with herbs like mint, lemon balm and basil."

SOUPE À LA CITROUILLE

Pumpkin soup

At Auberge Handfield, a country inn at St. Marc sur Richelieu, owner Conrad Handfield often serves his family's traditional recipes. This soup recipe belonged to his mother, Irene Janotte Handfield. Pumpkins grow so plentifully in this region that the neighbouring town of Iberville has a pumpkin festival each October.

---

4 cups (1 L) pumpkin, cut into 1-inch (2.5 cm) cubes*
3 cups (750 mL) chicken stock
2 tablespoons (25 mL) butter
2 tablespoons (25 mL) all-purpose flour
Pinch ground nutmeg and ground cloves
Salt and ground black pepper
1 cup (250 mL) light cream

* Pumpkin purée may be substituted; add 2 cups (500 mL) or 1 can (19 ounces/540 mL) to chicken stock base, then proceed with recipe.

In a saucepan, simmer pumpkin in 1 cup (250 mL) of chicken stock until tender. In another saucepan, heat butter, blend in flour and cook until bubbling. Blend in remaining chicken stock, stirring until thickened and smooth. Add pumpkin and cooking water, purée in a food processor or blender, then strain soup through a sieve.

Return soup to saucepan and season with nutmeg, cloves and salt and pepper to taste. Stir in cream, heat until hot but not boiling, and serve. Six servings.

Montérégie Menu

Head cheese
(page 156)

Crusty bread

Sorel fish stew
(page 154)

Cucumber salad

Butternut spice cake
(page 166)

Hostellerie Les Trois Tilleuls

Overlooking the Richelieu River, this century-old farmhouse has been expanded to include a modern wing. It's a comfortable, quiet place with a patio overlooking the river. Locally-crafted furnishings enhance the atmosphere. The principle activity is strolling the banks of the wide old river; a brisk walk may be in order if you wish to work off the expensive but excellent French cuisine. Both the owners and the chef are French-born and the wine list is impressive. There is cross-country skiing and skating on the river. A member of the prestigious Relais et Châteaux group of resort hotels, it has prices to match. (Rooms: 21, each with private bath; address: 290 Richelieu St., St. Marc sur Richelieu, Québec, J0L 2E0; telephone: (514) 584-2231.)

GALANTINE DE POULET
Jellied chicken loaf

The early Quebec cooking reflected its French roots with refined culinary preparations such as this tarragon-flavoured cold meat dish. The recipe belongs to Berthe Marcotte Gatien, who would make it each December to enjoy after Mass at the Christmas *Réveillon* or at the New Year's *jour de l'an* celebration.

---

1 tablespoon (15 mL) each vegetable oil and butter
1 large roasting chicken (about 5 pounds/2.5 kg)
1 veal shank, cut into pieces
1 stalk celery with leaves, chopped
1 large carrot, chopped
2 onions, quartered
1 clove garlic
1 tablespoon (15 mL) salt
½ teaspoon (2 mL) ground black pepper
1 bay leaf
¼ cup (50 mL) chopped fresh parsley
1 teaspoon (5 mL) dried tarragon or to taste
Cranberry sauce or jelly

In a large, heavy stock pot, heat oil and butter together. Quickly brown chicken on all sides and set aside. Brown veal shank pieces on all sides. Return chicken to stock pot, along with celery, carrot, onions and garlic. Cover with cold water. Season with salt, pepper and bay leaf. Bring to a boil and simmer, uncovered, for 1½ to 2 hours or until meat is very tender and falling off the bones. Let cool.

Strain stock and return to stock pot and heat until boiling, then simmer for 10 minutes.

Meanwhile, remove meat from bones and cut into small pieces. Add to stock along with parsley and tarragon. Simmer briefly and adjust seasoning with salt and pepper.

Rinse a 6-cup (1.5 L) ring mould with cold water.
Add meat mixture and fill to rim with stock.
Refrigerate until set, at least 4 hours or overnight.
Unmould and serve with cranberry sauce or jelly.
May be made 2 to 3 days in advance. Do not freeze.
Six to eight servings.

Soupe aux huîtres
Oyster soup

Oysters were so plentiful in the St. Lawrence River a
century ago, that this soup was a tradition at festival
meals. Thérèse Daigle remembers her mother,
Berthe Marcotte Gatien, serving it at the Christmas
Réveillon and other special holiday meals.

¼ cup (50 mL) butter
2 cups (500 mL) fresh shucked oysters with their
  juice
3 cups (750 mL) milk
½ cup (125 mL) whipping cream
1 tablespoon (15 mL) chopped fresh parsley
Pinch paprika
Salt and ground white pepper

Melt butter in a large, heavy saucepan. As soon as
butter is foamy, add oysters and their juice; poach
over medium heat until edges of oysters curl.

In another saucepan, heat milk and cream until
very hot; do not let boil. Add hot oyster mixture;
season with parsley, paprika and salt and pepper to
taste. Serve at once in warmed soup bowls
accompanied with crackers. Six servings.

The military connection

Military considerations
sparked a number of
developments in the placid
countryside of the Richelieu
River valley. French explorer
Samuel de Champlain first
journeyed up the river in
1609 to do battle with the
Iroquois Indians on Lake
Champlain. The first settlers
in the region were soldiers
from the regiment Carignan-
Salières, who were given
land in 1665, instead of
passage home to France.

The first fort on the river
was built in 1665 by Jacques
de Chambly as protection
against the Indians. Fort
Chambly was lost to the
British in 1760 and was
involved in skirmishes with
the Americans 15 years later.
After they captured Fort
Chambly, the British also
took Fort Lennox, built in
1759 at what is now St. Paul
de l'Île aux Noix near the
American border. Both forts
are now popular tourist
attractions.

GIBELOTTE DES ÎLES DE SOREL

Sorel fish stew

Many years ago, a small restaurant on one of the islands off Sorel began serving the day's catch of *barbotte*, the plentiful little catfish from the St. Lawrence, as part of a sustaining vegetable stew. The dish was called *gibelotte*, a term which the culinary Bible *Larousse Gastronomique* defines as rabbit stew and traces to the Old French *gibelet* or platter of birds. The island's fish dish became popular throughout the area. Families would simmer a variety of vegetables and fish, often perch, for several hours. Often they would make a convenient *gibelotte* with canned vegetables.

Today, the dish is celebrated each July at its own festival. Recently, the festival committee asked Montreal's Institut de tourisme et d'hôtellerie du Québec to refine the official recipe. Chef researchers used a variety of fresh vegetables cooked just until tender-crisp in the stew, which is served with pan-fried fish fillets in this modern adaptation of an old favourite.

½ pound (250 g) salt pork
2 onions, chopped
3 cloves garlic, finely chopped
6 medium potatoes, peeled and cubed
3 cups (750 mL) chicken stock
3 cups (750 mL) beef stock
Bouquet garni*
Salt and ground black pepper
¼ cup (50 mL) tomato paste
2 tomatoes, peeled, seeded and diced
1 cup (250 mL) frozen or canned corn kernels

Fish of the past

Sturgeon as long as a rowboat is wide (and eels even longer) were popular and plentiful in the Richelieu River as recently as the 1940s. Thérèse Daigle can remember her grandfather, Arsène Gatien, taking her trolling on the river. "We would never return without one of these fish or some *doré* (walleye), perch, whitefish or carp." The sturgeon would frighten her with its big teeth, "like a prehistoric monster," but it made a feast when it was baked with onions. Sturgeon is now so scarce in Quebec that it is usually imported.

Her grandfather, who came from Brittany and knew eels well, would skin this snakelike fish right in the boat. Later, he'd boil it to get rid of the oil, cut it in large pieces and roast it with onions and a dash of vinegar. Today, eels have faded in popularity and Quebec's catch is almost all exported to Europe.

Photo:
Salad with honey-broiled apples (page 158)

1 cup (250 mL) green and yellow beans, trimmed,
   cut into 1-inch (2.5 cm) lengths
½ cup (125 mL) frozen peas
2 carrots, peeled and diced
⅓ cup (75 mL) all-purpose flour
1 teaspoon (5 mL) paprika
1 teaspoon (5 mL) dry mustard
2 pounds (1 kg) fresh perch or catfish fillets
Butter and vegetable oil for frying

* Celery, thyme, bay leaf and parsley tied in a cheesecloth
  bag.

Soak salt pork in cold water for 1 hour, then cook in boiling water for 1 hour. Drain and cut into thin strips. In a large saucepan, fry salt pork until crisp. Add onions and garlic; cook until softened. Add potatoes, stock and bouquet garni; season with salt and pepper to taste. Bring to a boil, then simmer for 10 to 12 minutes. Stir in tomato paste, tomatoes, corn, beans, peas and carrots. Simmer until vegetables are tender, about 25 minutes. Keep warm.

In a large, shallow bowl, combine flour, paprika and dry mustard; season with salt and pepper to taste. Lightly coat fish fillets in seasoned flour. In a large, heavy frying pan, heat enough butter and oil to coat the bottom of the pan and fry the fillets over medium-high heat until golden on both sides.

To serve, ladle the hot vegetable stew into large, heated soup bowls and serve with fried fish fillets on the side. Six to eight servings.

Fisherman's paradise

When French explorer Samuel de Champlain paddled up the Richelieu River in 1603 from what is now Sorel to the lake that bears his name, he travelled a waterway that was so thick with fish, Indians would spear or hook their dinner from either the shore or their canoes. The richest fishing area was at the mouth of the Richelieu among islands and sand bars. Once seigneuries were allotted in this valley, beginning in 1672 with a grant to Sorel's namesake Pierre de Saurel from Dauphinée in southeastern France, fishing fees were imposed on tenants—two fish from every netful of shad caught. Nowadays, water pollution in the rivers is so extensive that trout farms have been established.

Photo:
Scallop soup (page 112)

TÊTE FROMAGÉE
Head cheese

This spiced type of country pâté is an example of the early custom of using every part of the pig to make good food. It's a staple of Quebec cuisine in every part of the province. This dish would be prepared by Berthe Marcotte Gatien for many special occasions. Her husband, a butcher in St. Marc sur Richelieu, sold the dish regularly at Montreal's Bonsecours Market.

½ pig's head, cleaned
1 pig's foot
1 veal shank
4 onions, quartered
1 large clove garlic
1 carrot, finely chopped
1½ teaspoons (7 mL) salt
1 teaspoon (5 mL) ground black pepper
½ teaspoon (2 mL) cinnamon
¼ teaspoon (1 mL) ground cloves
2 tablespoons (25 mL) chopped fresh parsley

Soak the pig's head, foot and veal shank in cold water for 30 minutes, then drain and dry. Wrap pig's head in cheesecloth and place in a large stock pot, along with pig's foot and veal shank. Cover with cold water. Add onions, garlic, carrot, salt and pepper. Cook over medium heat until the meat is very tender and falling off the bones, about 2 to 3 hours. Remove from heat and let cool.

Remove meats from stock pot, strain stock and reserve. Chop meat finely, discarding any fat or bones. Measure meat and place in a large saucepan. For every 1 cup (250 mL) of meat, add ½ cup (125 mL) stock, along with cinnamon, cloves and parsley; adjust seasoning with salt and pepper to taste. Simmer for about 5 minutes to blend flavours. Let

mixture cool. Set pan in a larger pan filled with ice
water and stir meat mixture until it begins to set.

Rinse 2 4-cup (1 L) moulds or small individual
moulds with cold water. Fill with meat mixture and
refrigerate, covered until set, about 4 hours or
overnight. To serve, carefully run a knife around the
edge of the moulds, dip in hot water and unmould
onto serving plates. May be frozen. Sixteen to twenty
servings.

SAUCISSES EN COIFFE
Spiced pork sausages

The natural casing to make these sausages would be
plentifully available after each pig was slaughtered.
Nowadays, to make this traditional recipe belonging
to Berthe Marcotte Gatien, you must visit a specialty
butcher shop to obtain the *crepine*, or casing. Serve
sausages with boiled or steamed potatoes (*anglaise*)
and home-made pickles and beets.

---

1 package (1 pound/500 g) casing, thawed if frozen
1½ pounds (750 g) ground pork
½ small onion, finely chopped
½ teaspoon (2 mL) ground cloves
Salt and ground black pepper

Soak casing in cold water for 15 minutes, drain and
pat dry.

In a bowl, combine pork, onion, cloves and salt
and pepper to taste. Form into medium-size
sausages. Using scissors, separate the rectangles of
casing and wrap around each sausage.

Place in a heavy, cold frying pan, without added
fat. Cover and cook sausages over medium heat,
turning to cook on all sides until golden brown and
no longer pink in centre. Six servings.

Salade d'automne pomme au miel tiède

Salad with honey-broiled apples

Two old houses on a residential street in St. Bruno have been made into one of this region's best restaurants, La Rabastalière. Quebec-born chef Claude Lépine likes to serve local products in light but classic dishes. His attractive salad shows off the region's apples and honey.

---

1 medium head Boston lettuce
A few leaves of red chicory or red-tipped leaf
    lettuce
2 large endives
4 apples (Melba, Spartan or McIntosh)
¼ cup (50 mL) liquid honey
Cider Vinegar Dressing (recipe follows)

Wash, trim and dry Boston lettuce and red chicory. Separate leaves of endives; wash and dry. Refrigerate in a bowl until shortly before serving time.

Peel apples, core and slice each into 4 equal rings. Drizzle with honey. Arrange on baking pan and grill briefly under hot broiler, turning once, until lightly browned.

Arrange 4 endive leaves, pointing outward, around edges of 4 serving plates. Place apple slices between endive leaves.

Toss lettuce and chicory with Cider Vinegar Dressing and arrange an equal amount in the centre of each plate. Four servings.

Cider Vinegar Dressing

---

1 tablespoon (15 mL) cider vinegar
1 tablespoon (15 mL) dry apple cider
1 teaspoon (5 mL) chopped dry shallots
Salt and ground black pepper
¼ cup (50 mL) olive oil

In a bowl, combine cider vinegar, cider and chopped shallots. Season with salt and pepper to taste, then beat in olive oil. Pour into a jar with a tight-fitting lid and refrigerate until needed. (It may be refrigerated for up to 2 week.) Bring to room temperature and shake well before serving. Makes about ⅓ cup (75 mL).

The *habitant*

Quebec's early farmers ate mainly bread, pork, dried peas and fresh vegetables from their garden or root cellar—in particular onions, cabbage and squash. A meal of game or fish relieved the routine of pea soup and salt pork, according to historian Allan Greer's book *Peasant, Lord, and Merchant: Rural Society in Three Quebec Parishes 1740-1840* (University of Toronto Press, 1985). Although they were enmeshed in the feudal society of Quebec's seigneurial system, the Richelieu River valley *habitants* that Greer studied were self-sufficient on their small farms. They would buy only salt, molasses and rum, if the budget permitted. By the 18th century, they ate more potatoes and marketed some of the wheat they had previously used in bread to generate income. Corn, beans and oats were other regular crops. All cooking was over the open hearth until the mid-18th century when cast-iron stoves became more widespread. Butter was a basic, but Greer found that cheese was made only after 1840.

TARTE AU SUIF DE MAMAN
Suet fruit pie

A rich dessert laden with dried fruit and walnuts and sweetened with maple syrup was always prepared by Berthe Marcotte Gatien to serve at the Christmas *Réveillon* in St. Marc sur Richelieu. Her daughter, Thérèse Daigle, carries on the tradition. She recommends using suet from beef kidneys.

½ cup (125 mL) finely chopped beef suet
1 cup (250 mL) currants
½ cup (125 mL) raisins
1 cup (250 mL) chopped walnuts
1 cup (250 mL) maple syrup
¼ teaspoon (1 mL) ground nutmeg
1 tablespoon (15 mL) cornstarch
2 tablespoons (25 mL) water
Pastry for double-crust, 8-inch (20 cm) pie

Place suet in a large, heavy frying pan and heat until it starts to melt. Add currants, raisins, walnuts, maple syrup and nutmeg. Cook over medium heat for 12 to 15 minutes, stirring occasionally.

Dissolve cornstarch in cold water and stir into fruit mixture. Cook for 1 to 2 minutes more or until thickened. Let filling cool.

Line an 8-inch (20 cm) pie plate with pastry. Pour in cooled fruit filling and cover with top crust, trim pastry, crimp edges to seal and cut steam vents.

Bake in a preheated 375°F (190°C) oven for 35 to 40 minutes or until crust is golden. May be frozen and reheated in oven. Six to eight servings.

MICROWAVE METHOD

Filling: In a 2-quart (2 L) glass measure or casserole, combine suet, currants, raisins, walnuts, maple syrup and nutmeg. Microwave at High (100 percent) for 4 to 5 minutes, stirring every minute. Blend cornstarch with water; stir into fruit mixture. Continue to microwave at High (100 percent) for 1 to 2 minutes more, or until filling thickens.

BETTERAVES MARINÉES
Pickled beets

This family recipe was passed on to Conrad Handfield, owner of Auberge Handfield at St. Marc sur Richelieu, by his mother Irene Janotte Handfield, and is regularly served with *tourtière* or cold meats at the inn.

---

4 to 5 medium whole beets
2 medium onions, sliced
7 whole cloves
1 cup (250 mL) vinegar
½ cup (125 mL) water
5 small, dry, hot red chilies
1 tablespoon (15 mL) coarse salt
5 whole black peppercorns
½ teaspoon (2 mL) dried thyme
1 bay leaf

Cook beets in boiling, salted water just until tender, about 40 minutes; drain, peel and either slice or cut into cubes. Arrange layers of cooked beets and raw onion slices alternately in a 1-quart (1 L) sterilized jar along with 2 cloves.

Prepare marinade by combining vinegar, water, chilies, the 5 remaining cloves, salt, peppercorns, thyme and bay leaf in a saucepan. Let simmer for 5 minutes, then strain. Pour over beets and onions in jar. Seal jar, refrigerate and let marinate for 1 month before serving. Makes 1 1-quart (1 L) jar.

CROQUIGNOLES DE GRAND-MAMAN
Grandmother's Fritters

These fritters are made according to a recipe that Thérèse Daigle obtained from her grandmother, the late Rose Anna Marcotte. They are flavoured with rum or brandy. The only other person that Mme Daigle knows who makes these special occasion treats this way is Soeur Monique Chevrier, a leading Montreal cooking teacher who grew up in Senneville on the western tip of Montreal Island.

½ cup (125 mL) butter
1 cup (250 mL) granulated sugar
3 eggs
5 cups (1.25 L) all-purpose flour
2 tablespoons (25 mL) baking powder
½ teaspoon (2 mL) salt
¼ teaspoon (1 mL) ground nutmeg
½ cup (125 mL) milk
½ cup (125 mL) light cream
2 tablespoons (25 mL) brandy or rum
Vegetable oil or shortening for deep frying
Icing sugar

In a bowl, cream butter and granulated sugar until fluffy. Beat in eggs, 1 at a time, until well combined. In another bowl, combine flour, baking powder, salt and nutmeg. Combine milk, cream and brandy; add to the creamed mixture, alternately with the dry ingredients to form a soft dough. Wrap dough well and let stand for 1 hour.

On a lightly floured surface, roll out dough to a ¼-inch (5 mm) thickness. Cut into rectangles, about 2½ × 2 inches (6 × 5 cm) in size. Cut 2 slits lengthwise in each rectangle. Heat oil in a deep-fat

You-pick directory

Food lovers can obtain a unique guide to the edible pleasures of this region. Called *Balade en Montérégie*, this annual directory lists over 125 farms where you can harvest, purchase or sit down and eat the local foods. Where to go to obtain strawberries or apples, tomatoes or corn, cheese or honey, rabbits or quail and many more specialties are listed in this handy publication. Maps, country fairs, food festivals and other tourist attractions are included. A project of the farm workers' union, Union des producteurs agricoles, it's available, in French only, from any branch of the Caisses Populaires Desjardins in Montreal and throughout the South Shore region.

fryer to 375°F (190°C). Fry no more than 4 or 5 at a time in the hot oil, turning the fritters once, until golden. Dry on paper towels and sprinkle with icing sugar. May be frozen and reheated. Makes about 60.

POMMETTES PAR LA QUEUE

Crab apples on the stem

The sour little apples from crab apple trees used to be made into this delicious dessert by Berthe Marcotte Gatien. "They were always the first apples of the season to ripen," her daughter, Thérèse Daigle, remembers.

---

3 cups (750 mL) small, early crab apples, with stems
3 cups (750 mL) boiling water
2 cups (500 mL) granulated sugar

Drop apples into boiling water and cook just until skins puff; do not overcook or skins will break. (Do not pierce with a fork to test for tenderness as this will cause the skins to tear.) Lift from boiling water with a slotted spoon and set aside.

Add sugar to liquid in pan and cook until slightly thickened and syrupy, about 10 to 12 minutes. Return apples to syrup and cook for 2 to 3 minutes more, then remove from syrup with a slotted spoon and let cool on a platter.

Continue cooking apple syrup until it has reduced and reached gel stage. To test, dip a chilled metal spoon into boiling mixture. When 2 drops run together to form 1 large sheet that drops off the spoon, the gel stage has been reached. Cool syrup until set. Serve cooled apples with jelly, 2 or 3 per serving, as a dessert or snack. Eight servings.

TARTE AUX OEUFS
Spiced custard pie

From the earliest days, settlers had plenty of eggs
from spring to fall. Berthe Marcotte Gatien of St.
Marc uses a partly baked pie shell to make this
dessert, which has links to the flan of northeastern
France. Other recipes call for brushing the uncooked
pastry with egg white before adding the warm
custard mixture. Although Mme Gatien uses dried
nutmeg, her daughter Thérèse Daigle likes to make
this recipe with the freshly grated spice.

---

2 cups (500 mL) milk
3 eggs
½ cup (125 mL) granulated sugar
½ teaspoon (2 mL) ground nutmeg, or ¼ teaspoon
   (1 mL) fresh, grated nutmeg
Pinch salt
Pastry for single-crust, 8-inch (20 cm) pie

Line an 8-inch (20 cm) pie plate with pastry. Trim
and crimp edge, then prick bottom and sides of pie
shell with a fork. Cover pie shell with a sheet of
aluminum foil and fill with uncooked rice. Bake
shell in a preheated 425°F (220°C) oven for 6
minutes, then remove foil with rice. Continue
cooking for 4 more minutes or until pastry is just set.
Set on rack to cool completely.

In a saucepan, heat milk until scalded. In a bowl,
beat eggs and sugar together well, then beat in hot
milk, nutmeg and salt. Pour custard mixture into
partly baked pie shell. Bake in a preheated 400°F
(200°C) oven for 15 minutes, then lower
temperature to 350°F (180°C) and continue to bake
for about 30 minutes more or until a knife inserted in
centre comes out clean. Let cool before serving. Six
to eight servings.

APPLESAUCE BREAD

At the Petch family orchard at Hemmingford, apple pies, apple doughnuts, apple butter and apple juice are made and sold to "you-pick" apple visitors each fall. Time-honoured family recipes include this bread, which Carol Petch likes to make with a large, red, striped, September apple called Wolf River. McIntosh and Cortland apples are alternatives.

---

1 cup (250 mL) raisins
1 cup (250 mL) walnuts, chopped
1¾ cups (425 mL) all-purpose flour
1 teaspoon (5 mL) baking powder
1 teaspoon (5 mL) baking soda
1 teaspoon (5 mL) ground nutmeg
1 teaspoon (5 mL) cinnamon
½ teaspoon (2 mL) ground allspice
½ teaspoon (2 mL) salt
½ cup (125 mL) shortening, softened
1¼ cups (300 mL) packed brown sugar
2 eggs, well beaten
1 cup (250 mL) thick, cold applesauce

Coat raisins and walnuts with ½ cup (125 mL) of the flour and set aside. Sift or mix together remaining flour with baking powder, baking soda, nutmeg, cinnamon, allspice and salt.

In a large bowl, cream shortening with brown sugar until fluffy. Add beaten eggs, beating in well. Add sifted dry ingredients alternately with applesauce until combined. Fold in floured raisins and walnuts. Spread batter evenly in a greased 9 × 5-inch (2 L) loaf pan.

Bake in a preheated 325°F (160°C) oven for 1¼ to 1½ hours or until a tester inserted in centre comes out clean. Cool in pan for 10 minutes, then turn out onto a rack to cool completely. Makes 1 loaf.

Not be be missed

Tourist attractions in the region include: the trails on Mont St. Hilaire, McGill University's mountain park; the wild animals at Parc Safari near Hemmingford; the Canadian Railway Museum, where more than 110 locomotives are on view at St. Constant; the beautiful old houses and churches of Varennes and Verchères; and the Musée Marcil in St. Lambert. There is an apple industry interpretation centre at Rougemont; and an 18th-century windmill on Île Perrot is also worth a visit.

BUTTERNUT SPICE CAKE

Carol Petch uses walnuts or pecans in this old
Hemmingford recipe because, although she has a
butternut tree, the nuts are hard to crack without
pulverizing the meat inside. The other name for this
light, spicy cake is Trumpour Cake, from the French
words for "misleading." Years ago, cakes were never
iced, only sprinkled with sugar, as this one is.

1 cup (250 mL) walnuts or pecans, finely chopped
2/3 cup (150 mL) butter, softened
1 1/3 cups (325 mL) brown sugar
2 eggs
2 cups (500 mL) cake and pastry flour
1 teaspoon (5 mL) baking soda
1 teaspoon (5 mL) cinnamon
1 teaspoon (5 mL) ground allspice
1/2 teaspoon (2 mL) nutmeg
1/2 teaspoon (2 mL) salt
1 cup (250 mL) buttermilk, or sour milk
Icing sugar

Generously butter a 9-inch (23 cm) tube pan and
sprinkle with half of the nuts so they are evenly
spread on the bottom and sides of the pan.

In a bowl, cream butter with brown sugar until
light and fluffy. Beat in eggs. Sift flour with baking
soda, cinnamon, allspice, nutmeg and salt. Stir dry
ingredients into butter mixture alternately with
buttermilk, making 3 additions of the dry ingredients
and 2 of the milk. Fold in the remaining nuts and
pour batter into prepared pan.

Bake in a preheated 350°F (180°C) oven for 45 to
50 minutes or until cake springs back when lightly
touched. Cool in pan for 10 minutes, then turn out
onto rack and cool completely. Just before serving,
sift icing sugar over top of cake.

MAURICIE-LANAUDIÈRE

 For centuries, the St. Maurice River was a north-south highway for Indians and explorers, *coureurs de bois* and woodcutters. Even though the water runs more calmly now and the forest is tamed, it's impossible to escape the feeling of wilderness. As I followed the river's spectacular shore between Grand-Mere and La Tuque, I had a sense that just back of a wooded cliff or up a tumbling stream, fish and game still flourished as they did before the river's power was harnessed and the region was opened to settlement.

Venison, hare and partridge still make the best *ragoût, cipaille* and *tourtière* in the Mauricie and its western neighbour Lanaudière. A *bouillabaisse* up La Tuque way is often based on trout; salmon pie is a regular supper dish, and mushrooms decorate many recipes.

Pollution in the rivers, the St. Lawrence in particular, has cut into the catch of two small but popular fish. One is perch, which Chef Joel Zaetta of Chez Claude in Trois Rivières' Motel Castel des Prés, likes to make into a terrine with sliced zucchini. The other is tommy cod, *poisson des chenaux* (fish of the channels), sometimes called *poulamon* (little cod).

The headquarters for the annual catch of these miniature cod has moved downriver in recent years to St. Anne de la Pérade. Each January and February, a village of fishermen's huts is dragged out onto the ice on the river and holes are cut. Each tiny hut has a stove and a crowd of men, women and children around the fishing hole. They drop lines laden with hooks and baited with pork liver. When a line is full, it is drawn up and the fish are removed and thrown out the window so nature can freeze the catch.

This stretch of the St. Lawrence is also duck country, according to Peggy Lafrenière of Trois Rivières, who told of the flocks of wild ducks on the islands off Berthierville. Hunters and bird watchers rate this area as a paradise for ducks, geese and other feathered visitors. A duck, wild or commercially raised, makes a special occasion meal in these parts. It is often accompanied by a fruit sauce, in particular the classic orange or one made with blueberries.

The best hunting in the region is to the north. In my quest for stories of the hunt, I drove north of Joliette, past the large, prosperous farms into the forest area just above St. Mélanie. Hunters in this village tell tales of an extra-large moose or illusive deer and proudly decorate their homes with a moose head or a stuffed wild bird.

The hunters suggest that this prized food be cooked simply so its delicate flavours can be appreciated. They opened freezers to show me their stock of carefully-wrapped venison and game birds. A wine marinade, a touch of the old-time salt pork seasoning, some fresh herbs and gentle cooking is what keeps the natural moisture in these lean meats.

When wild meats run short, cooks in these regions combine different varieties in interesting dishes. Venison and hare make a *civet*, or stew. Hare and partridge are layered into a *cipaille*, and hare is bolstered with plenty of onions and carrots in a *gibelotte*, a meal-in-one soup. When cooks run right out of wild foods, they make the same recipes with regular meats. For example, the traditional *perdrix aux choux*, which combines partridge with cabbage, is made with chicken breasts and renamed *fausses perdrix aux choux*. In La Tuque, another cabbage favourite is *cigares aux choux*, rolls filled with meat, rice and seasonings and baked in tomato sauce. This recipe is also found on the Côte du Sud.

The region has had a stable population with many farm families to maintain the early cooking traditions. Montrealer Renée Désy Audette, who grew up in Berthierville, remembers that meals were always governed by a combination of seasonal plenty and the Roman Catholic Church.

In spring, veal was the big meat. "My father was a butcher. We always ate veal in spring, for two weeks straight," said Renée. "Then, the day before Easter, we would have a big feast because Lent ended at noon. We always had ham at a minute past noon—smoked ham. And maple syrup would be served like a dessert, plain with a spoon to spread it on bread, or, if it was cold enough outside, made into fresh maple ice cream," she remembered.

The best desserts have always been made of fresh fruit, in Renée's opinion. "How about a rhubarb and strawberry pudding, or an apple purée flavoured with cinnamon and cloves between two layers of pastry? Or an apple turnover with a caramel sauce?" she suggested, remembering when her mother, Irène Plante Désy, made these dishes.

Strawberries are a big commercial fruit crop in Trois Rivières—raspberries come second. "But," said Arlene Letourneau, "everyone here makes strawberry jam."

Rhubard is made into a thick, syrupy pie filling. It's combined half and half with sugar, plus a little orange peel, and simmered, partly covered, over very low heat for four or five hours, until the fruit mixture is almost black. This method, so cooks told me, comes from the era of wood stoves when the fruit could be set to bubble away while other household tasks were accomplished.

SOUPE AUX TOMATES

Tomato soup

When Renée Désy Audette was growing up in Berthierville, her mother Irène Plante Désy would make a batch of this rosy red, onion-flavoured soup in the morning so it would mellow for the evening meal. Old-fashioned rolled oats provide the best flavour, says Mme Audette, who likes to add garlic for an extra tang.

Mauricie Menu

Potted pork
(page 171)

Crusty bread

Asparagus salad
(page 175)

Chicken breast with oyster
mushroom sauce
(page 182)

Rice Pilaf

Pancakes, Norman style
(page 188)

1 tablespoon (15 mL) butter or margarine
1 small onion, chopped
2 cloves garlic, crushed
4 cups (1 L) chicken stock or water
2 cups (500 mL) peeled, chopped tomatoes, or 1 can (19 ounces/540 mL) canned tomatoes, chopped, with the juice
1 carrot, peeled and chopped
¼ cup (50 mL) old-fashioned rolled oats
¼ teaspoon (1 mL) dried thyme or basil
1 teaspoon (5 mL) granulated sugar
Salt and ground black pepper

Heat butter in a large, heavy saucepan and sauté onion and garlic until softened. Add chicken stock, tomatoes, carrot, rolled oats, thyme and sugar; season with salt and pepper to taste. Bring to a boil. Partially cover and simmer soup gently for 45 minutes. Serve in heated soup bowls. Six servings.

MICROWAVE METHOD

In a 2-quart (2 L) casserole, microwave butter at High (100 percent) for 30 to 45 seconds. Stir in onion and garlic. Microwave at High (100 percent) for 3 minutes or until softened. Add chicken stock, tomatoes, carrot, rolled oats, thyme and sugar; season with salt and pepper to taste. Cook, covered, at High (100 percent) for 15 to 20 minutes, stirring once.

POTAGE LIVONIEN

Vegetable rice soup

Mixed vegetable soup, enriched with cream and
sometimes an egg yolk, makes a satisfying supper
dish for Henriette Caron of La Tuque.

---

2 tablespoons (25 mL) butter
½ cup (125 mL) finely chopped carrot
½ cup (125 mL) finely chopped celery, including
   leaves
¼ cup (50 mL) finely chopped turnip
1 medium onion, finely chopped
2 tablespoons (25 mL) chopped fresh parsley
2 tablespoons (25 mL) uncooked long grain rice
3 cups (750 mL) chicken or veal stock
1 cup (250 mL) light cream
1 egg yolk
Salt and ground black pepper
Thin slivers of mild cheese, such as Cheddar

Heat butter in a heavy saucepan and sauté carrot,
celery, turnip, onion, parsley and rice. Cook just until
vegetables begin to soften. Add chicken stock and
continue to cook, covered, until vegetables and rice
are tender, about 20 minutes. Beat cream and egg
yolk together; stir into hot soup. Season with salt and
pepper to taste. Heat gently; do not let boil or soup
will curdle. Ladle into warm soup bowls and sprinkle
with cheese slivers. Four to six servings.

MICROWAVE METHOD

In a 2-quart (2 L) casserole, melt butter at High (100
percent) for 30 to 45 seconds. Add carrot, celery,
turnip, onion, parsley and rice; stir well to coat in
butter. Microwave, covered, at High (100 percent) for
5 minutes, stirring once. Add chicken stock; continue
to microwave, covered, at High (100 percent) for 16

to 20 minutes or until rice is tender. Beat cream and egg yolk together; stir into hot soup. If necessary, reheat at Medium (50 percent) for 1 to 2 minutes. To serve, ladle soup into heated soup bowls and sprinkle with cheese slivers.

CRETONS

Potted pork

Quebec's favourite pâté should mature for at least two days in the refrigerator before you serve it. This recipe belongs to Gilberte Morin Martinson, a long-time resident of La Tuque. She likes to serve it sliced on a leaf of lettuce with pickles and tomatoes, and fresh, crusty bread. Her *cretons* will keep for four days in the refrigerator and two months frozen.

1½ pounds (750 g) shoulder of pork
1 pork kidney, trimmed
2 small onions, chopped
1 clove garlic, minced
¼ teaspoon (1 mL) ground allspice
Salt and ground black pepper
1 cup (250 mL) water

Grind pork and pork kidney in a meat grinder. Place in a heavy saucepan with onions, garlic, allspice and salt and pepper to taste. Add water; it should come ¾ of the way up the meat. Heat, stirring well with a wooden spoon, until mixture comes to a boil. Reduce heat and simmer gently for 2 hours.

Rinse small, individual bowls or a 1-quart (1 L) mould with cold water. Adjust seasoning of meat mixture, adding more salt and pepper, if desired. Pour mixture into bowls or mould. Cool to room temperature, then cover and chill in refrigerator. For best flavour, refrigerate for 2 days before serving. Serve in slices or as a spread. Makes about 4 cups (1 L).

Wilderness park

Tucked in a curve of the St. Maurice River, just north of Shawinigan, is a spectacular stretch of unspoiled wilderness—La Mauricie National Park. It's open year-round to naturalists, campers, and fishermen, as well as lazy tourists who wish to drive along its 63-km parkway. Visitor reception centres, located at each end of the parkway, direct newcomers to any of the 34 lakes or to the guided nature walks to see beavers building their dams, tumbling waterfalls and ancient Indian pictographs.

Inside the park, it is best to bring your own food. Or you could plan on eating—feasting may be the operative word—at the little town of St. Flore between Shawinigan Nord and the southeast entrance to the park. From fine cuisine to surf-and-turf and take-out crêpes, this spot caters to all types of taste buds, particularly at La Bombarde, a small headquarters for good food.

TERRINE DE PERCHAUDE ET COURGETTE VINAIGRETTE AU SIROP D'ÉRABLE

Perch and zucchini terrine with maple syrup dressing

At Chez Claude, an elegant oasis of gastronomy in a motel on the outskirts of Trois Rivières, owner Claude Gauthier and chef-partner Joel Zaetta offer local foods in classic but innovative dishes. This cool but flavourful *entrée* is one of their regional specialties.

3/4 pound (350 g) skinned, deboned fresh perch, cut into chunks
1½ teaspoons (7 mL) salt
Ground white pepper
1 egg
1 egg white
1 cup (250 mL) whipping cream
1 tablespoon (15 mL) butter
2 tablespoons (25 mL) white wine
1 pound (500 g) unpeeled, sliced zucchini
Maple Syrup Dressing (recipe follows)

In a food processor or blender, purée fish with salt, pepper, egg, egg white and cream until smooth. Chill for 30 minutes.

Meanwhile, melt butter in a heavy frying pan and add wine and zucchini slices; season with salt and pepper to taste. Cook this mixture over high heat for 1 or 2 minutes, just until zucchini has softened. Drain.

Butter a terrine mould or 8½ × 4½-inch (1.5 L) loaf pan. Spread a layer of fish mixture in bottom of mould to a depth of about ¼ inch (5 mm). Top with an equal depth of zucchini slices. Continue layering the 2 mixtures into the mould, finishing with a layer of the fish mixture. You should have 4 layers in all. Set mould in a shallow pan of hot water and oven-poach in a preheated 375°F (190°C) oven for about 1½ hours, or until set. Cool, then chill for at least 24 hours.

Slice into 1-inch (2.5 cm) slices and serve cold with Maple Syrup Dressing. Six servings.

Maple Syrup Dressing

---

2 tablespoons (25 mL) vegetable oil
2 tablespoons (25 mL) olive oil
2 tablespoons (25 mL) white vinegar
2 tablespoons (25 mL) tarragon-flavoured cider vinegar
¼ cup (50 mL) maple syrup
1 small, dry shallot, finely chopped
Salt and ground white pepper

In a jar with a tight-fitting cover, combine the 2 oils, the 2 vinegars, syrup, shallot and salt and pepper to taste. Cover jar tightly and shake well to mix vinaigrette. Refrigerate. Shake well before serving. Makes about ¾ cup (175 mL) dressing.

An historic walk

Trois Rivières, named after the three-way split of the St. Maurice River as it rounds two islands and enters the St. Lawrence, is a city of surprises. The second oldest settlement in the province was a fur-trading post during the period of New France. At its downtown core, Trois Rivières still has a small but charming old quarter of houses and religious buildings that date back two to three centuries. Only a handful of these architectural treasures survived a disastrous fire in 1908, but there are still some sights to take in on an hour's stroll.

Start on Rue des Ursulines. There, in 1697, French nuns built a convent that became a hospital and is now a museum for treasures of silver, furniture and embroidery. Two once-private houses can also be visited. Maison Hertel de la Fresnière, built in 1824, is now a wine shop; and Manoir de Tonnancour, originally constructed in 1722, has been restored as an exhibition centre. Nearby sights include churches, art galleries and a former prison that dates from 1816.

Auberge sur la Falaise

This is a modern, year-round resort sitting on the edge of the plain as it rises to the forested wilderness to the north, and it is developing a good reputation for comfort and cuisine. Auberge sur la Falaise is a member of the European hotel chain Relais du Silence, which has recently expanded to Quebec and specializes in tranquility. Just north of Rawdon and Joliette, off Route 343, the inn is on Lac Long. It has an indoor swimming pool and sauna with tennis and badminton, cross-country and downhill skiing nearby. Expensive. (Rooms: 25, each with private bath; address: 324 Lac Long Sud Rd, St. Alphonse, Québec, J0K 1W0; telephone: (514) 883-2269 or 1-800-363-1758.)

MOUSSELINE DE PERCHAUDE SUR COULIS DE HOMARD

Perch mousse with lobster sauce

Perch is a popular fish in this region and Gérard Michaud of the Auberge Grand-Mère in Grand-Mère likes to whip it into a light entrée. The lobster sauce may be replaced by a fish *velouté*, a cream sauce made with fish stock.

---

2 pounds (1 kg) perch fillets, skin and bones removed
Salt and ground white pepper
2 egg whites
1 cup (250 mL) whipping cream
1¾ cups (425 mL) hot lobster bisque*
Fresh chives, chopped

> * Freshly made lobster bisque may be replaced by 1 can (10 ounces/300 mL) of a reliable brand, diluted with ½ cup (125 mL) whipping cream.

In a food processor, purée fish fillets until smooth. Season with salt and pepper to taste. Add egg whites and purée until mixture is smooth. Add cream and purée for 30 seconds; do not process longer or mixture may become buttery.

Pile up 3 sheets of aluminum foil (2 sheets of heavy-duty foil may be used instead) 12 inches (30 cm) square. Butter the top sheet.

Spoon fish mixture evenly along one side of foil and form into a log shape. Roll up tightly in foil and seal ends. Fill a large, shallow saucepan or deep frying pan with enough water to cover foil package. Bring water to a full, rolling boil, add fish package, reduce heat to a gentle boil and simmer for 15 to 20 minutes, or until a meat thermometer inserted into fish reaches 140°F (60°C). Remove foil package carefully from water. Unwrap fish mousse and slice.

Heat lobster bisque and pour about ¼ cup (50 mL) onto each of 8 serving plates. Arrange slices of fish mousse on sauce and decorate with chopped fresh chives. Eight servings. (If desired, this dish may be used to serve 4 as a main course; reduce lobster bisque to 1¼ cups/300 mL.)

ASPERGES MARINÉES

Asparagus salad

Asparagus is the vegetable of choice in Mauricie and its popularity grows year by year. Suzanne Jobin of Trois Rivières likes to cook the spears and marinate them in a garlic-flavoured vinaigrette.

---

18 to 20 spears (1 pound/500 g) fresh asparagus,
  trimmed
2½ tablespoons (35 mL) cider vinegar
2 cloves garlic, finely chopped
1 teaspoon (5 mL) dried oregano
½ teaspoon (2 mL) salt
¼ teaspoon (1 mL) pepper
¼ teaspoon (1 mL) dry mustard
½ cup (125 mL) olive oil
Lettuce

Cook asparagus just until tender; do not overcook. Drain and place in a glass or china dish.

In a small bowl or jar, combine vinegar with garlic, oregano, salt, pepper and mustard. Pour in oil in a stream, blending well. Pour this dressing over warm asparagus, cover tightly and refrigerate for 2 to 3 hours, turning asparagus occasionally in marinade.

To serve, arrange lettuce on 4 salad plates and top with asparagus. Four servings.

RAGOÛT DE POISSON DES CHENAUX

Tommy cod stew

When the catch of these tiny fish was good in January and February, the late Maria de Bellefeuille Letourneau of Trois Rivières would make this layered fish and vegetable dish and cook it in her wood stove. She passed the recipe on to her daughter, Beatrice Letourneau Paradis of Quebec City, and her daughter-in-law, Arlene Letourneau of Trois Rivières.

---

2 to 3 pounds (1 to 1.5 kg) tommy cod*
5 medium potatoes, peeled, thinly sliced
½ cup (125 mL) chopped fresh parsley
Salt and ground white pepper
2 medium onions, thinly sliced
2 carrots, thinly sliced, blanched (optional)
3 cups (750 mL) water or milk
¼ pound (125 g) salt pork, diced, or 4 slices bacon, diced
Butter (optional)

* Smelts may be substituted.

Clean fish, removing heads and tails but not bones. In a heavy, 2-quart (2 L) casserole with a lid, arrange a layer of ¼ of the potatoes in the bottom of the casserole. Top with a layer of ⅓ of the fish. Season with parsley and salt and pepper to taste. Layer with ⅓ of the onions.

Repeat layers twice more. Add carrots at this point. Top with final layer of potatoes. Pour liquid slowly and carefully into casserole. Fry diced salt pork until crisp, then crumble. Sprinkle on top of potatoes. Dot with butter. Cover and bake in preheated 375°F (190°C) oven for about 30 minutes. Remove cover and bake for another 15 minutes to brown potatoes. Six to eight servings.

Pâté au saumon

Salmon pie

The combination of salmon and mashed potatoes in a pastry crust is a basic supper dish in Mauricie. Some recipes call for a double-crust pie. Hélène Beaudry of Trois Rivières uses only a top crust for her pie.

---

4 tablespoons (50 mL) butter
1 large or 2 small onions, chopped
2 tablespoons (25 mL) all-purpose flour
1 cup (250 mL) milk
1 can (15.5 ounces/439 g) salmon, drained, reserving liquid
1 teaspoon (5 mL) chopped fresh rosemary, or ¼ teaspoon (1 mL) dried
Salt and ground white pepper
3 cups (750 mL) seasoned, mashed potatoes (4 to 5 medium potatoes)
Pastry for single-crust, 9-inch (23 cm) pie

In a frying pan, melt 2 tablespoons (25 mL) of the butter and sauté chopped onions just until soft. In a medium saucepan, melt the remaining 2 tablespoons (25 mL) butter, blend in flour and cook until mixture is bubbling.

Blend in milk and salmon liquid and cook, stirring, over medium heat until sauce is thickened and smooth. Season with rosemary and salt and pepper to taste. Stir in onion mixture. Break salmon into chunks and fold in. Then fold in mashed potatoes.

Spread mixture evenly in a buttered 9-inch (23 cm) pie plate. Cover with pastry crust; trim, crimp edges and cut steam vents. Bake in a preheated 425°F (220°C) oven for 25 minutes or until crisp and lightly browned. Serve hot. Eight servings.

Controversy on the river

At the turn of the century, more than 500 *draveurs* worked on the big log drives on the St. Maurice River. Using a pole called a gaffe as a prod, these log drivers would skip from log to log, keeping the mass of lumber floating directly downriver to the waiting mills. Now most of the drive is controlled by a handful of operators who guide the logs downriver, through seven dams, by punching buttons that control sluice gates. The tall trees of early times have been replaced by four-foot logs to make the job more efficient.

Environmentalists say that this progress has been hazardous to the river's health. Fish spawning grounds have been destroyed and the water has been polluted by a murky, acidic mass of loosened bark and deadhead logs. A solution, which the lumber industry claims would be costly, would be to truck the logs directly to the mills, or at least to stop economizing on storage by leaving the logs in booms in the river for months. One proposed compromise is to share the river with the naturalists by channelling logs within booms so boats can navigate the shoreline.

CANARD À L'ORANGE

Duck with orange sauce

The Auberge Grand-Mère in Grand-Mère has had a reputation for fine food for generations and the inn maintains its reputation with Chef Gérard Michaud. He likes to give this classic treatment to either farm-raised wild ducks or domestic breeds, and serves the dish with potatoes and vegetables in season.

1 duck (4 pounds/2 kg)

Using poultry shears, cut duck into 4 pieces. With a sharp boning knife, cut breast meat away from breast bones and set aside to cook at last minute. Carefully debone legs, keeping meat in one piece. Cut remaining meat away from carcass and chop finely along with liver and heart to make stuffing.

Stuffing

Liver and heart of duck
1 teaspoon (5 mL) chopped onion
Salt and ground black pepper
Pinch mixed ground spices*
1 egg
¼ cup (50 mL) whipping cream
1 teaspoon (5 mL) Curaçao liqueur

* Ground cloves, cinnamon, ginger and nutmeg are suggested.

Mix chopped meat with onion, salt and pepper and spices until combined. Beat in egg, cream and liqueur.

Stuff legs with this mixture, and wrap first in parchment paper, then in aluminum foil.

1 small onion
1 small carrot
1 stalk celery
1 clove garlic, chopped
1 tablespoon (15 mL) butter
Orange Sauce (recipe follows)
4 thin strips of orange zest

Arrange duck bones in a casserole and lay the
wrapped legs on top. Add 2 inches (5 cm) of water to
the casserole, along with onion, carrot, celery and
garlic; season with salt and pepper to taste. Bring to a
simmer, cover and braise gently over low heat for 1½
hours.

Remove foil and parchment paper from stuffed
duck legs and grill briefly to brown the skin. Set
aside and keep warm.

In a frying pan, sauté duck breasts quickly in
butter, then transfer to a preheated 350°F (180°C)
oven for about 5 minutes or until meat is rare.

To serve, cut each leg into 4 slices and breasts into
thin strips. Pour Orange Sauce onto 4 warm serving
plates. Divide the meat among the plates and
decorate with orange zest. Four servings.

Orange Sauce

¼ cup (50 mL) granulated sugar
2 tablespoons (25 mL) white vinegar
1 cup (250 mL) orange juice
¼ cup (50 mL) brown sauce or chicken stock
½ clove garlic, finely chopped
1 tablespoon (15 mL) cornstarch
1 tablespoon (15 mL) water

Make a caramel sauce by boiling sugar and vinegar together until thickened and a rich golden colour. Add orange juice, brown sauce or chicken stock, and garlic. Blend cornstarch and water together and stir into sauce. Bring to a boil and cook sauce until thickened. Strain before serving. Makes about 1½ cups (375 mL) sauce.

MICROWAVE METHOD

Sauce: In a 4-cup (1 L) glass measure or casserole, combine sugar and vinegar. Microwave, uncovered, at High (100 percent) for 3 to 4 minutes or until mixture turns a deep golden colour. Carefully add orange juice, brown sauce or chicken stock, and garlic. Blend cornstarch with water until smooth and stir into sauce. Microwave sauce, uncovered, at High (100 percent) for 3 minutes, until sauce comes to a full boil and thickens, stirring once. Strain sauce before serving.

SOUFFLÉ AUX NAVETS

Turnip soufflé

Turnips, or rutabaga as the big yellow roots are often called, are a year-round basic throughout Quebec. Shirley Rousseau of Trois Rivières makes this inexpensive vegetable dish to serve with roasted or cold meats and a green vegetable or salad.

6 cups (1.5 L) peeled, cubed turnips
4 tablespoons (50 mL) butter, melted
2 eggs, beaten
3 tablespoons (45 mL) all-purpose flour
1 tablespoon (15 mL) brown sugar
1 teaspoon (5 mL) baking powder
3/4 teaspoon (4 mL) salt
Pinch ground black pepper
Pinch nutmeg
1/3 cup (75 mL) fine, dry bread crumbs

Cook turnips in boiling, salted water just until tender. Drain, then mash until smooth. Blend in 2 tablespoons (25 mL) of the melted butter and the beaten eggs. (This step may be done the day before and the turnips refrigerated, covered. Allow 5 to 10 minutes extra baking time.)

In a bowl, combine flour, brown sugar, baking powder, salt, pepper and nutmeg. Add dry ingredients to turnips and mix well. Butter a 2-quart (2 L) baking dish. Spread turnip mixture evenly in dish. Blend together bread crumbs and remaining melted butter; sprinkle over the turnips. Bake in a preheated 375°F (190°C) oven for 25 to 30 minutes or until golden-brown. Six servings.

MICROWAVE METHOD

In a 2-quart (2 L) casserole, combine turnips with 3/4 cup (175 mL) water. Microwave, covered, at High (100 percent) for 16 to 20 minutes or until tender. Drain and let stand for 5 minutes.

Prepare soufflé as directed in recipe. Microwave soufflé, uncovered, at High (100 percent) for 5 minutes. Rotate dish and microwave at Medium (50 percent) for 6 to 8 minutes more or until just puffed in the centre. (If turnips were cooked ahead and refrigerated, increase cooking time by 4 to 6 minutes at Medium (50 percent).)

Life in the woods

North of Grand-Mere at Grandes-Piles is a model community of 25 buildings duplicating life in an old-style lumber camp. Called Le Village du Bûcheron, it shows how the woodcutters worked and lived and includes a restaurant where typical fare is served. The menu, which includes soup, meat pie, baked beans, home-style bread and sugar pie, is written in a lively blend of English and French and lists such items as *steak de jobber* and *assiette du cook*. The village is open daily from the beginning of June to Labour Day, and weekends until Thanksgiving.

Suprême de volaille aux pleurottes du Québec

Chicken breasts with oyster mushroom sauce

A variety of mushrooms have long been harvested in the woods of the St. Maurice River valley. This recipe is a specialty at Chez Claude, the excellent French restaurant in the Motel Castel des Prés on the outskirts of Trois Rivières.

---

4 single, boneless chicken breasts, skins removed
1 tablespoon (15 mL) butter
Salt and ground black pepper
Oyster Mushroom Sauce (recipe follows)
4 sprigs fresh thyme

Flatten chicken breasts slightly. Heat butter in a large, heavy frying pan and brown chicken quickly on both sides. Season with salt and pepper to taste. Transfer chicken to a baking dish and bake in a 350°F (180°C) oven for about 15 minutes or until done.

To serve, divide Oyster Mushroom Sauce among 4 heated serving plates; arrange chicken breasts on top with a sprig of thyme. Four servings.

Oyster Mushroom Sauce

¼ pound (125 g) oyster mushrooms, chopped
1 large dry shallot, finely chopped
¼ cup (50 mL) dry white wine
½ cup (125 mL) veal stock (or use additional chicken
   stock)
¼ cup (50 mL) chicken stock
½ cup (125 mL) whipping cream
1 teaspoon (5 mL) chopped fresh thyme, or
   ¼ teaspoon (1 mL) dried
Salt and ground black pepper

Add mushrooms, shallot and wine to frying pan in
which chicken was browned. Over medium heat,
cook gently until softened. Add veal and chicken
stock; cook over high heat until reduced by half. Add
cream; continue to reduce until sauce thickens
slightly. Season with thyme and salt and pepper to
taste.

MICROWAVE METHOD

Chicken: Brown chicken in a frying pan as directed
in recipe. Place breasts on a microwave roasting rack,
cover loosely with waxed paper and microwave at
High (100 percent) for 3 to 4 minutes or until no
longer pink inside. Let stand, covered, while making
sauce as directed in recipe.

RÔTI DE PORC
ET PATATES JAUNES
Roast pork with pan-browned potatoes

A pioneer village

Near Rawdon, which is situated in a beautiful part of Lanaudière on the Ouareau River, there is a model community of some 20 buildings which date from the period 1835 to 1884. Visitors can tour houses, a general store, a chapel, a schoolhouse, a mill and a blacksmith's forge. Furniture, tools and clothing of the period add to the atmosphere. Called the Canadiana Village, it was originally a project of antiquarian Earl Moore. Groups can dine in the mill if they reserve in advance. The village is open from mid-May to the end of September.

This cold weather combination of garlic-flavoured pork and pan-browned potatoes turns up throughout the province, but it's more popular in Mauricie than anywhere else. In other regions, the meat can be seasoned with savoury, cloves or rosemary. Micheline Mongrain-Dontigny of La Tuque, a cooking teacher and cookbook author, considers this a Sunday dish. She suggests serving her recipe with hot buttered beets and a green vegetable or salad.

---

1 roast loin of pork (3 pounds/1.5 kg)
3 cloves garlic, halved
1 piece, about 3 inches (8 cm) square, of pork rind, fat removed
1 medium onion, sliced
Salt and ground black pepper
2 tablespoons (25 mL) butter, softened
1 tablespoon (15 mL) dry mustard
½ teaspoon (2 mL) dried marjoram
1 cup (250 mL) water
4 to 6 medium potatoes, peeled

Using a sharp-tipped knife, make 6 incisions in the roast and insert halves of garlic cloves. Place pork rind in a shallow roasting pan. Arrange onion slices on rind and place roast on top. Season roast with salt and pepper to taste. Blend butter with mustard and brush lean parts of roast with this mixture. Sprinkle with marjoram and pour water into bottom of pan. Roast, uncovered, for 1 hour at 350°F (180°C).

Arrange potatoes around roast. Continue roasting another 1½ to 2 hours, turning potatoes once during cooking, and basting meat every 15 minutes. (If pan juices evaporate during roasting, add a little more water.)

Transfer roast and potatoes to a heated serving platter. Skim fat from pan and transfer remaining juices to a gravy-boat to serve with meat and potatoes. Four to six servings.

OATMEAL LACE COOKIES

Rolled oats, linked with a sweet syrup, make these cookies crisp and light. Originally a Scottish recipe, it comes from Mrs. George Matte of La Tuque. It's one of a batch of British recipes in a French-language cookbook published by the churchwomen's group Le Cercle AFEAS de St. Zéphirin de La Tuque.

½ cup (125 mL) old-fashioned rolled oats
1/2 cup (125 mL) granulated sugar
1/2 cup (125 mL) all-purpose flour
¼ teaspoon (1 mL) baking powder
⅓ cup (75 mL) melted butter or margarine
2 tablespoons (25 mL) corn syrup
2 tablespoons (25 mL) whipping cream
2 teaspoons (10 mL) vanilla

In an bowl, combine rolled oats, sugar, flour and baking powder. Stir in butter, corn syrup, cream and vanilla, mixing well.

Using a ½-teaspoon (2 mL) measuring spoon as a measure, drop dough onto ungreased baking sheets, 4 inches (10 cm) apart. Bake in a preheated 375°F (190°C) oven for 6 to 8 minutes or until lightly browned. Let stand for a few seconds until firm enough to remove from baking sheets. Cool on rack. Makes about six dozen 2-inch (5 cm) cookies.

Veau aux fines herbes

Braised veal with herbs

Elisabeth Carré of Trois Rivières serves this veal dish with buttered noodles or potatoes, and mushrooms and carrots. Quebec's new "heavy", grain-fed veal would suit this recipe.

---

2 tablespoons (25 mL) olive oil
2 tablespoons (25 mL) butter
1½ pounds (750 g) veal cutlets, or 6 chops
Salt and ground black pepper
¼ cup (50 mL) chopped onion
1 clove garlic, minced
1 cup (250 mL) sliced, fresh mushrooms
¼ cup (50 mL) finely chopped fresh parsley
½ teaspoon (2 mL) dried thyme
½ teaspoon (2 mL) dried *fines herbes**
¼ teaspoon (1 mL) dried savoury
2 tablespoons (25 mL) finely chopped fresh chives
½ cup (125 mL) white wine
½ cup (125 mL) chicken stock
¼ cup (50 mL) whipping cream
1 tablespoon (15 mL) cornstarch

* Choose from such herbs as thyme, tarragon, chervil, parsley and chives.

In a heavy frying pan, heat oil and butter over medium heat. Quickly brown meat on both sides. Transfer to a flameproof casserole with a lid and season with salt and pepper to taste. Use pan drippings to sauté onion, garlic, mushrooms and parsley together just until softened. Season onion mixture with thyme, *fines herbes*, savoury and chives. Add wine and chicken stock; bring to a boil and pour over meat in casserole.

Cover and bake in a 325°F (160°C) oven for about 45 minutes or until meat is tender. Blend cream and

Photo:
Lamb and vegetable stew (page 193)

cornstarch together; stir into sauce around the meat. Heat gently, stirring, until sauce is thickened and smooth. Add more salt and pepper, if necessary. Six servings.

BEIGNES AUX DATTES DE MA MÈRE
Mother's date doughnuts

Dried fruit has always been a part of dessert-making throughout Quebec, particularly when there's snow on the ground. Doughnuts are another long-standing favourite. Pauline Lemire of Trois Rivières makes this family recipe as a dessert or snack.

---

2 eggs, beaten
3/4 cup (175 mL) granulated sugar
1 tablespoon (15 mL) melted butter
2 1/2 cups (625 mL) all-purpose flour
2 1/2 teaspoons (12 mL) baking powder
1/2 teaspoon (2 mL) salt
1/4 teaspoon (1 mL) ground nutmeg
1 cup (250 mL) chopped dates
1 cup (250 mL) milk
1 teaspoon (5 mL) lemon extract
Vegetable oil or shortening for deep-frying

In a bowl, combine beaten eggs, sugar and melted butter; beat well. In another bowl, combine flour with baking powder, salt and nutmeg. Fold in dates. Add dry ingredients to egg mixture alternately with milk and lemon extract.

Heat oil in deep-fat fryer to 375°F (190°C). Drop batter by tablespoonfuls (15 mL), 2 or 3 at a time, into hot oil and fry until crisp and brown, about 3 minutes' frying time, turning once. Drain on paper towels. Makes from 3 to 4 dozen.

Photo:
Oatmeal bread (page 206)

CRÊPES NORMANDES

Pancakes, Norman style

The paper-thin pancakes of Normandy and Brittany
were endlessly varied in the early days of New
France. They would frequently be made of
buckwheat flour and, when food was scarce, often
made a meal. The crêpes would be fried in lard and
served with molasses. This recipe from Adrienne
Cloutier of La Tuque is a deluxe version calling for
plenty of butter and rum.

¾ cup (175 mL) all-purpose flour
1 tablespoon (15 mL) granulated sugar
¼ teaspoon (1 mL) salt
2 cups (500 mL) milk
2 eggs, beaten
Melted butter
Rum Sauce (recipe follows)
¼ cup (50 mL) dark rum

In a bowl, combine flour, sugar and salt. Using a
whisk, beat in milk, then eggs to make a very smooth
batter. Strain batter through a fine sieve and let stand,
covered, at room temperature for 1 hour.

Heat an 8-inch (20 cm) crêpe pan and brush the
bottom of the pan lightly with melted butter. Pour a
scant 3 tablespoons (45 mL) of batter into the bottom
of the pan, tilting pan quickly to spread the batter
evenly. Cook the crêpes until golden, but not
browned, about 1 minute per side. Repeat until all
the crêpes are cooked (about 18 in all), stacking
them on a platter between pieces of waxed paper to
prevent them from sticking together.

To serve, fold the crêpes into quarters. Arrange on
an ovenproof serving plate, cover loosely with
aluminum foil and reheat in a 350°F (180°C) oven
for 15 to 20 minutes. Pour hot Rum Sauce over

warmed crêpes and bring dish to the table. Heat the ¼ cup rum in another small saucepan, pour over crêpes and flame. Six servings.

Rum Sauce

⅓ cup (75 mL) butter
½ cup (125 mL) instant dissolving sugar
1 tablespoon (15 mL) lemon juice
¼ cup (50 mL) dark rum

Make sauce just before serving. In a saucepan, melt butter with sugar and boil for 1 minute or until sugar is dissolved. Stir in lemon juice and rum. Serve hot.

MICROWAVE METHOD

Prepare the crêpes as directed in recipe. Arrange on a large serving plate, cover with paper towels and microwave at Medium (50 percent) for 2 to 4 minutes or until warmed through.

In a bowl, microwave butter and sugar at High (100 percent) for 1 to 2 minutes or until boiling and sugar is dissolved. Stir in lemon juice and rum; pour over the warm crêpes.

In a glass measure, heat ¼ (50 mL) rum at High (100 percent) for 30 to 45 seconds, pour over crêpes and flame.

The first stoves

Ironmakers of Trois Rivières played a part in the formation of the cuisine of French Canada by introducing the cast-iron stove to Canada. The ironworks, established in 1730, was the first in the country and operated for 150 years. Called Les Forges du Saint-Maurice, it's now an historic site, located on Boulevard des Forges on the north side of the city near the St. Maurice River.

Affluent settlers along the St. Lawrence River had these stoves by the mid-18th century. The majority owned one, or even two, by 1800, and these handsome box-type structures were used for heating the house rather than for cooking in the early days. Most cooking was done on the open hearth and bread was baked in the field-stone ovens in the cellar or outside the house. The stoves worked so well that visitors from Europe would complain about the excessive heat in French Canadian farmhouses. The forge is open daily for tourists from mid-May to Labour Day, and from Wednesday to Sunday until Thanksgiving.

TARTE AUX POMMES ET AU MIEL

Apple honey pie

Apple pie is a favourite dessert in Mauricie, as it is in the rest of Quebec. This variation calls for a mixture of honey and orange rind to be added to a lattice-topped pie in the final minutes of baking. The recipe belongs to Marie St. Arnaud of Trois Rivières.

¾ cup (175 mL) granulated sugar
1 teaspoon (5 mL) ground nutmeg
6 cups (1.5 L) peeled, sliced cooking apples
2 tablespoons (25 mL) butter
½ cup (125 mL) liquid honey
1 tablespoon (15 mL) grated orange peel
Pastry for double-crust, 9-inch (23 cm) pie

Roll out half of the pastry to line the bottom of a 9-inch (23 cm) pie plate. Roll out remaining dough and cut into ½-inch (1 cm) strips to make a lattice topping.

In a bowl, combine sugar and nutmeg; toss with sliced apples. Place apple mixture in pastry-lined pan and dot with butter. Moisten edge of pastry shell. Arrange lattice topping on pie and seal edges. Cover rim of pie with aluminum foil.

Bake in a preheated 450°F (230°C) oven for 10 minutes, then lower heat to 350°F (180°C) and continue baking for about 30 to 35 minutes longer or until lightly browned. Combine honey and orange peel. Pour mixture into pie through holes in lattice. Bake for another 5 minutes. Six to eight servings.

ESTRIE

In the massive retreat from Montreal each Friday night, some of the cars crossing the Champlain Bridge to the Eastern Townships are heading for the United States. But most of us are hurrying, bumper-to-bumper, to our most beautiful corner of Quebec.

The townships, or Estrie as the Quebec government has renamed this southeast region, were first settled as a result of a retreat of a different kind. The Abenaki Indians had been in the area since the 1680s. But beginning in 1785, the first United Empire Loyalists came, mainly New England frontier families fleeing the new American regime. Over the next 30 years, thousands more crossed the new border in search of homesteads in what became, in 1791, Lower Canada. These hardy pioneers created modest, self-sufficient communities as they carved homesteads from the forests, cleared the river valleys for crops and took over the hillsides for their livestock. (It's frequently said to this day that the townships' biggest crop is rocks.)

The settlers' cuisine was English with a New England accent and economical in the extreme. Later came the "great migrations" of Scots and Irish, which peaked in the 1840s. The newcomers soon added their stamp to the earliest cooking style.

The wilderness of these rolling hills and mountains helped provide food, just as it did in other regions. Deer and hare, wild birds and speckled trout are still lavishly available in what's viewed as a paradise for hunters and fishermen.

I've been a part-time townshipper, as we anglophones call ourselves, for about 20 years now and I still get a thrill out of the sight of the graceful, white-tailed deer munching on grasses by the side of my road, or leaping away into the woods when my dog barks. As I walk along the Yamaska River on a beautiful winding stretch that my neighbour has named the Primrose Path, I'm often surprised by the sudden beating of wings as a partridge or pheasant departs. And it's easy to spot rabbit tracks in the snow when I cross-country ski along that stretch.

I can pick fiddleheads on certain spring days in these woods, and steam them to tenderness to serve with a roast duckling from the nearby Brome Lake duck farm. In late summer, a quick drive to André Marcotte's corn farm near Dunham means we can sit down to the new "peaches and cream" cobs, so sweet they could almost be a dessert. The best late summer desserts are made with raspberries, picked wild beside fields and streams.

Along with British dishes such as mincemeat, lamb stew, oatmeal bread, tea biscuits, scones and fruit cake are New England basics such as corn or fish chowder, Boston baked beans and brown bread, pumpkin pie and Johnny cake.

After the Anglo-Saxons, the next people to vary Estrie's complexion were the French. Even before the seigneury system was abolished in 1854, long-time settlers on lands along the St. Lawrence River began venturing south to join the English-speaking farmers, small merchants and a smattering of professional men.

Joining the ethnic mix in this century were Europeans—Germans, Austrians, Swiss, Dutch and others—who found the combination of mountains and streams reminiscent of home. "I call our cooking a combination of English, Welsh, Scottish, Irish and French—a mixture that's developed over the years," said Hilda Mitchell Luce of Knowlton. A retired teacher, she helped research the cuisine of Brome county for a cookbook of old-time dishes. "The French people have given us pea soup, *tourtière*, baked beans and meatballs. Other Europeans have given us recipes too. Our cooking is an amalgamation of many cuisines," said Mrs. Luce.

The latest influx is of chefs, who have poured in from Montreal and even France, to run inns and restaurants in this burgeoning resort region. Chefs such as Yves Prod'homme, who opened L'Aubergade, an elegant and expensive French restaurant in a new little shopping centre in Cowansville. His cuisine rivals the best of Montreal or Quebec City.

I like the contrasts in culinary experiences available in these parts. Nothing beats a hot smoked meat sandwich and French fries with a cold beer at the Knowlton Pub, either after skiing or on a trip to see fall leaves on the scenic highway between Sutton and the Missisquoi River valley.

East toward Mont Megantic near the village of Notre Dame des Bois is a tiny little inn called Aux Berges de l'Aurore. Whether you've come to see the stars at the mountain's observatory or cross-country ski—the snow there lasts into May—this inn offers *nouvelle cuisine québecoise* of a calibre to win it an award as the top Estrie restaurant of 1988.

On a simpler level, the townships are rich in church bake sales and fund-raising suppers. Such English favourites as fruit cake, plum pudding and shortbread cookies sell at fall sales. Come strawberry season, which starts later than the usual Quebec opening date of St. Jean Baptiste Day June 24, the "strawberry social" is the place for shortcake.

Ragoût d'agneau

Lamb and vegetable stew

This lamb and vegetable stew is a family recipe belonging to Constance Richard of West Brome. It was printed in a collection of traditional township dishes called *100 Recettes d'Antan*, published in 1976 by the Cercle de Fermières de Cowansville. Mint jelly or preserved pears flavoured with cinnamon are recommended to serve with the lamb.

---

3 to 4 pounds (1.5 to 2 kg) fresh lamb shoulder
¼ cup (50 mL) all-purpose flour
¼ cup (50 mL) bacon fat or vegetable oil
1 onion, chopped
2 carrots, peeled and chopped
2 stalks celery, chopped
2 tablespoons (25 mL) chopped fresh parsley
½ teaspoon (2 mL) dried thyme
1 bay leaf
Salt and ground black pepper
1 can (10 ounces/284 mL) green peas, drained

Cut lamb into 1-inch (2.5 cm) cubes and dredge in flour. In a heavy, large saucepan or Dutch oven, heat the bacon fat and brown the meat on all sides. Drain off excess fat.

To the pan, add onion, carrots, celery, parsley, thyme and bay leaf. Season with salt and pepper to taste; add just enough water to cover.

Simmer stew, covered, over low heat for 1½ hours or until meat is tender. Just before end of cooking time, add drained peas and cook until heated through. Remove bay leaf before serving. Six to eight servings.

Estrie Menu

Dandelion salad
(page 201)

Spinach-stuffed veal with mushroom sauce
(page 194)

Buttered noodles

Steamed broccoli

Molasses custard
(page 210)

Auberge Hatley

Built at the turn of the century as the country house of affluent Americans from the southern United States, this large inn overlooks Lake Massawippi. Proprietors Robert and Liliane Gagnon have decorated it with antique Quebec pine furniture and work in tandem with their chef to maintain their membership as a Relais et Châteaux hotel with contemporary cuisine based on fresh, local foods. Expensive, it has an outdoor pool and is near golf and English summer theatre. Cross-county ski trails start at its door and the Mont Orford downhill centre is nearby. (Rooms: 22, many with private bath; address: P.O. Box 330, North Hatley, Québec, J0B 2C0; telephone: (819) 842-2325.)

PORTEFEUILLE DE VEAU AUX PLEUROTTES

Spinach-stuffed veal with oyster mushroom sauce

French-born Yves Prod'homme, chef-proprietor of Restaurant L'Aubergade in Cowansville, obtains tender veal from nearby Dunham. He flavours the cream sauce with oyster mushrooms and port in this elegant but easy recipe.

4 boneless veal loin chops (7 ounces/200 g each),
  1 inch (2.5 cm) thick
2 tablespoons (25 mL) butter
2 cups (500 mL) packed, fresh spinach, trimmed
Salt and ground black pepper
Mushroom sauce (recipe follows)

Have butcher slit chops horizontally to make a pocket for stuffing. Heat 1 tablespoon (15 mL) of the butter in a saucepan and add spinach. Cook over low heat, turning in the butter, for about 2 minutes or until spinach begins to wilt. Remove from heat, season with salt and pepper to taste and set aside.

In a large, heavy frying pan, heat remaining tablespoon (15 mL) butter until bubbling hot and sear veal chops on both sides. Continue cooking for about 2 minutes per side or until meat is still rare. Remove from heat; let cool slightly. Stuff veal chops with spinach and arrange in a single layer in a shallow baking pan.

Ten minutes before serving time, place stuffed veal chops in a preheated 400°F (200°C) oven for 10 minutes or until hot. To serve, arrange stuffed veal chops on heated plates and pour hot Oyster Mushroom Sauce over. Four servings.

Oyster Mushroom Sauce

¼ pound (125 g) fresh oyster mushrooms, finely
   chopped
1 dry shallot, finely chopped
¼ cup (50 mL) port wine
½ cup (125 mL) whipping cream
Salt and ground black pepper

Add chopped mushrooms and shallot to the frying
pan in which the veal was cooked and sauté just until
soft and very lightly browned. Add port wine, then
stir in cream and season with salt and pepper to taste.

MICROWAVE METHOD

Veal: Place 1 tablespoon (15 mL) butter and the
spinach in a 2-quart (2 L) casserole. Microwave,
covered, at High (100 percent) for 1 to 2 minutes or
until wilted, stirring once.

   Brown veal in frying pan as directed in recipe.
Stuff with spinach and arrange on a roasting rack.
Microwave, covered with waxed paper, at Medium
(50 percent) for 5 to 7 minutes. Let stand, covered,
while preparing sauce as directed in recipe.

GRAM'S CHICKEN AND BISCUITS

Rena Marsh of Knowlton recommends a free-range chicken be used in her family's chicken fricassee recipe, but says today's less flavourful broiler-fryer will make an acceptable version of this easy dish.

---

1 chicken (3 pounds/1.5 kg), quartered
1 tablespoon (15 mL) chopped onion
1½ teaspoons (7 mL) granulated sugar
½ teaspoon (2 mL) salt
¼ teaspoon (1 mL) dried sage
¼ cup (50 mL) all-purpose flour
Biscuits (recipe follows)

Place chicken in a large saucepan and add water to cover. Bring to a boil, cover and let simmer for 1 hour or until tender. Reserving stock, cool in pan overnight, then remove meat from bones, discarding skin, bones and fat. Chop chicken; set aside.

Measure chicken stock—there should be 2 cups (500 mL). Add water if necessary. Return stock to saucepan and bring to a boil. Add onion, sugar, salt and sage. Mix flour with enough cold water to form a paste and stir into boiling stock, stirring until thickened. Simmer for 5 minutes. Add chicken pieces to gravy and heat through.

To serve, split biscuits and arrange on serving plates; pour chicken and gravy over. Four servings.

Biscuits

---

2 cups (500 mL) all-purpose flour
4 teaspoons (20 mL) baking powder
1½ teaspoons (7 mL) granulated sugar
½ teaspoon (2 mL) salt
¼ cup (50 mL) lard or shortening
¾ cup (175 mL) milk (approximate)

In a large bowl, combine flour, baking powder, sugar and salt. Cut in lard with a pastry blender or 2 knives until mixture resembles coarse crumbs. Stir in enough milk to make a soft, but not sticky, dough.

Knead dough on a lightly floured surface for 3 minutes. Roll out to ¾-inch (2 cm) thickness and cut out 1½-inch (4 cm) circles.

Arrange circles of dough on a greased baking sheet and bake in a preheated 400°F (200°C) oven for 12 to 15 minutes. Makes 12.

MICROWAVE METHOD

Chicken: Place cut-up chicken with 1 cup (250 mL) water in a large casserole. Microwave chicken, covered, at High (100 percent) for 14 to 18 minutes until tender and juices run clear. Reserve stock.

Let chicken cool overnight. Remove meat from the bones and discard skin, bones and fat. Chop chicken and set aside.

Measure chicken stock. There should be 2 cups (500 mL). Add more water, if necessary. Pour into a 2-quart (2 L) casserole. Add onion, sugar, salt and sage. Microwave, covered, at High (100 percent) for 5 to 7 minutes or until boiling. Combine flour with enough water to make a smooth paste and stir into the stock. Microwave, uncovered, at High (100 percent) for 3 to 5 minutes until sauce boils and thickens, stirring twice. Add the chicken and microwave, covered, at High (100 percent) for 3 to 5 minutes until heated through.

A shopper's paradise

Estrie is rich in crafts, and each area has its own shop selling local ceramics, weaving, knitting, quilts, jewellery and woodwork. The Noirmouton Farm Shop, long associated with the late cookbook author Jehane Benoit, is the best-known source for sheepskin clothing and rugs made from her husband Bernard's flock. On Benoit Road at the foot of Mont Echo, the shop is next door to the area's busiest cross-country ski centre, called the Farmer's Rest.

Auberge La Girandole

A tiny jewel of a place between Knowlton and Magog, this inn is a latter day dream come true for co-proprietors Marcel Breton, an optometrist-turned-maître d'hôtel, and Paulette Lepage, a former Montreal caterer, who is the inspired chef. A Victorian clapboard house in a pretty garden, it's been restored and decorated with antiques from the period. There are comfortable bedrooms under the eaves, each with bathroom but neither television nor telephone to mar a peaceful holiday. Prices are moderate; there's a five-course *table d'hôte*, which changes daily, and the wine list is respectable. (Rooms: 6; address: Route 245, Bolton Centre, Québec, J0E 1G0; telephone: (514) 292-5070.)

TRUITE À LA CRÈME DE CRESSON

Trout in cress-flavoured cream sauce

At Auberge Hatley, the prize-winning inn on Lake Massawippi, rainbow trout from a nearby trout farm is served with a creamy watercress purée as the sauce.

---

4 dry shallots, chopped
4 rainbow trout (10 ounces/284 g each)
Salt
⅓ cup (75 mL) dry white wine
⅔ cup (150 mL) fish stock (see page 112)
½ bunch fresh watercress, stems removed
⅓ cup (75 mL) whipping cream
Ground white pepper

Butter a baking dish large enough to hold the fish in a single layer. Add chopped shallots to the dish and arrange fish on top. Season lightly with salt to taste. Pour wine over the fish and cover with a sheet of buttered parchment paper. Bake in a preheated 400°F (200°C) oven for 8 to 10 minutes.

Meanwhile, combine fish stock and watercress in a blender or food processor and purée until smooth. Pour into a heavy saucepan and cook over medium heat for 10 minutes. Keep sauce warm.

Remove fish from baking dish and transfer to a heated platter; keep warm. Pour cooking liquid from baking dish into watercress mixture. Stir in cream and cook sauce just until heated through. Season with salt and pepper to taste. Remove skin from trout and debone; serve with sauce. Four servings.

MICROWAVE METHOD

Arrange trout, heads and tails removed, in a shallow baking dish just large enough to hold them in a single layer. Pour wine over and cover with vented plastic wrap. Microwave fish at High (100 percent) for 5 to 6 minutes or until fish just flakes when tested with a fork. Let stand, covered, while preparing sauce.

Purée watercress with fish stock and place in a 4-cup (1 L) glass measure. Microwave, uncovered, at High (100 percent) for 3 to 4 minutes. Add cooking liquid from fish along with the cream. Microwave, uncovered, at High (100 percent) for 6 to 8 minutes until sauce reduces and thickens slightly. Serve sauce and fish as directed in recipe.

CREAM SALAD DRESSING

When Flora Primmerman Rhicard was growing up in Stanbridge East, salad meant lettuce from the garden with a cream dressing flavoured with mustard. Mrs. Rhicard's cooking is a blend of Townships' traditions. Her forbears were United Empire Loyalists of German background and her mother, Marie Chevalier Primmerman, a French-speaking Quebecer. Some families made their salad dressing with vinegar they made from sugar maple sap, Mrs. Rhicard remembers.

¼ cup (50 mL) granulated sugar
Pinch salt
½ to ¾ teaspoon (2 to 4 mL) prepared mustard
1½ teaspoons (7 mL) cider vinegar
½ cup (125 mL) light cream (approximate)

Using a measuring cup, combine sugar, salt, mustard and vinegar. Add enough light cream to make ¾ cup (175 mL), blending well. Cover and refrigerate for up to 1 week. Makes ¾ cup (175 mL) dressing.

Garden pleasures

Gardeners must be determined in the townships, for the region has rigorous winters, rock-filled land and a short growing season. Nevertheless, one of the largest garden clubs in Canada flourishes in Brome County.

Filet de Porcelet aux Échalotes et au Sirop d'Érable

Pork tenderloin with shallots and maple syrup

The tender, white meat of the piglet makes a delicious pork dish when trimmed with a sauce flavoured with cider vinegar and maple syrup. A creation of French-born chef Guy Bohec, this recipe is on the menu at Auberge Hatley.

---

1 tablespoon (15 mL) butter
4 small pork fillets (6 ounces/170 g each)
Salt
4 dry shallots, chopped
4 green onions, minced
1/4 cup (50 mL) cider vinegar
1/3 cup (75 mL) maple syrup
2/3 cup (150 mL) pork or chicken stock
Ground black pepper

Heat butter in a frying pan until foaming. Sprinkle pork fillets with salt to taste and sear on both sides in hot butter until golden. Transfer to a buttered baking pan and bake in a preheated 375°F (190°C) oven for 10 minutes.

Add shallots and green onions to frying pan and cook just until softened. Deglaze pan with vinegar and reduce by half. Add maple syrup and pork stock; simmer for 10 minutes.

Slice each of the pork fillets in 6 slices and serve hot with shallot sauce. Four servings.

MICROWAVE METHOD

Brown pork fillets as directed in recipe. Place on a roasting rack and microwave, covered with waxed paper, at Medium (50 percent) for 6 to 9 minutes or until no longer pink in centre. Let stand, covered, while making sauce as directed in recipe.

SALADE AUX PISSENLITS
Dandelion salad

On the first of May, when dandelion leaves are young and tender, this salad is part of a traditional spring meal in the southeastern part of Estrie. A similar salad, sometimes including potatoes, can be found in the Champagne region of northern France. This recipe comes from a collection published by the Cercle de Fermières of St. Edwidge. It is traditionally served with cheese and fresh bread.

---

8 cups (2 L) trimmed, fresh dandelion leaves
6 thin slices salt pork (about ¼ pound/125 g)
1 small onion, finely chopped
3 to 4 tablespoons (45 to 50 mL) white vinegar
Salt and ground black pepper

Arrange dandelion leaves in a large salad bowl. In a heavy frying pan, fry salt pork until crisp. Remove from pan with slotted spoon and drain on paper towels. To fat in pan, add onion and vinegar; bring to a boil. (Instead of using the pork fat, the onions and vinegar may be cooked in ½ cup (125 mL) vegetable oil.) Remove from heat and let stand for 1 minute, then pour over dandelion leaves. Season with salt and pepper to taste. Add crisp, fried pork, toss to mix, and serve at once. Six servings.

First spring lettuce

Rena Tibbets Marsh of Knowlton recalls the pleasure of the first spring lettuce 50 years ago when she gardened on her West Bolton farm. "I'd pick leaves when they were half the size of my hand, sprinkle them with a little white sugar and roll them up like cabbage rolls. We'd eat them with our fingers with no dressing."

An architectural tour

The townships are a region of clapboard buildings, and nowhere are they more attractive than on the eastern edge of Cowansville, on the main street of what was once the town of Sweetsburg. Victorian mansions, set back from rue Principale with big, old trees still shading their lawns, are beautifully maintained here.

If red brick is your taste, drive around Dunham and Bedford, where the roads are lined with handsome Victorian brick houses. They're decorated with well-maintained gingerbread, the architect's term for the fancy wooden trim on eaves and windows.

To help self-guided tours, the Brome County Historical Society in Knowlton has published directories to the old roads. The Missisquoi Museum at Stanbridge East is another source. Both are open during the summer.

CANARD AUX RAISINS ET AU MIEL

Duckling with raisins and honey

At the Knowlton restaurant Le Saint Martin Chef Jean-Claude Fortier prepares duckling from the nearby Brome Lake duck farm by roasting and deboning it, then adding a fruit and port wine sauce and a dash of honey for sweetness. Proprietor André Charbonneau serves it with fresh vegetables in season, such as green beans, carrots cut in tiny strips and whipped potatoes, and recommends the red St. Emilion, Château du Roy with this dish.

½ cup (125 mL) seedless raisins
⅔ cup (150 mL) port wine
1 duckling (about 4 pounds/2 kg)
Salt
2 cups (500 mL) chopped vegetables (onions, carrots and celery)
½ cup (125 mL) water
1 teaspoon (5 mL) *beurre manié**
3 tablespoons (45 mL) honey
Fresh fruit in season

* A mixture of an equal amount of soft butter and all-purpose flour.

Marinate raisins in ¼ cup (50 mL) of the port wine for 24 hours and set aside.

Prick duckling all over with a fork, truss, and sprinkle with salt. Spread chopped vegetables in a roasting pan and set duckling on top. Place in a 325°F (160°C) oven and roast, uncovered, for 2 hours, basting every 30 minutes with pan juices.

Remove from oven, cool duckling sufficiently to handle, then cut in half and debone, if desired, being careful to keep each half intact. Set duckling aside and keep warm.

Skim all fat from pan juices and discard. Transfer pan juices and vegetables to a heavy saucepan. Add remaining port wine and water; simmer gently for 8 to 10 minutes.

Strain vegetable-port mixture through a fine sieve and return to saucepan. Blend in *beurre manié*, stirring until sauce thickens slightly. You should have about ½ cup (125 mL) sauce. Add raisins to sauce along with 1 tablespoon (15 mL) of the honey. Heat over very low heat just until blended and keep warm.

Place duckling halves in roasting pan, skin side up, and baste with the remaining honey. Roast in a 400°F (200°C) oven for about 10 to 15 minutes, just to glaze and crisp the skin.

Arrange duckling halves on 2 warm serving plates and trim with a little fresh fruit in season (strawberries, apple slices, etc.). Serve with sauce. Two servings.

A memorable picnic

Huge boulders act as landmarks throughout the townships. One large rock on Miltimore Road near West Brome is engraved with a little piece of local history. The founders of the Brome County Historical Society rolled it out of the nearby woods in 1899 to mark the spot where Henry Collins, first settler to obtain a land grant in the county, put up the first log cabin in these parts in 1795. Records kept in the society's museum in Knowlton reveal that a celebratory picnic had been held on that spot two years earlier, on August 18, 1897, when the society was founded. On the menu, so it is speculated, would have been pork sandwiches, doughnuts, butternut cake, Duchess apples, and—to wash it all down—apple cider, ginger beer or raspberry vinegar.

CHAUDRÉE D'HIVER
Vegetable stew

This sustaining vegetable stew makes a warming lunch or supper dish with crusty homemade bread. It's an old-time recipe from St. Edwidge.

---

2 potatoes, peeled and cubed
2 carrots, peeled and cubed
1 onion, chopped
1 tablespoon (15 mL) melted butter or vegetable oil
1 tablespoon (15 mL) all-purpose flour
Salt and ground black pepper
1 cup (250 mL) ripe tomatoes, peeled, seeded, chopped, or 250 mL canned tomatoes, chopped, with juice
1 cup (250 mL) milk

Cook potatoes and carrots in boiling water; drain and set aside. In a large, heavy saucepan, sauté onion in melted butter until softened. Stir in flour and season with salt and pepper to taste; cook until bubbly. Add tomatoes and heat to boiling point, stirring. Add milk, cooked potatoes and carrots. Heat until piping hot. Adjust seasoning with salt and pepper, and serve in warm soup bowls. Three to four servings.

MICROWAVE METHOD

In a 2-quart (2 L) casserole, combine potatoes and carrots with ½ cup (125 mL) water. Microwave, covered, at High (100 percent) for 7 to 9 minutes or until tender. Drain and let stand, uncovered.

In another casserole, microwave butter and onion at High (100 percent) for 2 minutes. Blend in flour; stir in tomatoes. Microwave, covered, at High (100 percent) for 2 to 3 minutes or until thickened. Add cooked potatoes, carrots and milk. Microwave, covered, at High (100 percent) for 4 to 6 minutes or until piping hot. Season with salt and pepper to taste.

CURRANT BUNS

This traditional Scottish recipe has often won prizes for Ethyl Marsh of Foster. She flavours these buns with cinnamon or lemon rind.

---

1 package (1 tablespoon/15 mL) active dry yeast
½ cup (125 mL) lukewarm water
1 cup (250 mL) milk
2 tablespoons (25 mL) butter
¼ cup (50 mL) granulated sugar
½ teaspoon (2 mL) salt
½ cup (125 mL) currants
1 egg, beaten
½ teaspoon (2 mL) cinnamon, or grated rind of
   1 lemon
3 cups (750 mL) all-purpose flour (approximate)

In a small bowl, dissolve yeast in water and let stand until foamy, about 10 minutes.

In a saucepan, heat milk until scalded. Add butter, sugar, salt and currants; stir until butter melts. Let cool to lukewarm.

In a bowl, combine the milk mixture with the dissolved yeast, beaten egg and cinnamon. Add 2 cups (500 mL) of the flour, beating in well. Add enough of the remaining flour to make a soft dough that leaves the sides of the bowl.

Turn out onto a lightly floured surface and knead until smooth and elastic, about 5 minutes. Place in a large greased bowl, turning dough in bowl to grease on all sides, cover and let rise in a warm place (cold oven with light on) until double, about 1½ hours.

Punch down dough and shape into 8 balls. Arrange balls side by side in a greased 8- or 9-inch (20 or 23 cm) round baking pan. Cover and let rise again until amost double in bulk, about 1 hour.

Bake in a preheated 375°F (190°C) oven for 15 to 20 minutes or until golden. Turn out onto rack to cool. Makes 8 buns.

A-berrying we go

Although strawberries and raspberries can be harvested with ease at townships' "you-pick" farms, some of the region's favourite fruits are still obtained from the wild, just as they were in the early days. Pails full of wild raspberries can be picked in the corners of fields and along quiet county roads. Tiny wild blueberries grow thickly on hills and mountainsides, particularly where a fire has burned off the brush. Currants, gooseberries, chokecherries and high bush cranberries have their patches.

In Brome county, the location of a stand of blackberries is often a well-kept secret, for blackberry pie is a category in the cooking contest at the annual Big Brome Fair. Veteran contestants know that a blackberry patch can produce generously for four or five years and then suddenly there won't be enough fruit to fill a thimble. Scouting out this fruit in advance, when it's still coloured as red as raspberries, is a regular August routine in preparation for "Fair", as the Labour Day weekend exposition is always called.

OATMEAL BREAD

When maple syrup was cheap and maple sugar plentiful, Rena Tibbets Marsh would sweeten this traditional Scottish bread recipe with maple from her West Bolton farm. Now living in Knowlton, she uses molasses instead. Mrs. Marsh acquired this recipe many years ago from Lena Bobo of the neighbouring town of Waterloo.

---

1 package (1 tablespoon/15 mL) active dry yeast
1 teaspoon (5 mL) granulated sugar
1 cup (250 mL) lukewarm water
2 cups (500 mL) boiling water
2 cups (500 mL) old-fashioned rolled oats
1 teaspoon (5 mL) salt
5 tablespoons (75 mL) lard or butter
½ cup (125 mL) granulated sugar
2 tablespoons (25 mL) molasses
2 cups (500 mL) water
½ cup (125 mL) skim milk powder
2 eggs, beaten
8 cups (2 L) all-purpose flour (approximate)

In a bowl, sprinkle yeast and 1 teaspoon (5 mL) sugar over the water. Let stand until yeast is dissolved and foamy, about 10 minutes.

Place rolled oats and salt in a large bowl and pour in the boiling water. Add lard, ½ cup (125 mL) sugar and molasses; stir until lard is melted. In another bowl, combine 2 cups (500 mL) water with skim milk powder and beaten eggs. Beat by hand or with an electric mixer until frothy.

Combine dissolved yeast and egg mixture with the rolled oats. Gradually stir in 7 cups (1.75 L) of the flour, until dough starts to form a ball and leave the sides of the bowl. Turn dough out onto a heavily floured board and knead dough until smooth and

For hot weather thirst

Haying is motorized now and the cooling drink offered between tractor loads is likely to be mixed from flavoured powder. In days gone by, however, the refresher at haying time was oatmeal water, say local history buffs. It was made by soaking old-fashioned rolled oats in water along with sugar, vinegar, ginger and maple syrup. Some families skipped the oatmeal in their recipe. Imperial drink was another midsummer cooler. It was made by combining lemon juice and rind with sugar, epsom salts and some tartaric and citric acid.

elastic, about 10 minutes, working in the remaining flour, if necessary, to prevent dough from sticking to the board.

Place dough in a greased large bowl, turn to grease on all sides and cover. Set in a warm place (in a cold oven with light on) and let dough rise until double in bulk, about 1½ to 2 hours.

Knead again on a lightly floured board for 2 to 3 minutes, adding more flour if necessary if dough is sticky.

Have ready 4 greased 8½ × 4½-inch (1.5 L) loaf pans. Divide dough into 4 pieces and shape each portion into 2 balls. Set 2 balls in each pan, then cover and let rise until almost double in size.

Bake in the upper third of a preheated 350°F (180°C) oven for 25 to 30 minutes, then turn heat off and leave loaves in oven for 10 minutes more. Remove loaves from pans and let cool on racks. Makes 4 loaves.

Glaze

---

3 tablespoons (45 mL) icing sugar
2 tablespoons (25 mL) water
1 tablespoon (15 mL) butter
1 teaspoon (5 mL) orange or lemon juice

Combine icing sugar, water, butter and juice in a small saucepan and heat until smooth.

Either brush loaves with glaze, or melted butter or margarine.

MICROWAVE METHOD

Glaze: Place ingredients for glaze in a bowl and microwave at High (100 percent) for 20 to 30 seconds.

BISCUITS AU SIROP D'ÉRABLE

Maple cookies

When Pauline Jacques, who runs the Granby cooking school Les Ateliers de Pauline, was growing up, she remembers both her mother and grandmother making these cookies to serve with Maple Mousse (see page 209). The maple syrup came from her grandfather's maple woods in South Stukeley. The family recipe is based on one from a treasured cookbook, *Cuisinière de la Reverende Mère Caron*, published in 1908 by the director of Quebec's first domestic science school, which was run by the Ursulines at Roberval on Lac St. Jean.

---

1 cup (250 mL) butter or shortening, at room
   temperature
1 cup (250 mL) brown sugar
2 eggs, beaten
⅓ cup (75 mL) maple syrup
1 teaspoon (5 mL) vanilla
3½ cups (875 mL) cake and pastry flour
   (approximate)
2 teaspoons (10 mL) baking powder
½ teaspoon (2 mL) salt

In a large bowl, cream butter with brown sugar until fluffy. Beat in beaten eggs, maple syrup and vanilla until well combined.

In another bowl, sift or mix together 3 cups (750 mL) of the flour with baking powder and salt.

Beat dry ingredients into creamed mixture, along with enough of the remaining ½ cup (125 mL) flour, until dough leaves the sides of the bowl and forms a ball. Cover dough and chill until firm, about 2 hours. On a lightly floured surface, roll out dough thinly and cut into desired shapes.

Place on lightly greased baking sheets and bake cookies in a preheated 350°F (180°C) oven for 8 to 10 minutes or until edges are lightly browned and crisp. Place on racks to cool. Makes about 5 to 6 dozen cookies, depending on size.

MOUSSE À L'ÉRABLE

Maple sauce

Sometimes called a mousse, this sauce is more like a *meringue italienne*, says Pauline Jacques, who considers it a perfect topping for Maple Cookies (see page 208). She makes the latter in the shape of maple leaves.

---

1 cup (250 mL) maple syrup
1 egg white
Pinch cream of tartar

Make sauce no more than an hour before serving.

In a small saucepan, bring maple syrup to a boil over medium-high heat. Let boil until syrup reaches the firm ball stage—248°F (120°C) on a candy thermometer.

In a bowl, beat egg white with cream of tartar until stiff peaks form. Pour the boiling syrup into the beaten egg white, in a thin steady stream, continuing to beat at high speed for 3 to 4 minutes or until sauce is smooth and shiny. Spoon into individual serving dishes and serve accompanied with Maple Cookies. Makes about 1 cup (250 mL) sauce.

The museum scene

Two museums of note are at Stanbridge East and Knowlton. At Stanbridge East, the Missisquoi Museum is housed in a mill on the Pike River. Dating from 1830, it is partly decorated as a late 19th-century country house. The grounds contain a smithy with forge and bellows, a station, a cobbler's shop and a school. In Knowlton, at the Brome County Historical Museum, the old school building dates back to 1854. A store, a courtroom and a museum, where a First World War German airplane is displayed, are included. The Tibbets Hill Pioneer Schoolhouse is run by the Knowlton museum. Located on a hillside to the west of the village, the tiny, stone one-room school, built in 1844, replaced an earlier log cabin structure. Another townships museum is at Melbourne—a farmhouse furnished as it would have been a century ago. These museums are open only in the summer months.

The food supply

When Rena Tibbits Marsh goes shopping in one of Knowlton's supermarkets, she sometimes recalls how they got provisions years ago on her West Bolton farm. "You didn't go to the store once a week. You raised your own food. When you wanted a chicken, you went out to the henhouse. You'd have an idea of which hen you were after. If a hen hadn't been laying, her name was Damn Her and you grabbed her. If you wanted a fish dinner, you took a rod to the river. Everyone kept pigs and so a lot of people cooked with lard. You made your own bread or you went without. You would make sugar biscuits with your own milk, cream and eggs. You used what you had."

CRÈME BRÛLÉE
Molasses custard

This simplified version of the burned cream dessert comes from a group of early recipes in a cookbook called *Nos Recettes Préférées* published by the Cercle de Fermières in St. Edwidge.

---

6 tablespoons (75 mL) cold water
6 tablespoons (75 mL) all-purpose flour
2 cups (500 mL) milk
1 cup (250 mL) molasses
½ teaspoon (2 mL) almond extract

In a medium saucepan, combine water and flour; stir briskly to blend. Whisk in milk and cook over medium heat, stirring continuously, until thickened and smooth. Keep warm.

In a small saucepan, bring molasses to a boil and simmer until it thickens and almost caramelizes. Remove from heat and cool slightly. Stir into warm custard, blending well. Flavour with almond extract. Pour into serving dishes. Serve warm or cool. Four to six servings.

MICROWAVE METHOD

In a 2-quart (2 L) glass measure or casserole, blend water and flour together until smooth; stir in milk. Microwave, uncovered, at High (100 percent) for 5 to 6 minutes until mixture comes to a boil, thickens and sauce is smooth, stirring every minute.

In another 2-quart (2 L) glass measure or casserole, microwave molasses, uncovered, at High (100 percent) for 6 to 7 minutes until reduced and thickened. Stir into milk sauce along with the almond extract until combined. Pour into serving dishes.

QUEEN ELIZABETH CAKE

Dates and nuts are always part of this Townships cake. The icing usually contains brown sugar and more nuts. Coconut is an option. This recipe wins prizes for Linda Bresee of Sutton Junction at the annual Labour Day weekend fair run by the Brome County Horticultural Society.

---

1 cup (250 mL) boiling water
1 cup (250 mL) chopped dates
1 teaspoon (5 mL) baking soda
¼ cup (50 mL) butter or margarine
1 cup (250 mL) granulated sugar
1 egg, beaten
1 teaspoon (5 mL) vanilla
1½ cups (375 mL) all-purpose flour
1 teaspoon (5 mL) baking powder
¼ teaspoon (1 mL) salt
½ cup (125 mL) chopped walnuts
Broiled Icing (recipe follows)

Pour boiling water over dates and add baking soda. Let stand until lukewarm.

In a bowl, cream butter with sugar, then beat in beaten egg. Add date mixture along with vanilla. In another bowl, combine flour with baking powder and salt. Stir dry ingredients into creamed mixture until combined. Fold in walnuts.

Pour batter into a greased, 9-inch (23 cm) square baking pan. Bake in a preheated 350°F (180°C) oven for 40 to 45 minutes or until a tester inserted in centre comes out clean.

While cake is still warm, spread with Broiled Icing and place under a preheated broiler for 2 to 3 minutes or until lightly browned.

A royal cake

A cake called Queen Elizabeth Cake or Gâteau Reine Elisabeth turns up in recipe collections in Estrie and beyond. It contains dates and nuts, sometimes walnuts, and has a brown sugar icing which sometimes includes coconut along with nuts. The cake can be made with milk, cream or condensed milk.

It's a relatively new tradition, according to Annie McElrea Goodfellow of Sherbrooke, who has been making this cake since the Second World War. That's when it first appeared, shared by Queen Elizabeth, later the Queen Mother, with members of the Quebec Women's Institutes. Her Majesty reportedly stirred the cake up herself and decreed that the recipe was not to be passed on freely, but sold for charitable purposes. It has its own category in the cooking contest each Labour Day weekend at Big Brome Fair.

Broiled Icing

---

5 tablespoons (75 mL) brown sugar
3 tablespoons (45 mL) butter
2 tablespoons (25 mL) whipping cream
½ cup (125 mL) coconut
½ cup (125 mL) chopped walnuts (optional)

In a small saucepan, combine brown sugar, butter, cream, coconut and nuts, if desired. Bring to a boil over medium heat; boil for 3 minutes. Makes about 1¼ cups (300 mL).

MICROWAVE METHOD

Cake: Prepare batter as directed in recipe and spread in a lightly greased, 9-inch (23 cm) round baking dish. Microwave, uncovered, at Medium (50 percent) for 5 minutes. Rotate dish and microwave at High (100 percent) for 3 to 5 minutes more, or until a tester inserted in centre comes out clean, rotating dish once. Let stand on counter top for 10 minutes before spreading with Broiled Icing.

Icing: Place brown sugar, butter, cream, coconut and walnuts in a 4-cup (1 L) glass measure or dish. Microwave at High (100 percent) for 3 minutes until sugar dissolves and mixture boils, stirring twice. Spread on warm cake. Broil cake, if desired, as directed in recipe.

INDEX

APPETIZERS:
  Cod tongues with almonds, 130
  Crab custard with lemon butter sauce, 6
  Fish salad with smoked salmon dressing, 34
  Garlic fried smelts, 68
  Head cheese, 156
  Jellied chicken loaf, 152
  Leek tart, 10
  Old fashioned calves' liver pate, 9
  Perch and zucchini terrine with maple syrup dressing, 172
  Perch mousse with lobster sauce, 174
  Potted pork, 171
  Puff pastry with vegetables in coriander sauce, 96
  Scallop flower appetizer, 8
  Smelt pie, 71
  Smoked salmon with endives and zucchini, 111
Apple cream, 127
Apple dumplings, 79
Apple honey pie, 190
Apple maple pudding, 63
Apple maple upside-down tart, 126
Applesauce bread, 165
Asparagus salad, 175
Auberge Benedict Arnold, 60m
Auberge des Peupliers, 68m
Auberge du Gargantua, 135m
Auberge Hatley, 194m
Auberge La Girandole, 198m
Auberge La Goeliche, 7m
Auberge Le Coin du Banc, 145m
Auberge Le Presbytere, 35m
Auberge Otter Lake Haus, 91m
Auberge sur la Falaise, 174m
Aunt Gertie's meat pie, 131

Baked stuffed ouananiche, 29
BEANS:
  Bean soup, 27
  Cream-topped bean soup, 67

Pork and beans, 52
  Pureed bean soup, 86
BEEF:
  Aunt Gertie's meat pie, 131
  Beef pastry roll, 49
  Boiled beef and vegetable dinner, 73
  Braised beef tongue with vegetables, 122
  Cipaille/Layered meat pie, 120
  Cipâte/Layered meat pie, 77
  Grandmother's beef in a cast iron pot, 90
  Old-fashioned beef in red wine, 18
  Saguenay meat pie, 28
Beef pastry roll, 49
BEETS:
  Jellied pork aspic with beets, 87
  Pickled beets, 161
Blackberry jam, 121
Blueberry oat crumble, 38
Blueberry pie, 37
Blueberry upside-down pudding, 41
Boiled beef and vegetable dinner, 73
Bouquet garni, 94m
Braised beef tongue with vegetables, 122
Braised veal with herbs, 186
BREAD:
  Applesauce bread, 165
  Currant buns, 205
  Oatmeal bread, 206
  Whole wheat bread, 58
Breast of guinea hen with thyme and honey, 115
Buckwheat pancakes, 105
Butternut spice cake, 166

CABBAGE:
  Cabbage salad, 11
  Grandfather's partridge, 92
  Partridge and cabbage, 138
CAKES:
  Butternut spice cake, 166
  Joe Louis cakes, 60
  Johnny cake, 80

214 A TASTE OF QUEBEC

Pumpkin cake, 102
Queen Elizabeth cake, 211
CANDY:
Grandmother's molasses taffy, 104
Cap Chat bouillabaisse, 132
CASSEROLES (including stews):
Boiled beef and vegetable dinner, 73
Braised beef tongue with vegetables, 122
Braised veal with herbs, 186
Cap Chat bouillabaisse, 132
Cipaille/Layered meat pie, 120
Cipâte/Layered meat pie, 77
La Coulée Douce bouillabaisse, 136
Gram's chicken and biscuits, 196
Grandfather's partridge, 92
Grandmother's beef in a cast iron pot, 90
Ground meat pie, 31
Lamb and vegetable stew, 193
Maple-flavoured hare and partridge
casserole, 70
Meatball and pork hocks stew, 12
Old-fashioned braised hare, 94
Partridge and cabbage, 138
Pork hocks stew with dumplings, 47
Rabbit vegetable casserole, 74
Saguenay meat pie, 28
Seafood pie, 40
Sturgeon in cream sauce, 113
Tommy cod stew, 176
Vegetable stew, 204
Cauliflower souffle, 33
CHICKEN:
Chicken breasts with oyster mushroom
sauce, 182
Cipaille/Layered meat pie, 120
Gram's chicken and biscuits, 196
Jellied chicken loaf, 152
Maple-baked chicken breasts, 62
Saguenay meat pie, 28
Cipaille/Layered meat pie, 120
Cipâte/Layered meat pie, 77
COD:
Cod tongues with almonds, 130
Gaspé style cod, 143
COOKIES:
Maple cookies, 208
Molasses cookies, 39
Oatmeal lace cookies, 185
Corn soup, 46
Country style date nut pie, 22
Crab apples on the stem, 163

Crab custard with lemon butter sauce, 6
Cream salad dressing, 199
Cream-topped bean soup, 67
CUCUMBERS:
Maple-flavoured cucumber pickles, 57
CURRANTS:
Currant buns, 205
Suet fruit pie, 160

Dandelion salad, 201
DATES:
Country style date nut pie, 22
Mother's date doughnuts, 187
Queen Elizabeth cake, 211
DESSERTS:
Apple cream, 127
Apple dumplings, 79
Apple honey pie, 190
Apple maple pudding, 63
Apple maple upside-down tart, 126
Blueberry oat crumble, 38
Blueberry pie, 37
Blueberry upside-down pudding, 41
Buckwheat pancakes, 105
Country style date nut pie, 22
Crab apples on the stem, 163
Economy dessert, Saguenay style, 40
Economy pudding, Matane style, 146
Fleur-Ange's sugar pie, 103
Grandmother's fritters, 162
Lemon pudding, 145
Madeleines with honey ice cream, 106
Maple cookies, 208
Maple sauce, 209
Maple syrup tart, 125
Molasses custard, 210
Molasses pie, 101
Pancakes, Norman style, 188
Poached pears with wine custard, 20
Raspberry Bavarian cream, 82
Spiced custard pie, 164
Suet fruit pie, 160
Sugar pie, Gaspé style, 148
Tante Lise's sugar pie, 81
Drunkard's soup, 26
DUCK:
Duckling with raisins and honey, 202
Duck with orange sauce, 178
Wild duck with garlic leaves, 114

Economy dessert, Saguenay style, 40
Economy pudding, Matane style, 146

EGGS:
Cauliflower souffle, 33
Crab custard with lemon butter sauce, 6
Eggs in maple syrup, 53
Turnip souffle, 180
ENDIVE:
Smoked salmon with endives and
zucchini, 111

Fiddleheads, garlic-flavoured, 137
FISH (see also SEAFOOD):
Baked stuffed ouananiche, 29
Cap Chat bouillabaisse, 132
Cod tongues with almonds, 130
La Coulée Douce bouillabaisse, 136
Lac St. Jean salmon pie, 32
Fish salad with smoked salmon dressing,
34
Fish stock, 112
Fisherman's hash, 123
Garlic fried smelts, 68
Gaspé style cod, 143
Gaspé whelk soup, 134
Indian fish pie, 36
Manor-style fish fillets, 54
Perch and zucchini terrine with maple
syrup dressing, 172
Perch mousse with lobster sauce, 174
Salmon pie, 177
Smelt pie, 71
Smoked salmon with endives and
zucchini, 111
Sorel fish stew, 154
Stuffed baked mackerel, 142
Sturgeon in cream sauce, 113
Trout fillet, Coulibiac style, 98
Trout in cress-flavoured cream sauce, 198
Walleye in pastry with chive butter sauce,
55
Fleur-Ange's pork pie, 88
Fleur-Ange's sugar pie, 103
Fruit vegetable relish, 15

GAME: see individual game meats
GUINEA HEN, PHEASANT,
PARTRIDGE,etc.
Game bird stock, 114m
Game birds with mushroom and onion
sauce, 78
Garlic-flavoured fiddleheads, 137

Garlic-fried smelts, 68
Gaspé style cod, 143
Gaspé whelk soup, 134
Gram's chicken and biscuits, 196
Grandfather's partridge, 92
Grandmother's beef in a cast iron pot, 90
Grandmother's fritters, 162
Grandmother's molasses taffy, 104
Green tomato ketchup, 91
Ground meat pie, 31
GUINEA HEN:
Breast of guinea hen with thyme and
honey, 115
Game birds with mushroom and onion
sauce, 78
Île d'Orléans guinea hen with red
currants, 16

HARE: see also RABBIT
Hare in red wine with morel sauce, 116
Maple-flavoured hare and partridge
casserole, 70
Old-fashioned braised hare, 94
Head cheese, 156
Herbs, salted, 26m
Hostellerie Les Trois Tilleuls, 152m

ICE CREAM:
Madeleines with honey ice cream, 106
Île d'Orléans guinea hen with red currants,
16
INNS:
Auberge Benedict Arnold, 60m
Auberge des Peupliers, 68m
Auberge du Gargantua, 135m
Auberge Hatley, 194m
Auberge La Girandole, 198m
Auberge La Goeliche, 7m
Auberge Le Coin du Banc, 145m
Auberge Le Presbytere, 35m
Auberge Otter Lake Haus, 91m
Auberge sur la Falaise, 174m
Hostellerie Les Trois Tilleuls, 152m
L'eau à la Bouche, 87m
Manoir des érables, 127m

JAM: see PRESERVES
Jellied chicken loaf, 152
Jellied pork aspic with beets, 87
Joe Louis cakes, 60
Johnny cake, 80

LAMB:
  Lamb and vegetable stew, 193
  Lamb meatballs in herb-flavoured sauce, 118
  Leg of lamb flavoured with juniper berries, 72
Layered meat pie/Cipaille, 120
Layered meat pie/Cipâte, 77
Layered salmon pie, 139
L'eau à la Bouche, 87m
Leek tart, 10
Lemon pudding, 145

Madeleines with honey ice cream, 106
Manoir des érables, 127m
Manor-style fish fillets, 54
MAPLE:
  Apple maple pudding, 63
  Apple maple upside-down tart, 126
  Eggs in maple syrup, 53
  Maple-baked chicken breasts, 62
  Maple cookies, 208
  Maple-flavoured cucumber pickles, 57
  Maple-flavoured hare and partridge casserole, 70
  Maple sauce, 209
  Maple syrup tart, 125
  Perch and zucchini terrine with maple syrup dressing, 172
  Pork tenderloin with shallots and maple syrup, 200
  Suet fruit pie, 160
MEAT: see BEEF, PORK, LAMB etc.
Meatball and pork hocks stew, 12
Molasses cookies, 39
Molasses custard, 210
Molasses pie, 101
Mother's date doughnuts, 187
MUSHROOMS:
  Braised veal with herbs, 186
  Chicken breasts with oyster mushroom sauce, 182
  Game birds with mushroom and onion sauce, 78
  Hare in red wine with morel sauce, 116
  Spinach-stuffed veal with mushroom sauce, 194

Oatmeal bread, 206
Oatmeal lace cookies, 185
Old-fashioned beef in red wine, 18
Old fashioned braised hare, 94

Old-fashioned calves' liver pate, 9
ONIONS:
  Drunkard's soup, 26
Oyster soup, 153

PANCAKES:
  Buckwheat pancakes, 105
  Pancakes, Norman style, 188
  Potato pancakes, 17
PARTRIDGE:
  Grandfather's partridge, 92
  Maple-flavoured hare and partridge casserole, 70
  Partridge and cabbage, 138
  Saguenay meat pie, 28
PASTRY:
  Charlevoix pastry, 75
  Pastry for seafood pie, 140
Pea soup, Beauce style, 45
PEPPERS:
  Wintertime salad, 59
Perch and zucchini terrine with maple syrup dressing, 172
Perch mousse with lobster sauce, 174
PHEASANT:
  Game birds with mushroom and onion sauce, 78
PICKLES, see PRESERVES
Pickled beets, 161
PIES, meat and vegetable (for sweet pies, see DESSERTS):
  Aunt Gertie's meat pie, 131
  Charlevoix meat pie, 76
  Cipaille/Layered meat pie, 120
  Cipate/Layered meat pie, 77
  Fleur-Ange's pork pie, 88
  Ground meat pie, 31
  Indian fish pie, 36
  Lac St. Jean salmon pie, 32
  Layered salmon pie, 139
  Leek tart, 10
  Potato pie, 89
  Quebec pork pie, 14
  Saguenay meat pie, 28
  Salmon pie, 177
  Seafood pie, 140
  Smelt pie, 71
Poached pears with wine custard, 20
PORK:
  Aunt Gertie's meat pie, 131
  Charlevoix meat pie, 76

Cipaille/Layered meat pie, 120
Cipate/Layered meat pie, 77
Fleur-Ange's pork pie, 88
Ground meat pie, 31
Head cheese, 156
Jellied pork aspic with beets, 87
Meatball and pork hocks stew, 12
Pork and beans, 52
Pork hocks stew with dumplings, 47
Pork liver and bacon with tea sauce, 100
Pork tenderloin with cranberry cream
  sauce, 50
Pork tenderloin with shallots and maple
  syrup, 200
Pork turnovers, 69
Potted pork, 171
Quebec pork pie, 14
Roast pork with pan-browned potatoes,
  184
Saguenay meat pie, 28
Spiced pork sausages, 157
POTATOES:
  Fisherman's hash, 123
  Potato pancakes, 17
  Potato pie, 89
  Roast pork with pan-browned potatoes,
  184
  Saguenay meat pie, 28
Potted pork, 171
POULTRY: see CHICKEN, TURKEY,
  DUCK, GUINEA HEN, etc.
PRESERVES:
  Blackberry jam, 121
  Fruit vegetable relish, 15
  Green tomato ketchup, 91
  Maple-flavoured cucumber pickles, 57
  Pickled beets, 161
Puff pastry with vegetables in coriander
  sauce, 96
Pumpkin cake, 102
Pumpkin soup, 151
Pureed bean soup, 86

Quebec pork pie, 14
Queen Elizabeth cake, 211

RABBIT:
  Hare in red wine with morel sauce, 116
  Maple-flavoured hare and partridge
  casserole, 70
  Old fashioned braised hare, 94

Rabbit vegetable casserole, 74
Saguenay meat pie, 28
Raspberry Bavarian cream, 82
RELISH, see PRESERVES
RICE:
  Trout fillet, Coulibiac style, 98
  Vegetable rice soup, 170

SALADS, including dressings:
  Asparagus salad, 175
  Cabbage salad, 11
  Cream salad dressing, 199
  Dandelion salad, 201
  Fish salad with smoked salmon dressing,
  34
  Jellied pork aspic with beets, 87
  Salad with honey-broiled apples, 158
  Smoked salmon with endives and
  zucchini, 111
  Strawberry spinach salad, 23
  Wintertime salad, 59
SALMON:
  Fish salad with smoked salmon dressing,
  34
  Lac St. Jean salmon pie, 32
  Salmon pie, 177
  Smoked salmon with endives and
  zucchini, 111
Salted herbs, 26m
SAUCES:
  Chive butter sauce, 56
  Lemon sauce, 7
  Maple sauce, 209
  Maple syrup dressing, 173
  Orange sauce, 179
  Tomato bechamel sauce, 48m
SCALLOPS:
  Scallop flower appetizer, 8
  Scallop soup, 112
SEAFOOD:
  Cap Chat bouillabaisse, 132
  Crab custard with lemon butter sauce, 6
  Gaspé whelk soup, 134
  La Coulée Douce bouillabaisse, 136
  Oyster soup, 153
  Scallop flower appetizer, 8
  Scallop soup, 112
Smelt pie, 71
Smoked salmon with endives and zucchini,
  111
Sorel fish stew, 154

SOUFFLES:
  Cauliflower souffle, 33
  Turnip souffle, 180
SOUPS:
  Bean soup, 27
  Corn soup, 46
  Cream-topped bean soup, 67
  Drunkard's soup, 26
  Fish stock, 112m
  Game bird stock, 114m
  Gaspé whelk soup, 134
  Lamb stock, 119
  Oyster soup, 153
  Pea soup, Beauce style, 45
  Pumpkin soup, 151
  Pureed bean soup, 86
  Scallop soup, 112
  Tomato soup, 169
  Vegetable rice soup, 170
Spiced custard pie, 164
Spiced pork sausages, 157
SPINACH:
  Strawberry spinach salad, 23
Strawberry spinach salad, 23
Stuffed baked mackerel, 142
Suet fruit pie, 160
Sugar pie, Gaspé style, 148
Sturgeon in cream sauce, 113

Tante Lise's sugar pie, 81
Tomato bechamel sauce, 48
TOMATOES:
  Green tomato ketchup, 91
  Tomato bechamel sauce, 48
  Tomato soup, 169
  Wintertime salad, 59

Vegetable stew, 204
Tommy cod stew, 176
TOURTIÈRE: see PIES
Trout fillet, Coulibiac style, 98
Trout in cress-flavoured cream sauce, 198
Turnip souffle, 180

VEAL:
  Braised veal with herbs, 186
  Ground meat pie, 31
  Meatball and pork hocks stew, 12
  Saguenay meat pie, 28
  Spinach-stuffed veal with mushroom
    sauce, 194
VEGETABLES (see also individual
  vegetables):
  Fruit vegetable relish, 15
  Green tomato ketchup, 91
  Puff pastry with vegetables in coriander
    sauce, 96
  Vegetable stew, 204
  Vegetable rice soup, 170
  Wintertime salad, 59

Walleye in pastry with chive butter sauce,
  55
Whole wheat bread, 58
Wild duck with garlic leaves, 114
Wintertime salad, 59

ZUCCHINI:
  Perch and zucchini terrine with maple
    syrup dressing, 172
  Smoked salmon with endives and
    zucchini, 111